Praise for *Walking the Little Way of Thérèse of Lisieux*

"Br. Joseph Schmidt reflects on the words and formative events of one of the most popular and beloved of modern saints, guiding us to appreciate more deeply St. Thérèse's 'little way' of love and showing us how we might make it our own."

Most Rev. Emil A. Wcela
Auxiliary Bishop Emeritus, Rockville Centre, New York

"I encourage everyone to read this book if they wish to know more about St. Thérèse, a Doctor of our Church, as declared by Pope John Paul II. Blessed John Paul said, 'Thérèse is a living icon of God,' which personifies what Thérèse said about herself: 'My vocation is love.'"

Most Rev. Robert P. Maginnis, DD, VG
Auxiliary Bishop Emeritus of Philadelphia

"St. Thérèse has been a real spiritual sister to me for many years, especially during my twenty-five years as bishop. I have found her powerful but totally gentle message of love, joy, trust, and self-surrender a continual source of inspiration. Joseph Schmidt has the great gift of opening up the saint's rich teaching for the ordinary reader. He does this beautifully in this present book, which I strongly recommend."

Most Rev. Hugh Slattery, MSC
Bishop Emeritus of Tzaneen, Sout

"As he did in his previous books on ... lt has mined the depth and lessons of Thérèse's ... der grow in God's transforming love. This book ... se who do a daily examination of consciousness."

Sr. Mary Lavin, OCD
Former Prioress, Carmel of the Holy Family, Cleveland Heights, Ohio

"This presentation on St. Thérèse is a down-to-earth understanding of the complexity of her affection. The author brings us a deeper and passionate appreciation of the humanness of this saint. While being absorbed in this gifted writer's book, you will open and deepen that personal relationship with God that dwells within your own heart."

Deacon Sal Lema
Editor, *Carmelite Review* Magazine

"*Walking the Little Way* is an extraordinary book, beautifully written. Although Thérèse's words are the foundation of the book, the author's reflections help enlighten the journey of the 'little way' from violence to love. In a world filled with violence and abuse of power, Thérèse's way offers an alternative. For someone seeking to live more reflectively, more intentionally, with inner freedom, and to grow in a personal relationship with God, this inspirational book offers a 'little way' with flesh. The reader understands why Thérèse is described as the 'human saint' and someone who 'democratized' holiness. It is no wonder why Thérèse has become so popular and her message appeals to Christians and non-Christians. Even if you have read other books about Thérèse of Lisieux, this book offers significant insights into this saint of our time."

Br. Bernard LoCoco, FSC
Former President of Christian Brothers University, Memphis, Tennessee; Past Director, School of Applied Theology Sabbatical Program, Berkeley, California

"This book offers new, deeper, and practical insights into the spirituality of St. Thérèse so that we can follow her path in our daily lives. As in his previous writings, and especially in his biography of Thérèse, *Everything is Grace*, Joseph Schmidt brings a freshness and a heartfelt way of easily identifying with Thérèse. Schmidt is an insightful guide to those who wish to live by her spirituality."

Fr. Bob Colaresi, O Carm
Society of the Little Flower, Darien, Illinois

"This beautiful book is filled with helpful insights for the daily life of unconditional, nonviolent love. We are to love ourselves, one another, our neighbors, and our God, but how do we do this? Using the lessons of St. Thérèse, a Doctor of the Church, this book teaches us 'the path of love.' May it be read, studied, and practiced far and wide in the hope that we may make many new discoveries in universal love."

Fr. John Dear, SJ
Author of *The Questions of Jesus, Living Peace,* and *Transfiguration*

"A refreshing, inspirational, and challenging understanding of Thérèse's spiritual journey, this book will change your idea of Thérèse and her 'little way.' It invites us to pray and challenges us to grow in love. Readers learn from Thérèse how to know what actions flow from love."

Sr. Joan Sue Miller, SCL
Former Major Superior, Sisters of Charity of Leavenworth, Kansas

"*Walking the Little Way of Thérèse of Lisieux* brings to life Thérèse as an influence for us in this twenty-first century. In this study of Thérèse's path of love, we see her dealing with her own tendencies and gently pointing out to us our tendencies to violence in thought, feelings and speech toward ourselves and others."

Sr. Patrice Kerin, OSF
Former General Superior, Sisters of St. Francis of Sylvania, Ohio

"This excellent book highlights the simplicity, holiness, and method of Thérèse's spirituality. It brings to light six unique 'heart qualities' of Thérèse that we, in our own spiritual journey, can reflect upon and integrate into our own lives of love."

Br. Steven Grazulis, SM
Formation Director, Zambia

"Br. Joseph Schmidt bridges centuries and cultures to bring this nineteenth-century French woman to us today. Thérèse's responses to the psychological and spiritual challenges she encountered can offer hope to any modern reader."

Sr. Doris Gottemoeller, RSM
Former President of the Sisters of Mercy of the Americas

"Pray this book, and please don't rush it. Or maybe it's better to say, live it—as a contemporary, deeply penetrating reflection on the doctrine of our newest Doctor of the Church, one of God's incredible surprises. Born into what we would judge exactly the wrong culture, she went on to get everything right. She teaches, and we can do no better than listen."

Sr. Miriam Pollard, OCSO
Prioress, Santa Rita Abbey, Sonoita, Arizona

"Br. Joseph Schmidt provides here a detailed and thorough analysis of the 'science of love' as practiced by St. Thérèse of Lisieux. He explains as never before the precise steps that brought Thérèse to extraordinary sanctity by her very ordinary 'little way.' In this, he gives the reader ready access to the precise practices that can bring us to her everyday kind of holiness of life."

Thomas Groome
Professor of Theology and Religious Education, and Chair of the Department of Religious Education and Pastoral Ministry at Boston College School of Theology and Ministry, Boston, Massachusetts
Author of *Will There Be Faith?*

"This study graphically brings to life Thérèse's path from codependency to saintly maturity. The *Story of a Soul* becomes 'the path of love.'"

Abbot Owen Purcell, OSB

St. Benedict's Abbey, Atchison, Kansas (retired)

"Joseph Schmidt offers an unusual and creative perspective on Thérèse's inner world as she struggles to know if the love in her heart is authentic. Packed with insights and fresh intuitions and written in an engaging, lively style, this book give us a beautiful introduction to the 'Doctor of Love,' who, going against the currents of the spirituality of her time, prophetically articulates a vision of God that unmasks the hidden violence of conventional religion and the toxic versions of spirituality. Thérèse, through Schmidt's able hands, leads us on a love path to acquire the heart qualities so needed today in our contemporary 'culture of death' to resist violence in any of its forms. Don't miss this invitation to embark on a fascinating journey with Thérèse herself as guide, interpreted through the lens of one of the best current English-language commentators on Thérèse's thought and spirituality."

Fr. Eamonn Mulcahy, CSSP, STD

International Retreat Director and Professor of Systematic Theology at Tangaza College, Catholic University of Eastern Africa, Nairobi, Kenya

Walking the Little Way of Thérèse of Lisieux

Discovering the Path of Love

Joseph F. Schmidt, FSC

Published by The Word Among Us Press
7115 Guilford Drive
Frederick, Maryland 21704
www.wau.org

16 15 14 13 12   1 2 3 4 5
ISBN: 978-1-59325-205-2
eISBN: 978-1-59325-439-1

Cover Image: Photograph of Thérèse at twenty-two years old in 1895.
Copyright © Office Central de Lisieux
Cover design by Faceout Studio

Library of Congress Cataloging-in-Publication Data

Schmidt, Joseph F.
  Walking the little way of Thérèse of Lisieux : discovering the path of love /
Joseph F. Schmidt.
     p. cm.
  Includes bibliographical references.
  ISBN 978-1-59325-205-2
  1. Thérèse, de Lisieux, Saint, 1873-1897. I. Title.
  BX4700.T5S345 2012
  282.092—dc23
                    2012018530

Other books by Joseph F. Schmidt, FSC

Praying Our Experiences

Praying with Thérèse of Lisieux

Everything Is Grace:
The Life and Way of Thérèse of Lisieux

A Note about Thérèse's Words

The words that Thérèse said or wrote are printed in italics throughout the book. They come from her autobiographical manuscripts *Story of a Soul* and her letters, poems, and prayers, as well as from words attributed to her in *St. Thérèse of Lisieux: Her Last Conversations*, in the memoirs of her sister Céline, and in the testimonies given during the process of her beatification and canonization.

List of Illustrations

Contents

Source Abbreviations

CCC: *Catechism of the Catholic Church*

CP: *Collected Poems of St. Thérèse of Lisieux*, translated by Alan Bancroft

DAS: *Divini Amoris Scientia*, Apostolic Letter of His Holiness Pope John Paul II

DUC: *Saint Thérèse of Lisieux: Doctor of the Universal Church* by Steven Payne, OCD

EIG: *Everything Is Grace: The Life and Way of Thérèse of Lisieux* by Joseph F. Schmidt, FSC

FGM: *St. Thérèse of Lisieux: Her Family, Her God, Her Message* by Bernard Bro, OP

GC: *General Correspondence*, Volumes I and II, translated by John Clarke, OCD

HF: *The Hidden Face: A Study of St. Thérèse of Lisieux* by Ida Friederike Görres

HLC: *St. Thérèse of Lisieux: Her Last Conversations*, translated by John Clarke, OCD

HLTT: *St. Thérèse of Lisieux: Her Life, Times, and Teaching*, edited by Conrad de Meester, OCD

MSST: *My Sister St. Thérèse by Sister Geneviève of the Holy Face* (Céline Martin)

PST: *The Prayers of Thérèse of Lisieux*, translated by Aletheia Kane, OCD

STL: *St. Thérèse of Lisieux by Those Who Knew Her*, edited and translated by Christopher O'Mahony, OCD

SS: *Story of a Soul*, translated by John Clarke, OCD

TLMT: *Thérèse of Lisieux and Marie of the Trinity* by Pierre Descouvemont

Foreword

St. Thérèse is recognized as a great intercessor before God, and many favors are reported through prayers to this amazing saint. Statues of St. Thérèse usually project the image of a charming young Carmelite letting fall her promised shower of roses. She is familiarly known as the "Little Flower." In my youth, I attended Little Flower High School in Philadelphia, where Thérèse was held up to us as a model for our lives. Over the years I have read many books describing her "little way" of spirituality. The true depth of her spirituality, however, unfolded itself for me only when, as a member of the Carmelite Forum with lectures to prepare for our annual Carmelite seminar, I delved more deeply into her writings.

While exploring what I called her "spirituality of imperfection" and observing from the text of her writings her development from child to young girl to teenager to mature woman, it was evident that Thérèse, like me, had struggled with all that being human entails. She bore the emotional scars of her early years and of her family upbringing, along with the distorted spirituality of her times.

Fortunately, woven into her years of struggle was the increasing gift of reflective self-observation. Instead of becoming self-centered, her increasing self-awareness became integral to her life with God and others. How her journey progressed as Thérèse struggled to discover the path of authentic love is the unique gift that Br. Joseph Schmidt opens up for us. Together with Thérèse, he helps us through her journey to discover our own path of love.

Thérèse's reflections on her family life through her growing years and her difficulties living in community during her years as a Carmelite, along with her personal interior struggles, are told with a charm and simplicity deceptive to superficial reading. Br. Joseph Schmidt is uniquely gifted with the ability to insightfully explore Thérèse's everyday life from both a psychological and spiritual perspective. In doing so, he artfully uncovers the genuine holiness and strength of character that emerged as Thérèse struggled to be a truly loving person. His book offers a profound understanding of why St. Thérèse was proclaimed the greatest saint of modern times by Pope Pius X and a Doctor of the Church by Pope John Paul II. Br. Joseph makes it possible for us to recognize the potential for holiness present in all the facets of our own life experiences.

Anyone who has read Br. Joseph's excellent book *Everything Is Grace: The Life and Way of Thérèse of Lisieux* will welcome *Walking the Little Way of Thérèse of Lisieux: Discovering the Path of Love*. As the reader will come to recognize, this book elaborates in further detail how St. Thérèse's very human limitations—the psychological wounds and shortcomings resulting from her early childhood experiences—became the place of God's transforming action in her. Themes relevant to Thérèse's ongoing growth as the path of love is revealed to her are skillfully woven through each chapter. As the various colors and threads of her life journey appear and reappear, new insights and the potential for greater self-knowledge emerge for the reader. Deep desires stir within us that we ourselves might grow with Thérèse on her Gospel path of love.

Especially remarkable for today is the author's ability to show how Thérèse, through her struggles, came to recognize that at times, she was actually doing violence to herself. Her penetrating insights challenge readers to become more personally self-reflective about their own entangled inner world. Thérèse demonstrates that every aspect of our being, as well as the winding ways of our life experiences, is integral to the struggle to live in a loving manner. Thérèse encourages us to recognize within ourselves, as she did, the experience of inner freedom, creativity, compassion, willingness, self-surrender, and gratitude that became for her the signs of authentic love.

This book models for us the insights that surface when an author explores themes through the classic writings of the mystics and lets the texts speak for themselves. When these texts are viewed through the lens of contemporary understandings in the fields of spirituality, Scripture studies, anthropology, psychology, and human development, fresh understanding comes forth that inevitably enriches our lives as we, too, walk the path of love.

Sr. Vilma Seelaus, OCD
Author of *Distractions in Prayer: Blessing or Curse?* and *St. Teresa of Ávila's Teachings in The Interior Castle*

Introduction

The science of Love, St. Thérèse of Lisieux wrote toward the end of her life, *ah, yes, this word, resounds sweetly in the ear of my soul, and I desire only this science* (SS 187–88).

From her early years, Thérèse had desired to be a saint, and the primary focus of her life was to walk the path of love, to discover *the science of love*, to do God's will. Yet as her life drew to a close, she asked herself, *Is pure love in my heart? Are my measureless desires* [to love] *only but a dream, a folly?* (SS 197).

Thérèse had, with a tender conscience and deep sensitivity, struggled persistently throughout her life with the ambiguity of her motivation and had tried to resist her tendency toward self-centeredness, which she knew compromised her desire to do God's will in love. She recognized that the path of authentic love was not always clear within her own heart. She also lacked confidence in the way the Gospel path of love was presented in the spirituality of her day.

So she continuously asked herself questions such as these: How do I know that I am loving authentically? What are the thoughts and feelings, the dispositions, the heart qualities that would tell me that I am living, to the best of my ability, a life of genuine love of God and selfless charity toward others? What are the psychological signs of love; what goes on in the mind and heart of one who authentically loves? What would God's love manifested in me really feel and look like? Am I on the path of authentic love?

Thérèse did not usually express explicitly such questions in her writings, but these were the kinds of questions that arose in her heart, especially during her prayer. They were the kinds of questions that had plagued her in youth during the eighteen months she battled scrupulosity and self-doubt. They were the questions that had surrounded her complete conversion experience as a teenager. They were also the kinds of questions that had arisen again after she had entered the Carmelite community and had relapsed into scrupulosity (GC 580–81, note 7; 585; 598; 767–68, note 5). And these were the kinds of questions that surfaced the evening before her profession of religious vows, when she suffered a brief panic attack. On that occasion, questioning her own sincerity and struggling with confusion, she wrote, *The darkness was so great that I could see and understand one thing only: I didn't have a vocation* (SS 166).

The year after Thérèse's profession of vows, Franciscan Father Alexis Prou, who preached the community retreat, gave her assurance of the way of love she already intuitively and tentatively had begun to follow. *He launched me full sail upon the waves of confidence and love which so strongly attracted me, but upon which I dared not advance,* Thérèse later wrote (SS 174). And yet just over a year after Fr. Prou's encouragement, she apparently sought additional reassurance from her long-time confessor, the Jesuit Father Pichon. In a letter, he replied to her, trying to calm her lingering self-doubts. Attempting finally to end her *martyrdom of scruples* (GC 568) and to confirm her path of love, he wrote, "Banish, then, your worries. . . . Fall asleep, tranquil and serene in the arms of Jesus" (GC 767).

And these same questions about *the science of love* disturbed Thérèse during her nine years of religious life when she made efforts to love the sisters with whom she lived. Although she had the best of intentions, she did not always feel love and was not confident that she was loving. Rather, sometimes she felt negative and resistant toward some of the community members.

These same questions also arose as she boldly tried to sort through the mistaken spirituality that contaminated the common teaching of her times. In this venture, she had little support or outside reassurance. The erroneous teaching about Gospel love and holiness was shared by most of the community members, was contained in most of the books in the community library, and was often presented during the annual community retreats.

As she neared the end of her life, these questions about the path of love were expressed in her fundamental concern: *Is God asking something more of me than my poor little actions and desires? Is He content with me? Is pure love in my heart?* (SS 191, 197).

Even as Thérèse matured in wisdom and became more confident of her "little way"—as she called her way of spirituality—questions about the sincerity of her motivation and the purity of her love continued almost obsessively to arise within her sensitive heart. Throughout her life, she remained a seeker of personal authenticity and truth, seeking her Beloved who called himself the Truth and who dwelt in the depths of her heart. *Yes, it seems to me I never sought anything but the truth,* she said in her final days (HLC 205).

In her youth Thérèse had already become aware that the ambiguity of her motivation could poison her heart and understood that purity of heart was essential to love. She knew the truth of Jesus' words: "This people honors me with their lips, but their hearts are far from me" (Matthew 15:8). She was certain that *it is the heart that the eyes of Jesus are always looking at,* and that our *heart . . . is what He longs for* (GC 496; 641–42). She was also aware of the warning of St. Paul, her most important scriptural teacher: "If I speak in human and angelic tongues but do not have love, I am a resounding gong or a clashing cymbal. . . . If I have all faith so as to move mountains . . . If I give away everything I own, and if I hand my body over so that I may boast but do not have love, I gain nothing" (1 Corinthians 13:1, 2, 3). It was not, therefore, only the fruits of her actions, however important they might be, that concerned Thérèse. It was her true motivation and, more specifically, the psychological indicators, the qualities of heart associated with pure love, that Thérèse desired to know.

This study is an attempt to journey with Thérèse as she struggled with and tentatively, intuitively answered her questions about the way of love. We will accompany her as she came to discover the personal dispositions, the heart qualities, that told her she was indeed learning *the science of love* and was walking the path of authentic love. We will notice, as she also noticed, six such heart qualities of love that unfolded within her over the years: inner freedom, creativity, compassion, willingness, self-surrender, and gratitude.

We will journey with Thérèse through three fundamental formative experiences that led her to address her questions about love, to learn *the science of love,* to discover these heart qualities of love, and to come to the realization of her little way of spirituality. These three formative experiences of Thérèse were

- her complete conversion that occurred just before her fourteenth birthday, in which she learned that there was more to love than simply trying to please and be good to others—she needed to respect and love herself as well;

- her nine-year struggle to live lovingly with her sisters in the Carmelite convent, during which she learned more clearly the vulnerability of the human heart to the negative, hostile feelings toward oneself and others that poison love;

- and her experience of staying true to the authentic spirituality of the Gospel, as she vigilantly made her way through the dark and dangerous thicket of the erroneous spirituality of her time that contained the pitfalls of Jansenism, Pelagianism, and perfectionism.

In chapters 2 to 5, after exploring several of Thérèse's experiences that preceded and were related to her youthful conversion, we will focus on the complete conversion experience itself and notice some of its immediate effects.

In chapters 6 to 12, we will examine Thérèse's experiences in the Carmelite community and her growth in authentic love. We will especially notice her attempts to love her superior and particularly some of the difficult members of the community in response to Jesus' call to "love your enemies" and "to love as I have loved you."

In chapters 13 to 16, we will study how Thérèse confronted and corrected the mistaken notions of the spirituality of her day, particularly the false understanding of the nature of God and the distorted ideal of holiness.

In chapters 17 to 20, we will examine more closely Thérèse's little way. We will focus on what led her to recognize this way of spirituality and how she lived and taught her way. We will then accompany her as she followed her little way into the deep mystery of Christ's redemptive suffering in the dreadfully painful final months of her dying.

In chapter 21, we will be attentive specifically to the six heart qualities that Thérèse had intuitively used as psychological indicators to guide her steps along the path of love. We will offer additional examples and details of these heart qualities. Walking her spiritual path mostly alone, without the support of the prevailing spirituality to guide her, Thérèse relied on these heart qualities to help her avoid any inner movement that tended to poison authentic love in her heart.

In our final Summary and Concluding Reflections in chapter 22, we will refocus and review some aspects of our study. We will note that Thérèse learned her little way of love particularly from Jesus and Paul and that her spirituality, being without violence, makes a contribution in our day to the Church's development of doctrine.

Her little way is, in some aspects, "new," as she claimed (SS 207). It also can rightly be called "little." It is a Gospel path of self-emptying that brought her *with empty hands* (SS 276; PST 53ff.) to the fulfillment of her vocation to love and that allowed her to proclaim at the end of her life, *O Jesus, my Love, . . . my vocation, at last I have found it. . . . MY VOCATION IS LOVE! . . . I shall be Love* (SS 194).

Thérèse's own ability for self-reflection will provide us the means for journeying with her as she grew in her understanding of *the science of love*. Whenever possible, therefore, we will allow Thérèse to speak for herself. (The words that she wrote or spoke are noted in italics throughout this study.) She is a master storyteller, sharing both the external details of situations as well as revealing her own thoughts, feelings, and motives. Having learned the heart qualities, the personal dispositions, that told her that she was actually walking the path of love, she left many stories of what loving looks like and what loving feels like. She also recognized the self-centered, sometimes resentful and hostile feelings and thoughts that compromise the human heart, and she has stories of them as well. She identifies them as red warning flags on the path of violence.

But before we begin our journey with Thérèse through her three formative experiences, we will, in chapter 1, give a brief overview of Thérèse's life and consider Thérèse's authority as a teacher of the path of love for our day.

Thérèse herself observed that one reason that more ordinary people, *"little souls"* like herself, sometimes do not realize deep intimacy with God and fail to attain full love in their hearts is that they are not properly taught about the human and divine realities of love. *Ah! how many souls*, she wrote, *would have reached sanctity had they been well directed!* (SS 113).

In this regard, Pope John Paul II noted in the apostolic letter making Thérèse a Doctor of the Church that "the power of her message lies in its concrete explanation of how Jesus' promises [of union in Christ] are fulfilled in the believer [Thérèse herself] who knows how confidently to welcome into . . . [her] own life the saving presence of God" (DAS 10). Thus, Thérèse in her life and teaching manifests Jesus' promise of our union with God. She is a personification of God's love, and her life and teaching are a model, a kind of revelation, an "icon," as the pope said (DAS 8), of the path of authentic sanctity, the way of love. Thérèse is a great gift to those seeking peace and love today, since she herself is the spiritual director who can help ordinary people realize more fully the union with God that constitutes authentic sanctity.

The Authority of
Thérèse's Teaching

CHAPTER 1

The Science of Love

DOCTOR OF THE CHURCH, TEACHER FOR OUR TIME, ICON OF GOD

St. Thérèse of Lisieux was only twenty-four years old when she died on September 30, 1897, and yet she has become a Doctor of the Church and one of the most popular saints in the history of the Catholic Church. She has captured the imagination of countless people concerned with religion and spirituality by having achieved great wisdom without academic degrees and for having attained great holiness without living a life of extraordinary spiritual experiences. And this she did during the era of the nineteenth century, when it was presumed that martyrdom was required to be recognized for sanctity in the Catholic Church or, if not martyrdom, then an extraordinary life of personal and spiritual gifts. That might mean great learning, skills of preaching, exceptional piety, notable ascetical practices, uncommon prayer experiences, spiritual visions or ecstasies, and even, perhaps, some status in the hierarchy, success in missionary work, or achievements in founding a religious community.

Thérèse experienced none of these. However, the gift that she did have, and which she gave to the Church, was to attain sanctity by living a simple, unremarkable life, responding to the demands of her day-to-day duties, attempting to do what God was asking of her at each moment, surrendering herself into God's providence, acting in peace, justice, and love.

The gift of her life and teaching has helped ordinary people know that there is an "ordinary sanctity"—a life of faith and love focused on God's presence in the usual experiences of life. She has "democratized" holiness, making it clear that holiness is within the reach of anyone willing to do God's will in love at each successive moment as life unfolds. Not everyone will be a canonized saint, certainly—not even a recognized saint; but everyone is called to holiness and everyone can become a saint.

A Very Ordinary Life

Born on January 2, 1873, Thérèse was the youngest of five girls in a very fervent, rather well-to-do Catholic family living in Normandy, France. Her mother, Zélie Martin, died of breast cancer when Thérèse was only four and a half, and Louis Martin, her father, assumed the responsibilities of raising the children alone. Thérèse entered the religious Carmelite community in Lisieux at the age of fifteen. Two of her older sisters, Marie and Pauline, had already entered the same convent, and another of her sisters, Céline, would enter several years later. Her fourth sister, Léonie, entered the Visitation Convent.

Within the cloistered convent, Thérèse lived the remaining nine years of her life with the twenty-six or so of her companion religious, all engaged in the prayer, the devotional activities, and the usual domestic duties of community life. Because of her sensitivities, excessive at times, Thérèse suffered much during her life in her interactions with others, in the aridity of her prayer, and with her own inner struggles. She also bore especially intense physical and emotional suffering during the last eighteen months of her life as she endured with great patience and without pain suppressants the ravages of tuberculosis.

Thérèse's prayerful reflections on her life experiences, and in particular on her interactions with the sisters of the community, formed an important foundation for her holiness. It was mostly from her own experiences that she learned the wisdom of *the science of love* and formulated her teaching. She was canonized a saint in 1925 by Pope Pius XI, twenty-seven years after her death—the most rapid canonization under the current procedures.

Her holiness consisted of a deep interior life of faith, centered on God and expressed in prayer and responding to God's will through inconspicuous acts of charity toward others. Although not recognized as exceptionally saintly by many of the equally devout religious women with whom she lived, Thérèse, who identified herself among the "*little ones*" (cf. SS 200, 208) of God's kingdom, came to be greatly appreciated as a very humble, wise, patient, and loving sister. Her holiness and wisdom were acknowledged by the community when she was given, at only twenty years of age, the responsibility of helping to mentor the newer candidates in the spiritual life of the convent.

She was not gifted with any unusual human or spiritual accomplishments, and after her death. her memory, like the memory of almost all holy people, would have simply vanished into the recesses of history. She has been saved from sure oblivion only by her writings and by the miracles attributed to her intercession that began very shortly after her death.

Thérèse had composed her autobiography near the end of her life at the request of her superiors, and she expected that they alone would read it. After her death, however, the superiors first distributed the manuscript to the other French Carmelite communities as a kind of obituary. It was published more widely later that year as *Story of a Soul*—a book that has since gone through ninety or so editions and has been translated into more than sixty languages. Still in print, the book continues to this day to be a religious best seller.

In her writings, she had promised to spend her heaven doing good on earth. Many who learned of her life were attracted to her spirituality and were touched by her promise of help. They prayed to her for favors, and many of their requests were answered. Through her intercession miracles began to happen, and miracles small and grand continue to this day: blessed coincidences, faith conversions, moral transformations, emotional healings, family reconciliations, and unexplainable physical cures.

The continued popularity of her writings cannot really be understood in strictly literary terms, and the flood of miracles also cannot be explained in any human way. It was as if God had singled out this virtually unknown young woman who had lived a very secluded, unnoticed, even isolated life to be especially regarded and appreciated after her death. She did quickly become known and admired, and because of the surge of popular devotion, she was rapidly canonized. Her universal popularity continues to the present day among believers and nonbelievers alike, among men and women, scholars and the illiterate, clerics and laity, rich and poor, young and old.

Those who have come to know Thérèse have embraced her as the "little saint" of the little way—the saint of the "ordinary" whom they are able to imitate. Her devotees understand that her greatness consists in her willingness to walk the path of faith and love in the daily responsibilities of life—the same path that they, too, are trying to walk in their own lives. She was a person who understood and lived the Gospel message of peace and charity in a way that is not beyond them. They especially appreciate the simplicity, wisdom, and love with which she engaged her lifelong struggles with her own natural flaws and spiritual weaknesses—struggles that they, too, experience in their own lives. And they fully agree with Pope Pius X that she is "the greatest saint of modern times" (DAS 10).

Doctor of the Church

Pope John Paul II proclaimed St. Thérèse of Lisieux a Doctor of the Church in October 1997, the year of the hundredth anniversary of her death. In granting Thérèse this distinction, the pope was responding to some sixty years of requests from the hierarchy and theologians from around the world who, within ten years of her canonization, had begun petitioning that she be made a doctor.

The title "Doctor of the Church" is bestowed on special saints who have lived and taught the message of Jesus in an outstanding way and whose teaching, in response to the signs of the times, has been universally received and appreciated by the faithful. This honor places Thérèse with only thirty-two other doctors in the entire history of the Church, including her among some of the greatest names in the theological and spiritual tradition of Catholicism. Even though she had little formal education, earned no academic degrees, and produced no doctrinal writings, nevertheless, she now stands equal as a teacher of authentic Catholic doctrine with such renowned saints and theologians as John Chrysostom, Jerome, Augustine, Thomas Aquinas, Bonaventure, Francis de Sales, Teresa of Ávila, and John of the Cross. She is the third woman to be named a doctor, is the youngest of all the Church Doctors, and is most contemporary to our day.

By conferring the eminent title "Doctor of the Church" on Thérèse, the pope surprised some of the Catholic faithful, including historians, Scripture scholars, and theologians. Some believed that since she died so young, she had nothing significant to teach the modern Church. Some thought that since she had attended only primary school and lacked any depth of official theological or scriptural training, her teaching carried no weight. Some felt that since she lived a cloistered life in a Carmelite convent, her message was limited and irrelevant to the current active age. Some thought that since she wrote no systematic theological treatises, her spirituality was more sentimental than solid. Some imagined that since she had no special revelations and had no new pious devotions to offer the Church, her teaching was unnecessary.

These misconceptions, however, were answered by Pope John Paul II in his apostolic letter *Divini Amoris Scientia* naming Thérèse a doctor. They have also been corrected by those who have studied Thérèse's life and writings in the context of the most recent Church documents and in light of the teachings of the Second Vatican Council. And above all, they have been brushed aside by the multitude of faithful who have identified with the essence of Thérèse's life and have correctly perceived that her teaching participates in the development of Christian doctrine, authentically expressing the Gospel for our time. Thérèse's spirituality is widely accepted as resonating with the sense that the faithful have of the Gospel message unfolding in the present life of the Church (cf. DAS 7).

In naming Thérèse a doctor, the pope noted that "many times during the celebration of the Second Vatican Council, the Fathers recalled her example and doctrine" (DAS 10). The pope added, "A sign of the ecclesial reception of the Saint's teaching is the appeal to her doctrine in many documents of the Church's ordinary Magisterium, especially when speaking of the contemplative and missionary vocation, of trust in the just and merciful God, of Christian joy, and of the call to holiness. Evidence of this fact is the presence of her doctrine in the recent *Catechism of the Catholic Church.* . . . She who so loved to learn the truths of the faith in the catechism deserved to be included among the authoritative witnesses of Catholic doctrine" (DAS 10). In the *Catechism of the Catholic Church* that appeared in the early 1990s as the reference text for the pastoral renewal following the Second Vatican Council, Thérèse is quoted more often than any other woman.

The title "Doctor of the Church" is equivalent to the designation "official teacher of the Church" but does not strictly depend on academic credentials or theological achievements. Rather, the title proclaims the holiness of Thérèse, but particularly testifies to the depth and orthodoxy of her wisdom and also to the universal appreciation given to her message.

"In the writings of Thérèse of Lisieux," the pope acknowledged in the context of Thérèse's lack of theological writings usually associated with being named a doctor, "we do not find, perhaps, as in other doctors a scholarly presentation of the things of God. . . . Thérèse does not have a true and proper doctrinal corpus; nevertheless a *particular radiance of doctrine* shines forth from her writings which, as if by a charism of the Holy Spirit, grasp the very heart of the message of Revelation in a fresh and original vision, presenting a teaching of eminent quality. . . . With her distinctive doctrine and unmistakable style, Thérèse appears as an *authentic teacher of faith and the Christian life.* In her writings, as in the sayings of the Holy Fathers, is found that life-giving presence of Catholic tradition (DAS 7, 8).

"One can say with conviction about Thérèse of Lisieux," Pope John Paul II noted, "that the Spirit of God allowed her heart to reveal directly to the people of our time the *fundamental mystery,* the reality of the Gospel. . . . Her 'little way' is the way of 'holy childhood.' There is something unique in this way, the genius of St. Thérèse of Lisieux. At the same time there is the confirmation and renewal of the most *basic* and most *universal* truth. What truth of the Gospel message is really more basic and more universal than this: God is our Father and we are his children? (DAS 10).

"The core of her message is actually the mystery itself of God-Love, of the Triune God," the pope emphasized. "It must be said that Thérèse experienced divine revelation, going so far as to contemplate the fundamental truths of our faith united in the mystery of Trinitarian life. At the summit, as the source and goal, is the merciful love of the three Divine Persons. . . . At the root, on the subject's part, is the experience of being the Father's adoptive children in Jesus. . . . At the root again, and standing before us, is our neighbor, others, for whose salvation we must collaborate with and in Jesus, with the same merciful love as his" (DAS 8).

The title "doctor" does not, of course, refer to the medical arena or to curing and healing. Yet perhaps to a degree surpassing many other Doctors of the Church, Thérèse is a special healer for our day. She has provided a healing presence and wisdom to those who have come to know her and have sought her intercessory powers. Her wisdom teaching comes from the understanding and empathy of one who has suffered and who offers compassion without condemnation. From her own experience, she presents the authentic teaching of the Gospel in a feminine way that is especially fresh and heartening to those who are burdened with personal emotional limitations, obsessive-compulsive tendencies, and moral weaknesses.

Thérèse conveys the challenge and the essence of the Gospel spirituality of love with an empathy and compassion that consoles and does not intimidate, much less terrorize. Among those seeking a life of peace and love in our time, she has planted seeds of healing and hope throughout the Church—indeed, throughout the world.

A Teacher for Our Time

By her writings, particularly *Story of a Soul*, but also by her letters, poems, and prayers, "Thérèse is a Teacher for our time," the pope pointed out, "a time which thirsts for living and essential words, for heroic and credible acts of witness. For this reason she is also loved and accepted by brothers and sisters of other Christian communities and even by non-Christians" (DAS 11).

Thérèse is a teacher for our time because she is virtually our contemporary, having lived in the cultural atmosphere of our day. She died young, but had she lived to be ninety years old, an age attained by two of her blood sisters, Pauline and Céline, Thérèse would have died in 1963.

As a contemporary of Freud, Jung, Darwin, Marx, Sartre, Nietzsche, and other formative thinkers and writers of our time, she lived in the climate of thought that has become the mentality of the modern and postmodern eras. The last half of the nineteenth century was *an age of inventions*, as Thérèse herself observed (SS 207). But it was not only an age of inventions; it was also an era of the establishment of many of the industrial, commercial, engineering, social, political, and economic projects, as well as much of the rapid developments and astonishing breakthroughs of science and technology, that are the foundation of our present way of life.

For our time, Thérèse's little way of spirituality contains the particular challenge to understand Jesus' message of God's love from a feminine perspective. Thérèse's "feminine genius" (DAS 11) supplements authentic contemporary masculine insights and brings to the Church's teaching a profound integration. The emphasis of her teaching provides a much needed corrective to any misreading of the Gospel and to any one-sided, mistaken views of theology and spirituality of our day.

In addition, Thérèse's life and teaching express the wisdom of a very sensitive, wise, mature young person who has endured the sufferings experienced by many of the hopeful youth as well as the tested elders of our time. She bore the painful contemporary sense of alienation and the search for true freedom, love, meaning, integrity, and peace. She faced the challenges of living a life of holiness with the inner conflicts of her own self-centeredness and willfulness. She endured the tension of remaining true to herself without being self-centered or subservient to the expectations of others. She addressed the issue of needing to be free from poisonous feelings of hostility, retaliation, and self-righteousness, which are the seeds of violence. She experienced the personal distress of abandonment and loneliness, and she engaged in the struggle of self-doubt and near despair. Feelings of helplessness and depression that many today experience in the grip of psychosomatic illnesses, addictions, and obsessions she also experienced.

During the last eighteen months of her life, dying of tuberculosis, she endured such physical pain, emotional distress, and spiritual darkness that she had momentary thoughts of suicide. She bore the felt experience of the atheist. The very modern and postmodern question of whether the afterlife really exists also invaded her own mind. She witnessed the uneasy interaction between science and religion as well as the disparity between spirituality lived as an expression of faith vision and religious observance lived as an expression of fear. The tension between faith and feelings, the ever-perplexing personal issue of how to live with difficult people, and the pressing problem of how to combat feelings of negativity and hostility toward oneself or others were all part of her experience.

Thérèse's life and teaching are especially significant for our time because she addressed a particularly contemporary question faced by all people, believers and nonbelievers alike, seeking love, justice, and peace. It is the question of how to cope with violence—the physical, moral, or psychological force that coerces and therefore diminishes or negates the free flourishing of human life and that produces emotional suffering, inflicts pain, or causes death to oneself or others.

During the last hundred years, there has been a dramatic display of violence on the personal and social level throughout the world. Some of this violence is itself an attempt to remedy grievous injustices and to confront violence. The violence of all-out war between states may be decreasing, but the violence associated with religious and political ideology, social uprisings, political corruption and greed, genocide, illicit drug use, human trafficking, sexism, racism, tribalism, abortion, poverty, domestic conflicts, and environmental destruction now exceeds previous periods of history. As Pope Benedict XVI said at the October 2011 Day of Reflection, Dialogue, and Prayer for Peace and Justice in the World held in Assisi, "Violence as such is potentially ever present, and it is a characteristic feature of our world."

Of course, Thérèse was not familiar with all of these aspects of violence, but she did recognize from her own experience and from the contemplation of the life of Jesus that authentic love is not compatible with violence of any kind. Authentic love is incompatible not only with the external violence of acts that inflict emotional pain, physical suffering, or death. Love is also incompatible with the toxic thoughts and feelings of fear, hostility, and self-centeredness that are at the root of external violence and that do internal violence to the human spirit of those who cultivate these attitudes.

Thérèse also recognized through each of her three formative experiences in *the science of love* that it is a mistake to think that there is a "holy," "good," or "sacred" violence that can be perpetrated in the name of God. She became aware that violence against oneself or others even in the attempt to produce good or end evil is incompatible with authentic love. She understood the practical ineffectiveness and ultimate spiritual incongruity of combating violence with more violence.

Violence is one of the "signs of our times." And when Pope John Paul II bestowed the title "Doctor" on Thérèse, he indicated an important contribution that the Doctors of the Church, and specifically Thérèse, make in helping the Church discern and address the signs of the times. He said that "the Lord has continued to reveal himself to the little and the humble" and that "in this way the Holy Spirit guides the Church into the whole truth . . . rejuvenating [the Church] with the power of the Gospel and enabling her [the Church] to discern the signs of the times in order to respond ever more fully to the will of God" (DAS 1). The pope went on to remark that "Thérèse's teaching expresses with coherence and harmonious unity the dogmas of the Christian faith." Her teaching thus contributes to "the understanding of the deposit of faith transmitted by the Apostles . . . [which] makes progress in the Church with the help of the Holy Spirit . . . through the contemplation and study of believers," of which Thérèse is the eminent example (DAS 7).

The example of Thérèse's life and the wisdom of her teaching contribute in a special way to the development of doctrine in the Church. By shedding a penetrating light on love and violence, Thérèse's "intimate sense of spiritual realities" (DAS 7) contributes to the progress that the Church makes in understanding the faith as well as discerning and responding to the signs of the times. Thérèse enables the Church, the hierarchy, and all the faithful "to respond ever more fully to the will of God" by revealing how Jesus' call to love contained in the Apostolic faith, the "deposit of faith," might be lived today. Her life and teaching affirm that violence is incompatible with Christian faith and love.

A Living Icon of God

In the decree proclaiming Thérèse a Doctor of the Church, Pope John Paul II stated that one of her important contributions to the modern Church was correcting the lingering errors of Jansenism. "She has made the Gospel shine appealingly in our time; she had the mission of making the Church, the Mystical Body of Christ, known and loved; she helped to heal souls of the rigors and fears of Jansenism, which tended to stress God's justice rather than his divine mercy. In God's mercy she contemplated and adored all the divine perfections, because, [as Thérèse said] *even His Justice (and perhaps even more so than the other perfections) seems to me clothed in love* [SS 180]. Thus she became a living icon of that God who, according to the Church's prayer, 'shows his almighty power in his mercy and forgiveness'" (DAS 8).

Jansenism was recognized as contrary to authentic Catholic teaching and was officially condemned as a heresy as early as the seventeenth century. Jansenism promotes, among other errors, the false image of God as punitive and vindictive, and it advocates a morality of fear. By healing souls of the rigors and fears of Jansenism, as the pope said, Thérèse has also helped heal the Church of the errors of Pelagianism and perfectionism as well. Pelagianism and perfectionism also popularly speak of God's justice as vengeful. These three distortions of Christian spirituality, popular in the teaching of the Church in Thérèse's day, were intertwined to form a whip of acceptable violence in the hand of God. Thérèse's focus on the reality that God's justice is *clothed in love* (SS 180) and her emphasis on God's mercy make Thérèse "a living icon of God."

The pope's declaration that Thérèse has become "a living icon of that God who . . . shows his almighty power in his mercy and forgiveness" is a bold statement affirming that Thérèse is a revelation of God for our time. As St. Paul invited the early Christians to "be imitators of me, as I am of Christ" (1 Corinthians 11:1), Thérèse, as "a living icon of God," could, in truth, say the same thing to people today. For people to experience the presence of God today, to hear the word of God, and to glimpse the countenance of God, it is enough, according to the pope, to encounter Thérèse and embrace her little way. Thérèse has become God's self-revelation for modern people.

From Thérèse shine forth with particular clarity the feminine dimensions of God's perfections, especially God's mercy and forgiveness. Correcting any contemporary misunderstanding of the nature of God, Thérèse's wisdom provides a vivid expression of the reality of God's desire that people be healed and set free of oppression, coercion, suffering, division, and despair, and live in reconciliation, hope, and love. Thérèse is "one of the great masters of the spiritual life in our time," the pope noted (DAS 3).

"When the magisterium proclaims someone a doctor of the Church," the pope observed in his homily at the Mass of proclamation, "it intends to point out to all the faithful, particularly to those who perform in the Church the fundamental service of preaching or who undertake the delicate task of theological teaching and research, that the doctrine professed and proclaimed by a certain person can be a reference point, not only because it conforms to revealed truth, but also because it sheds new light on the mysteries of the faith, a deeper understanding of Christ's mystery" (cf. DUC 159).

As a Doctor of the Church, and more especially as a "living icon of God," Thérèse can be regarded as a unique teacher of Church doctrine, shedding new light and deeper understanding on the Church's authentic teaching of Christ's mysteries today. The essential aspect of her message—that the love Jesus proclaims is love without violence—therefore must be regarded as a lens through which to read Church teaching and to understand the Sacred Scriptures.

At this time of diverging opinions, Thérèse's teaching can be profitably included in any discussion of the fundamental meaning of Church doctrine and in any search for the deepest understanding of the biblical text. Her wisdom is not just of casual interest and clearly not some kind of passing fad. It is not limited to some special school of spirituality or formative for only a special group, such as religious or women or young adults. Her teaching is not even one opinion among many. Her teaching participates in the official teaching of the Church.

Nor is Thérèse's message relevant only to Christians; it possesses a universal quality and has, in fact, been accepted and treasured by people of goodwill around the world. "*Thérèse possesses an exceptional universality*," the pope acknowledged. "Her person, the Gospel message of the 'little way' of trust and spiritual childhood have received and continue to receive a remarkable welcome, which has transcended every border" (DAS 10).

Her popularity continues to endure and to spread. People of faith recognize in her wisdom a genuinely modern expression of Jesus' message, and people of goodwill everywhere intuit that her teaching of *the science of love* is an important expression of the deepest and most authentic tendency of the human heart.

Her path as a way of love and peace is an invitation to every person of good-will and can be a challenge not only to individuals but also to societies.

Microcosm of the Science of Love

Thérèse lived most of her life in the confined physical, even isolated space of a cloistered, contemplative convent. Her relationships were few; perhaps not many more than fifty people knew her at the time of her death. Her interactions were limited, and they involved the very simple, ordinary give-and-take of daily life. In the usual routine and the relative seclusion of her life, Thérèse was able to concentrate her full and honest attention on the dynamics unfolding within her own heart. It was on these dynamics, in her own experiences of her daily interactions and responsibilities, that in faith she focused her great capacities for self-awareness and love. As she studied and prayed *the science of love* from the data of her own mundane experiences, her wisdom blossomed.

Through prayerful self-reflection on her spiritual journey, Thérèse came to know the depth of her self-centeredness, the extent of her God-inspired desires, and the role and significance of her thoughts, acts, and feelings in the spiritual life. Thérèse had a great self-confidence in her ability to be honest with herself and an enormous intuitive capacity about the ways of divine and human love. Under the microscope of faith and prayer, in her self-awareness, she came to learn universal truths about love: how love originates, how it is nourished or blocked, and how it grows. Her life became a microcosm of love; her teaching, a school of love.

As a microcosm, Thérèse's life reveals the essential dynamics of the flow of love in every human heart. Her teaching of *the science of love* sheds light on the lives of all those who seek peace and love. Her wisdom is particularly revealing to those who live with much more exterior complexity and whose responsibilities of productivity and leadership may far exceed her own. Thérèse calls those busy with exterior activities to come home to their hearts made in the image of Love, to express their deepest desires, to embrace a singular focus in their motivation, and to fulfill their destiny to love.

As a microcosm, Thérèse's life also sheds light on the grand social relationships that pervade societies and cultures. Her teaching has no schemes or formulas to solve the many difficult interactions and conflicts that pervade current societies and cultures and that sometimes result in violence. But a study of her wisdom regarding one-to-one human relationships may draw back the curtain on the question of what it might look like for the kingdom of God's love to begin to flourish within and among societies and cultures.

Thérèse's wisdom might suggest some answers to the question "What would be some of the patterns of desires, thoughts, feelings, and sentiments that must prevail in the human heart and be incorporated into the priorities of societies and cultures if peace is to begin to blossom in the world?"

Authentic peace and love on any scale, from the personal to the societal, are never without difficulties, and what love might involve can never be subjected to a formula or be completely determined in advance. But Thérèse came to understand what authentic love will not involve. Following the example of Jesus, she discerned that divine love and authentic human love do not endorse or promote any human violence or coercion that diminishes or eliminates the flourishing of human life. Thérèse's proclamation of love without violence, a modern expression of the Gospel, is *the* challenge for everyone of goodwill in our day seeking peace and love on the personal and social levels.

The Science of Love

To understand as well as live *the science of love* was the singular focus of Thérèse's desire and the quest of her entire life. Toward the end of her life, having gained a depth of wisdom, she wrote: *I desire only this science* [of love]. *. . . I understand so well that it is only love which makes us acceptable to God that this love is the only good I ambition. Jesus deigned to show me the road that leads to this Divine Furnace* [of God's love] *and this road is the surrender of the little child who sleeps without fear in its Father's arms* (SS 187–88).

When making her a Doctor of the Church, Pope John Paul II noted that "during her life Thérèse discovered *new lights, hidden and mysterious meanings* [SS 179] and received from the divine Teacher that *science of love* which she then expressed with particular originality in her writings. This science is the luminous expression of her knowledge of the mystery of the kingdom and of her personal experience of grace. It can be considered a special charism of Gospel wisdom which Thérèse, like other saints and teachers of faith, attained in prayer" (DAS 1).

Although Thérèse understood that she was called to practice *the science of love* in a spirit of self-surrender and gratitude of the little child without fear in the arms of God's love, she was continually challenged as she actually walked the path of love in the very ordinary experiences of life. At each step on the path of love, she was constantly learning what love might look like at any given moment. The details and particulars of how she might love arose unexpectedly and creatively. At the same time, the ambiguity of her motivation to love and her failures to feel, think, and act in love also surfaced unexpectedly. She became vigilant, constantly concerned that she might have strayed from the path of love, and she never assumed that her love path was ever finally completed. In fact, as she came to the end of her life, she found herself still preoccupied with the quest, and she asked explicitly the question that she had pondered her entire life: *Is God asking something more of me? Is He content with me? Is pure love in my heart? Are my measureless desires* [to live a life of love] *only but a dream, a folly?* (SS 191, 197).

Having canonized Thérèse a saint and having named her a Doctor of the Church, the Church has answered her questions and affirmed her life of love. Thérèse had indeed learned and lived *the science of love*. God's *pure love* did flow in her heart. She had taken *the road* of self-surrender into God's loving *arms*, and her *measureless desires* to live a life of love were not a dream or a folly. Her desires had been fulfilled and the quest of her life had been attained. Her prayer at the end of her life had been answered. She had prayed, *Jesus, my Love; . . . my vocation, at last I have found it. . . . MY VOCATION IS LOVE! . . . I shall be Love* (SS 194). And to the present day, God's love continues to radiate from her as from an icon.

Thérèse had desired to read *in the book of life* (SS 187) the depths of *the science of love*, and that is what she has done. By prayerful self-reflection on her daily experiences, especially by being aware of her feelings, thoughts, and actions, Thérèse learned whether she was actually living the vocation of love or whether she was acting out of self-centered egoism. We now follow her in her journey of walking the path of love by exploring in detail in the next chapters Thérèse's three core experiences on that path. We will notice in particular Thérèse's heart qualities that helped her stay true to the path of love, that enlightened her to attain the wisdom of *the science of love*, and that empowered her to fulfill her vocation to love.

Thérèse's Experience of Complete Conversion

Thérèse (right) at eight years old with her
sister Céline in 1881

CHAPTER 2

Is Pure Love In My Heart?

PRACTICING VIRTUE IN A STRANGE WAY

Thérèse's spiritual life, her path of love, was clearly developmental. Actually, her path was not as linear as it was spiral. Returning again and again to the same basic issues surrounding how to love, her path spiraled down into greater depths of self-awareness and simultaneously spiraled up into more sublime clarity of insights into *the science of love* and into the reality of God's love embracing her. She learned through her own experiences each day, not only the deep spiritual wisdom of love, but also the transcendent potential for love in the simple, ordinary experiences of life. She also recognized the ways that love was blocked in her heart and learned that she sometimes stepped off the path of love. She grew in her ways of cultivating love in her thoughts and feelings even as she continued throughout her life to ask herself, "Am I living in love or living in secret self-centeredness? *Is pure love in my heart?*" (SS 197).

And above all, she came at the end of her life to know that when she loved authentically, her love was really not "her" love at all but was divine love in her. In the act of authentic love, her self-centered ego was dissolved, and she lived and loved now, no longer her, but Christ in her (cf. Galatians 2:20). This reality, which allowed her to surrender into the depths of confidence and love, became the heartbeat of her little way of spirituality.

Practicing virtue in a strange way

Thérèse's education in *the science of love* began in her childhood years. She was taught early in life that as an expression of love, she should be self-giving especially to her parents, to her four older sisters, and to her relatives. A week before her fourteenth birthday, she had a very special experience, however, that alerted her to aspects of her motivation and to the dimensions of love that she had not fully noticed before. That experience, which Thérèse called her "*complete conversion*," she fully described in her autobiography and referred to it again in one of her late letters. Both references were almost ten years after the event had occurred (SS 97–98; GC 1016). She clearly believed that her conversion radically changed the course of her life. It was an experience utterly private, personal, and transformative. It was an experience that she prayerfully treasured and pondered for the rest of her days, entering into the reality of its profound meaning.

That Thérèse needed a *complete conversion* at this early childhood age, as she ended her thirteenth year, no one but Thérèse herself knew. Those in the household thought that Thérèse was just about perfect, and her father, who affectionately called her his "little queen," had already canonized her as a saint. Only Thérèse herself knew at the time that something had been going wrong within her heart. She had, however, no clear insight into exactly what the issue might be. All she recognized was that during the last several years, she had not been fully at peace. She was also beginning to notice two sources of her inner disturbance, two red flags that warned her that all was not well.

One source of her unrest was a certain ambiguity in her motivation. She wrote later, *I had a great desire, it is true, to practice virtue, but I went about it in a strange way* (SS 97). Fulfilling a desire that had arisen within her as a young child, she tried consciously to do everything to please God; however, she noticed a contrary pattern at work within her.

When her older sister Céline was away, *I'd bring in her plants*, she wrote. *But . . . it was for God alone I was doing these things and should not have expected any thanks from creatures. Alas,* she saw with misgivings, *it was just the opposite. If Céline was unfortunate enough not to seem happy or surprised because of these little services, I became unhappy and proved it by my tears* (SS 97).

On the one hand, Thérèse was consciously trying to practice virtue to please God alone. On the other hand, she recognized that she felt disappointed when her acts of virtue were not noticed and her sister was not grateful. This Thérèse experienced as *a strange way to practice virtue,* and indeed, it was this strange inability to have a singular motivation that became her first warning signal that something was amiss within her heart.

The truth was that Thérèse's acts of kindness carried some subtle and disguised self-centeredness, and this emerging recognition was disturbing her peace. Thérèse's ambiguous motives were prompted by her personal hidden needs—needs to be noticed and so to feel connected, secure, and approved. She was caught in the clutches of not wanting to displease others in the family lest she experience the distress of not feeling connected, supported, and appreciated.

She also naturally wished to conform to the prevailing family pattern of pleasing others at almost any price, a pattern that further disguised the ambiguity of her motives. Her so-called virtues as practiced *in a strange way* did not really issue from love, and so were precisely microexamples of St. Paul's comments about not doing the good that he wanted to do but rather doing what he hated, even seeming to have all faith and moving mountains but without charity (cf. Romans 7:15; 1 Corinthians 13:1ff.).

In addition, Thérèse's own natural grace-given inclination was to accommodate and please others. However, this tendency, unbalanced and excessive, was becoming a dominant feature in Thérèse's expressive style. Who she really was, in the complexity of her being, was being undermined by the benefits gained from simply pleasing others. She was finding her sense of identity, security, and self-worth in the affirmation of others, but in doing so, she was losing her true self and inner freedom. She was beginning to move along a human path that would come to be called codependency. She had only the vaguest sense, however, that her lack of peace had to do with her taking small steps in not being true to herself, in compromising her fundamental desire to please God alone.

God was pleased all through my life to surround me with love

Thérèse's inner peace was disturbed not only by her awareness that she was practicing virtue *in a strange way*. There was a second red flag as well. Her second and related awareness that something was not right within her heart was her inability to manage her excessive feelings. Her mother had died when Thérèse was four and a half years old, and since that time, the power of Thérèse's feelings had been a constant source of distress for her.

Everyone who knew Thérèse as a child believed that she had had a favored childhood. Truly she had been gifted with a pleasant, loving nature, and from birth she had been embraced with love. She had been surrounded by affection and protection, and as the youngest of a family that had already lost four young children, she had been particularly treasured by her parents and her four sisters. But other emotional dynamics had also been at play within the child's heart.

Because of breast cancer, her mother, Zélie, had not been able to breast-feed the infant Thérèse. Advised by her doctor, therefore, her mother gave little Thérèse, only three months old, to Rose Taillé to be nursed. Rose had nursed two of Zélie's previous infants, and although both had died, Thérèse's mother still maintained great confidence in her. Zélie later acknowledged that Rose had indeed saved Thérèse's life. Thérèse lived with Rose and her family at the Taillé family farm from her third month until her fifteenth month.

Rose truly loved Thérèse with a constant, tender affection, but during that year with Rose, the infant Thérèse experienced subtle emotional insecurity. Thérèse was no longer with her mother; she had the natural feelings of separation and abandonment. Also, as part of Rose's thoughtful care for the young child, she brought Thérèse, usually weekly, from the farm to the town to be with her mother and family. At these times, Rose herself was busy at the market selling her farm produce and buying her supplies. In these circumstances, Thérèse was experiencing herself being loved but by two mothers and being welcomed but into two homes. So for all of the affection Thérèse received during those first months, the separation from her own mother, family, and home, compounded by the ambiguous message the infant received from the weekly back-and-forth visits, weakened Thérèse's emotional stability.

After the year of separation, when she returned permanently to her family, Thérèse's conduct toward her mother testified to the powerful need the infant had to establish the security of unwavering maternal attachment. At that time also, Thérèse's behavior toward all the family members focused on her need to maintain the feeling of unambiguous bonding to compensate for the fear of again being abandoned and to hold firmly to the certainty of being "home" (cf. EIG 52–55; 62ff.).

Welcomed back to her own family by her four sisters and loving parents, and now surrounded by the warmth and security of home, Thérèse entered a time of great personal joy. During the next three years before her mother's death, Thérèse gradually gained emotional balance and lived a life of increasing contentment, peace, and childhood bliss. Remembering those early years, she wrote, *God was pleased all through my life to surround me with love, and the first memories I have are stamped with smiles and the most tender caresses. . . . He [God] also sent much love into my little heart, making it warm and affectionate* (SS 17).

But what Thérèse did not remember were the feelings of having been abandoned nor the feelings of insecurity she had experienced during those twelve months that she had lived in the Taillé household apart from her own mother and family. Thérèse was not consciously aware of these difficult feelings, and she did not write about them in her memoirs. Nevertheless, the sensitive heart of Thérèse had been emotionally wounded, not because of the malice of anyone, but by the inevitable sufferings of the human condition. No child emerges without wounds from childhood, and Thérèse was not exempted. The wound in her heart continued to affect her for the rest of her life, and in a providential way, it influenced her unique spiritual path.

Neither did I speak to anyone about the feelings I experienced

With the death of her mother, Thérèse at four and a half years old again experienced the eruption of those early, primal feelings of having been abandoned, of separation and loss, that had taken hold of her heart during those first fragile, formative fifteen months of her life. These feelings erupted in what Thérèse later referred to simply as *extreme touchiness* (SS 97) and *excessive sensitivity* (SS 34). They often surfaced in episodes of melancholy and weeping.

My happy disposition completely changed after Mamma's death, she wrote. *I, once so full of life, became timid and retiring, sensitive to an excessive degree. One look was enough to reduce me to tears, and the only way I was content was to be left alone completely* (SS 34–35). The passing of her mother ended Thérèse's three years of childhood happiness. Over the next ten years, she would constantly seek to recapture that happy childhood of spontaneity, self-confidence, and pervading, carefree joy. With the loss of her mother, Thérèse also lost a part of herself.

Years later, Thérèse recalled the scene standing beside her mother's open casket. *Papa took me in his arms and said: "Come, kiss your poor little Mother for the last time." Without a word I placed my lips on her forehead. I don't recall having cried very much, neither did I speak to anyone about the feelings I experienced. I looked and listened in silence*, she wrote with a touch of sadness for that young child. *No one had any time to pay any attention to me, and I saw many things they would have hidden from me* (SS 33).

Thérèse refused to make known her own needs to be consoled, even as feelings of insecurity, abandonment, and isolation were sweeping over her. Having seen her father sobbing at her mother's last sacramental anointing, Thérèse was sensitive to his sorrow, but also, perhaps, she feared that her own cry for help would simply have been lost in the family anguish. The least hint of not being understood would have only deepened Thérèse's terrible sadness. Grief overwhelmed her. She tightly held her feelings in secret, and Thérèse's heart plunged into a dark tunnel.

To calm her pain and to try to find her way through her distress, Thérèse became withdrawn, timid, and shy. Those rich, joyful, spontaneous qualities of her childhood nature completely vanished. She took the first step on a ten-year solitary path into a pervasive gray sadness that she later would call *the winter of my soul* (SS 34; cf. EIG 72ff.).

I'd begin to cry again for having cried

Her mother's death thrust Thérèse into what she described as *the second period of my existence, the most painful of the three* [periods of her life]. . . . *This period extends from the age of four and a half* [the time of her mother's death] *to that of fourteen* [the experience of her complete conversion], *the time when I found once again my childhood character* (SS 34).

Reflecting back on this time, Thérèse remembered, *Before I entered* [the convent of Carmel, the ten years following her mother's death], *when I woke up in the morning I used to think about what the day could possibly have in store for me, happy or troublesome, and if I foresaw only troubles, I got up depressed* (TLMT 104).

During this period she did have some times of delight and happiness, but the state of joy and the childhood spirit of carefree peace that had filled Thérèse's early years had vanished into an encompassing gloominess, a mild lingering depression. Thérèse was now controlled by feelings of loss and insecurity that surfaced as melancholy, withdrawal, and *extreme touchiness* (SS 97).

Just two months before Thérèse's complete conversion and almost ten years after her mother's death, she described a visit she took with the family to the site of her mother's grave. *I cannot express the tears I shed on Mamma's grave because I had forgotten to bring the bouquet of corn-flowers I had gathered especially for her. I really made a big fuss over everything!* . . . *I was still only a child who appeared to have no will but that of others, and this caused certain people . . . to say I had a weak character* (SS 91).

She was upset when she noticed what others had been saying about her, but more important, she knew within herself that she needed to grow in self-control and not make *a big fuss over everything*. However, she felt helpless by her inability to cope with her powerful feelings and excessive sensitivity. *I was really unbearable because of my extreme touchiness,* she wrote, describing this period (SS 97).

She recognized her excessive sensitivity when she reflected on experiences in which her reactions were out of proportion. She gave an example: *If I happened to cause anyone I loved some little trouble, even unwittingly, instead of forgetting about it and not crying, which made matters worse, I cried like a Magdalene and then when I began to cheer up, I'd begin to cry again for having cried* (SS 97). Her distress at her extreme sensitivity and at the automatic behavior that flowed from it then became the source of more distress. She was finding herself in that cyclic, obsessive pattern that characterizes addiction and compulsivity.

Now within a week of her fourteenth birthday, Thérèse saw herself as *still in the swaddling clothes of a child!* (SS 97). She was a child in the grip of her feelings, always on the edge of losing herself to the control of her *extreme touchiness*. She knew she was not growing emotionally or spiritually.

During the ten years since her mother's death, she had been calming her upsetting feelings by engaging in the family pattern of pleasing others in her neediness to feel close, bonded, and secure. Her contribution to the family pattern also allowed her father and sisters to assume their roles in the pattern as well, taking care of her emotionally, affirming her, and even pampering her.

Everyone in the family was too ready to help Thérèse. Here was a responsive, genuinely good and pleasing child who was experiencing a pervading melancholy. She was sometimes in poor health; she had nearly died from a strange illness; she was burdened by headaches and had endured a period of scruples; she was often on the verge of tears and constantly on the threshold of sadness. All of this moved her four loving sisters and her father to overlook Thérèse's moodiness and to accommodate her excessive sensitivity (cf. EIG 67–120).

The family attributed to her the best of intentions and adjusted to her pervading emotional immaturity. No one in the family except her Uncle Isidore doubted that Thérèse's *extreme touchiness* was a quality of nature, even a gift of nature. They believed that as she grew older, she would either grow out of her touchiness naturally, or if it were truly a gift, she would integrate it appropriately.

Thérèse herself had noticed this family pattern of accommodating her. She was especially aware that *Céline wanted to continue treating me as a baby since I was the youngest in the family* (SS 98). She recognized that her father also enjoyed the teenage Thérèse in her role as the baby, his little queen. Thérèse was too kind and too needy to confront this characterization of herself that *I was still only a child who appeared to have no will but that of others* and that certain people said *I had a weak character* (SS 91). It had begun to disturb her, but she was also benefiting from it.

Some of her important needs were met by taking on the role of the baby. At the mercy of her excessive feelings, she could not stand her ground emotionally, and this weakness was precisely the red flag signaling to Thérèse that she needed to grow up and be true to herself.

Even after noticing that she was being controlled by her feelings, Thérèse could have continued in secret on this mistaken path. However, two personal and interrelated gifts had been developing within her since her mother's death, and these surfaced to her rescue: her sensitive conscience and her longing for the truth (cf. SS 25). Thérèse would not deny her conscience, and her desire for personal authenticity and truth was actually the graced longing to be filled with the Spirit of truth, the Holy Spirit (cf. EIG 64ff.). At the end of her life, she would pray, *O my God, I really want to listen to you. I beg you to answer me when I say humbly: What is truth? Make me see things as they really are. Let nothing cause me to be deceived. Yes, it seems to me I never sought anything but the truth* (HLC 105; MSST 21; cf. GC 862). But for now, at some level of consciousness, she knew that she had strayed from the path of truth.

This terrible fault

As Thérèse searched for her true self at one with the Spirit of truth, that Spirit, already possessing her, was crying out in her flood of frequent tears. Her tears were actually welling up in opposition to this false pattern she had been following since the loss of her mother. Her weeping was trying to reveal and bring peace to the war within herself—the conflict between the longing of her true self to do everything freely for God and her weakness of being controlled by her excessive feelings. She was glimpsing the truth that in her *extreme touchiness*, she really no longer had her feelings; rather, at such times her feelings had her in their power. Her loss of inner freedom to her feelings and her lack of peace warned her of the inner war between her true self and her self-centered, self-indulgent ego.

In the delicacy of her sensitive conscience, Thérèse was experiencing the conflict and admitted both her own helplessness and the latent seriousness of the pattern: *I was quite unable to correct this terrible fault* (SS 97). She was also aware that her *extreme touchiness* that contributed to her inability to manage her feelings involved some degree of culpability. By constantly giving way in self-indulgence to excessive feelings, she was allowing herself to make *a big fuss over everything*. Thérèse recognized that by permitting Céline *to continue treating* [her] *as a baby*, she was responsible and knew furthermore that this was not a minor matter.

Under the influence of sheer grace, she began to see her situation as a *terrible fault*, a personal compromise tearing at her heart, a conflict within herself diverting her from the path of being authentic to herself. At her mother's grave, she had also gotten a brief glimpse of the fact that her inner conflict was fueled by the feelings of disappointment, confusion, and hostility that she felt against herself for still having a *weak character*, for making a *big fuss over everything*. She wept in embarrassment and distress.

Most important, she accepted her responsibility, and further, she was aware of her helplessness in the grip of her powerful feelings. She had tried in vain for almost ten years to pull herself out of her enduring dark tunnel of *extreme touchiness*, melancholy, and self-preoccupation. She had tried also with her best efforts to overcome her timidity and her propensity to permit *one look . . . to reduce me to tears*, and she had struggled with the illusion that *the only way I was content was to be left alone completely* (SS 34–35). Powerless, she knew that only the power of God could rescue her. She expressed herself simply: *God would have to work a little miracle to make me grow up* (SS 97). And God had already been preparing Thérèse to receive that little miracle.

CHAPTER 3

I Was Still in the Swaddling Clothes of a Child!

NEEDING A LITTLE MIRACLE

In her memoirs, Thérèse identifies many personal heroes, Joan of Arc among them, but she compares herself most often with Mary Magdalene. Thérèse thought of Magdalene when she wrote about her need of a miracle to be free from the oppression of her excessive feelings. *I cried like a Magdalene,* Thérèse noted at this time. Describing herself as being overwhelmed by her *extreme touchiness*, she explained that *when I began to cheer up, I'd begin to cry again for having cried.* Then, noticing that even her good judgment and reason were powerless in the control of her feelings, she added, *All arguments were useless* (SS 97).

Jesus has forgiven me more than Saint Mary Magdalene

Thérèse also identified with Magdalene when she reflected on an experience with a friend that had occurred four or so years before her conversion. She was about ten years old and was attending the Benedictine Abbey school as a day student. That experience also alerted her to her *extreme touchiness.*

Her school years were another time of difficult feelings for her. In her shyness and continuing melancholy and having never associated with peers who were so rough and rude, Thérèse was unprepared for the petty malice that she would encounter in her relationships with her schoolmates. Although outstanding academically, socially she was a failure. She became the object of jealousy and childish cruelty and recalled later that *I didn't know how to defend myself and was content to cry without saying a word and without complaining* (SS 53). Even though she was being supported and sometimes even protected by her sister Céline, who also attended the school, nonetheless, Thérèse later wrote that *the five years I spent in school were the saddest in my life* (SS 53).

During her school experience, Thérèse did manage to begin to establish one peer friendship, which, however, proved to be short-lived. But importantly, the relationship was revelatory. On one occasion early in the relationship, separated from her little girlfriend for a few months, Thérèse became characteristically sad. She described her experience when her friend returned. *When I saw my companion back,* Thérèse noted passionately, *again my joy was great, but all I received from her was a cold glance. My love was not understood* (SS 82). Her friend had simply forgotten about her. Thérèse had given her heart to her friend, and her friend had not noticed. For Thérèse, this was another experience of being emotionally abandoned, an experience of loss, separation, and of being paid no attention. The childhood wound in her affectionate heart was reopened (cf. EIG 106–8).

Thérèse again withdrew emotionally as she had withdrawn after her mother's death. In her desire not to complain or disturb others and to avoid further pain, she again hid her own needs and took her own counsel. She did not discuss her hurt feelings with anyone, not even her family, and did not even mention them to her friend. She did not blame her friend. Her reticence, however, was not denial, nor was it just because of her timidity or simply the fear of experiencing further separation. She seems to have had an intuition that speaking carelessly about her feelings might have defused the power of the truth about herself that the feelings could reveal.

Recalling her experience of her First Communion, which occurred at about this same time, she wrote that *there are certain things* [profound joys] *that lose their perfume as soon as they are exposed to the air* and that *there are deep spiritual thoughts which cannot be expressed in human language without losing their intimate and heavenly meaning* (SS 77). Perhaps she had a similar intuitive sense that the same was true of deep personal hurts: that speaking of them would dissipate their important personal revelatory meaning.

During her five years at the school, she had many personal experiences of ridicule, gossip, and negative comments among her classmates. She may have suspected that talking of her hurt even to her friend would have resulted in an exchange of rationalizations, excuses, subtle blaming, and apologies that would have contaminated the inner processing that she needed to do alone. Thérèse, with or without full consciousness, did not want anything to destroy the power of the *intimate and heavenly meaning* hidden in that experience of loss and rejection. She prayerfully pondered her experience silently within the solitude of her own heart, and there she reaped *deep spiritual thoughts.*

Thérèse understood that in this childhood relationship with her friend, she could have easily fallen into the false love of infatuation that would have undermined her true self. *My heart, sensitive and affectionate as it was,* she later recognized, *would have easily surrendered had it found a heart capable of understanding it* (SS 82).

As Thérèse recalled this experience some twelve years later, she again compared herself with Mary Magdalene. In light of the scriptural teachings of her day, Thérèse would have imagined Magdalene stumbling on that most dangerous path of compromising herself even into adultery until she met Jesus. Thérèse described her experience with her classmate: *I was preserved from it* [infatuation and emotional attachment] *only through God's mercy! I know that without Him, I could have fallen as low as St. Mary Magdalene.* Then she added, *I also know that Jesus has forgiven me more than St. Mary Magdalene since He forgave me in advance by preventing me from falling* (SS 83).

He has forgiven me not much but ALL

Through the rejection of her little friend, Thérèse became more aware that with her heart so sensitive, she could have allowed herself *to be taken and my wings to be clipped, and then how would I have been able to "fly and be at rest"?* [Psalm 55:7] (SS 83). She recognized that she was capable of walking the path of personal compromise. *My heart, sensitive and affectionate as it was, would have easily surrendered* (SS 82), she had written, and she knew that such a surrender would have been a complete loss of personal inner freedom.

The feeling of rejection by her friend could be considered a small event in Thérèse's life, and apparently her friend thought nothing of it. For the sensitive Thérèse, however, it was an experience that resulted in a personal awareness and a spiritual revelation. She came to appreciate more fully her own personal weakness and the reality of God's preventive, protective love in her life, which had saved her from being *taken,* of compromising herself even in this slight way. *How can I thank Jesus for making me find only bitterness in earth's friendships!* (SS 83).

Years later, still reflecting on this failed friendship and continuing to compare herself to Mary Magdalene, Thérèse composed the parable of the caring physician, embodying the theme of God's loving in advance. In the first scenario of her parable, a physician's child stumbles on a stone in his path and breaks a limb. The father immediately attends to the child, and he is cured. The child is grateful. In the second scenario, the father sees the stone before the child does and removes it without the child's noticing. Not knowing his father's love in advance, the child does not express any appreciation, but when he learns of the father's loving foresight, he loves his father even more. *Well, I am this child*, Thérèse said, *the object of the foreseeing love of a Father who has not sent His Word to save the just, but sinners. He wants me to love Him because He has forgiven me not much but ALL. He has not expected me to love Him much like Mary Magdalene, but He has willed that I know how He has loved me with a love of unspeakable foresight in order that now I may love Him unto folly!* (SS 84).

Thérèse would have seen Mary Magdalene as having been both a great lover and a great sinner. Most important, Thérèse would have thought of her as wasting her youthful passion in falseness and self-deception. Mary Magdalene was the woman in the Gospel who tried to overcome her feelings of neediness and to establish her identity, security, and self-worth in compromising relationships. Magdalene had been on the verge of selling her soul. She had been living a lie until Jesus came into her life. Jesus raised Mary Magdalene to her own dignity as a child of God and as a person called to live in personal authenticity without compromise. Thérèse would have believed that Magdalene was physically promiscuous, and Thérèse identified with Magdalene. She understood that she herself could also easily have become promiscuous—not in the physically compromising way of Magdalene, but in a spiritual, emotional way.

Like Magdalene, Thérèse shed copious tears over her state of complete weakness and personal inability to change. She needed to meet Jesus in a way that would transform her.

Years later, as she continued to learn from this childhood experience of her relationship with her little friend as well as from her failed attempts to befriend some of her teachers, Thérèse posed to herself this question: *How can a heart given over to the affection of creatures be intimately united to God?* With the self-knowledge of her own natural tendencies, with her weaknesses and gifts, with her own inner wounds and limitations, she believed that she would have to answer that question in the negative: *I feel this is not possible* (SS 83).

Thérèse understood that this was a discernment only about herself. She did not denounce others who were more capable of legitimate and deep friendships. She had seen others, particularly her own family members, in healthy relationships. She knew, however, that she was excessively prone to attachments, and thus, she reflected, *a heart given over to the affection of creatures . . . was not* [possible] *for me, for I encountered only bitterness where stronger souls met with joy, and they detached themselves from* [any temptation] *through fidelity* (SS 83). After several years of experience in the convent observing the relationships among the sisters, Thérèse wrote, *Without having drunk the empoisoned cup of a too ardent love of creatures, I feel I cannot be mistaken. I have seen so many souls, seduced by this false light* [of false friendship] (SS 83).

It was only near the end of her life, when *God . . .* [gave] *me the grace to understand what charity is* (SS 219), that Thérèse would trust herself to human friendships beyond her family members. Having come to a greater capacity for detachment, Thérèse came to know that love of God and love of neighbor are not two different loves. The grace of that knowledge was the blessing of freedom and joy that blossomed in her human friendships with the sisters.

He frightened me

Now Thérèse, acutely aware of her weaknesses and helplessness and nearing her fourteen birthday, simply prayed for a miracle of *complete conversion* that would allow Jesus to embrace her with his transforming power. Thérèse's need for a miracle was not a matter of her avoiding a particular sin and acquiring a particular virtue. She was not deliberately opposing grace. She prayed that God would move her from the path bordering on compromising herself to the path of personal authenticity, inner freedom, and integrity. Her identity, security, and self-worth needed to be established in her relationship with God alone. Only the inner strength of union with God would allow her to bear in peace the distressing, lingering primary feelings of having been abandoned, of separation and loss that were at the core of her excessive neediness and sensitivity.

Thérèse's Uncle Isidore seems to have been the only person besides Thérèse herself who sensed that she was wallowing in some kind of emotional mire. Although Thérèse knew that her uncle had a deep fondness for her—*he used to call me his little ray of sunshine*, she remembered—she never seemed to feel completely at ease in his presence. *I didn't like it when he asked me questions*, she wrote (SS 42). Later in her life, she would respect him as a saint (GC 908), but as a child, she found him to be brusque, without the supporting, bonding attitude she so desired and needed.

When Uncle Isidore placed *me on his knee and sang Blue Beard in a formidable tone of voice*, he scared Thérèse half to death. *He frightened me*, she wrote (SS 42, 35; GC 765). By contrast, when her mild and accommodating father took her on his lap, he would gently rock her, and she delighted listening to him sing *in his beautiful voice, airs that filled the soul with profound thoughts* (SS 43). Isidore, moreover, thought that Thérèse was softhearted, of a weak character, and sentimental. She was humiliated by this assessment.

A short time after the rejection by her little friend, Thérèse experienced another minor but highly significant "rejection," this time by her uncle. She and Céline were staying at his home while their father was away on a pilgrimage. Her uncle had occasion to talk with Thérèse about her mother's death, which had occurred almost six year before. By then, Isidore had brought peace to his own feelings over the loss of his sister. He wanted to share with his niece fond memories of her mother and invited Thérèse to speak with him about her own sentiments. She experienced her uncle's invitation as a rejection of her sensitivities, reopening all the enduring painful memories and distressing feelings of loss and abandonment lingering in her heart. Thérèse began to weep uncontrollably.

Isidore was troubled by Thérèse's crying, but more so, he was annoyed at what he considered her maudlin, childish behavior. He thought his niece was allowing her feelings to control her, and in his irritation, he suspected that she might be doing this out of a kind of self-indulgence.

This may not have been the first time he entertained the idea that Thérèse might not be perfect; that she might have a dark side to her nature and that she might indeed bear some responsibility for her melancholic state. He was the only family member to seriously consider this possibility. Now breaking the family pattern of simply trying to please, he was not afraid to tell her bluntly that she *was too soft-hearted*. He announced that he would help her overcome her brooding. He had decided, Thérèse remembered, *that I needed a lot of distraction, and he was determined to give us* [Thérèse and her sister Céline] *a good time during our Easter vacation. He and Aunt would see to it* (SS 60).

Uncle Isidore had resolved that on that very evening, in spite of Thérèse's weeping, he would take her, Céline, and his own daughters to the Catholic Circle meeting, a social club for young adults, and give them an opportunity for some dancing and socializing (cf. GC 348). He thought that it would do them all a great deal of good to forget any sadness they might still be carrying. Of course, socializing, music, and dancing were the last things that Thérèse wanted in her present state of disturbance, and besides, by this time, she was nurturing a growing desire to enter the convent. The entire episode was a complete break in the family pattern of being sensitive, accommodating, and pleasing. Thérèse was terrified. She again withdrew into herself as into a fortress, and the episode precipitated a traumatic illness in her that lasted seven weeks and from which she was finally rescued by the smile that she saw on the face of her bedside statue of the Virgin Mary (cf. EIG 90–95).

Her interaction with her uncle, like the interaction with her little classmate friend, had hurt Thérèse, and both were personal revelations that alerted her to her own weakness. She had learned much from her little friend's rejection, but she was too frightened to learn deeply from her uncle. And neither incident was enough to move Thérèse from her misguided path.

The need to grow up

Thérèse sensed that, with her mother's passing, she had lost her *strength of soul*. Now, as she approached her fourteen birthday, she realized that if she didn't regain her *childhood character*, she would eventually wither spiritually (SS 98, 34). Her real nature had to bud forth, with all its childlike simplicity and beauty, with all its originality, spontaneity, and creativity, with all its inner freedom, allowing her to be her true self with integrity and love. Then she would be on the authentic path of entering the realm of those possessing the spirit of children to whom Jesus promised the kingdom (cf. Matthew 19:14). She would be on the path of becoming the person that God called her to be. She spoke of this simply as the need to *grow up* (SS 97).

She recognized that *I was still in the swaddling clothes of a child!* (SS 97). It was the need to become more deeply her true self, "so that we may no longer be infants, tossed by waves and swept along by every wind of teaching" (Ephesians 4:14), as St. Paul wrote, but to be carried by the breath of the Holy Spirit. Only her true self could bear in peace the distressing, lingering primary feelings of separation and loss that were at the core of her excessive neediness and sensitivity.

When those early feelings of having been abandoned resurfaced within Thérèse, she thought she needed the security, recognition, and praise of others. What she really needed was the inner strength—*the strength of soul*—founded on her own conscience and established on the truth of her union with her loving God. She really needed to enfold her feelings into faith, and this she knew she was unable to do by her own efforts. She needed *a little miracle* (SS 97, 98).

CHAPTER 4

That Unforgettable Christmas Day

WELCOMING COMPLETE CONVERSION

Thérèse's lack of inner peace had alerted her that her fundamental orientation of love was being diverted from the authentic path of love and that she was, in some way, engaging in a *terrible fault* (SS 97). She had an intuition that the compass of love in her heart was off center. She also knew, after almost ten years of effort, that she herself could not set that compass right, because the only resource she could think to use to set it right was her own effort, and that itself was flawed and just off center. She recognized that *God would have to work a little miracle to make me grow up, and this miracle He performed on that unforgettable Christmas day* (SS 97).

Thérèse's conversion miracle was indeed a "little" miracle. It has none of the drama of the conversion stories that are found in the lives of the saints. But for Thérèse herself, it was a miracle of momentous proportions. It was really an ordinary experience, a casual remark that pierced through all of Thérèse's emotional defenses and broke her heart, and through that break, light shone on *hidden and mysterious meanings* (SS 179). The conversion was an inner transformation with few outward manifestations.

Those words which pierced my heart

On that *unforgettable Christmas day*, as Thérèse remembered it, she had just returned with her sister Céline and her father from Christmas midnight Mass. It was about 1:30 in the morning, and entering their living room from the starlit night, her father noticed the slippers that Céline had arranged by the fireplace. It was a custom similar to that of hanging stockings on the mantle, to be filled with sweets and trivial goodies. It was a custom that Céline had continued even into Thérèse's teen years, part of the family ritual for the amusement of their father and a way to continue treating Thérèse as the baby of the family.

On this evening as on past Christmas evenings, Thérèse would engage in a demonstration of childish enthusiasm as she took the gifts from the shoes, and by this feigned display of exuberance would engage and please her father. She was his "little queen" and he was her "king" (cf. EIG 124–29). Thérèse was a teenager pretending to believe in Santa Claus and playing the childish role of the baby of the family in petty fantasy and pretended delight to entertain her father. But on this Christmas, at this early morning hour and after the lengthy religious service, her father was tired and irritated. He was not his usual self, and he was not amused at the prospect of playing along with this childishness, even with his little queen.

Thérèse was on her way upstairs to her room to take off her coat and hat to prepare for the charade. Her father turned aside and said to Céline, who was lingering near the fireplace with him, "Well, fortunately, this will be the last year!" (SS 98). Sharing with Céline his frustration and criticizing Thérèse's immature style, he was saying, in effect, "When will Thérèse ever grow up?"

Her father did not intend that Thérèse would hear his remark, which was made in fatigue and annoyance. He would never have wanted to offend his little queen. But his little queen did hear and, as she said, the *words . . . pierced my heart.* Tears came to her eyes (SS 98).

Thérèse experienced her father's displeasure just as she had experienced her Uncle Isidore's criticism, which had also wounded her heart and prompted her weeping. She had never been sure of her safety with her uncle, and she had spontaneously defended herself against the impact of her uncle's force. This Christmas Day, however, she was stronger, and she was safe at home in the presence of her beloved father and her soul sister, Céline.

Thérèse let the truth of her father's words, even with its terrible pain, to invade her heart. Her father's remark was shocking; it was devastating. It tore the fabric of Thérèse's desires to show her love for her father, to be his pleasing little queen. To fail to show love for her father, particularly on a Christmas Day, the day God showed such great love, would have been unimaginable for Thérèse. Since her mother's death, her father had bonded with Thérèse as both a mother and father. How could she wound his heart, his *very affectionate heart* [that] *seemed to be enriched now with a truly maternal love* (SS 35)? He was the primary and most significant person in Thérèse's life. And she had hurt him.

Her father's words pained her deeply, not only because she had offended her father and been criticized by him, but because the words also threw her into the dreadful awareness that she was a failure in the area of her life in which she had tried to establish her sense of perfection, identity, and self-worth. She had imagined herself to be the good and virtuous one who loved others by pleasing them. This had been her ego-based identity, secured by the affirmation of the family and especially by her father, who loved her. If she were not the selfless, perfect, loving, pleasing young girl, who was she?

The criticism of her father shattered the self-image of who she thought she was. It destroyed her sense of self. It threatened her very survival. The ground of her existence was falling away, and she felt thrust to the very edge of a dark void, wavering on an abyss of nothingness. Separated from her father, with the foundation of her identity crumbling, her self-worth vanishing, and her body trembling, Thérèse was seized with fear.

Thérèse felt the annihilation of forfeiting everything. Her ego identity was being torn from her in an experience not unlike that of St. Paul's conversion as he was thrown to the ground and blinded; in that experience, his sense of identity as the perfect religious Pharisee had been stripped away (Philippians 3:8).

Thérèse 's heart was broken and tears were in her eyes. She had been emotionally shattered, but she continued to take the next step on the stairway. By sheer grace, as with St. Paul, Thérèse received in an instant the blessing to let go of the façade of who she thought she was. In that instant and for the first time in her life, she was absolutely certain that to be the acceptable, perfectly loving pleaser with *no will of her own* was not her real identity after all. And that awareness, at first terrifying, liberated her mightily.

In a flash of light, she recognized that her entire path—her focus of self-centered attention and her effort in trying to be the pleasing, perfect little girl—had been a grand illusion. She had not really been expressing her authentic virtue or inner freedom. Neither had she been deploying her real love. This path was fabricated and fictitious, partly foisted on her by the obligation to continue the family patterns and rituals and partly acceptable to her because she was secretly reaping the rewards of bonding affirmation. By grace stripped of falseness, Thérèse now saw herself more clearly mirrored in the eyes of God, a child of God. She recognized the real truth of herself instantaneously and with a sense of profound freedom and peace.

Thérèse suddenly recognized an even further dimension of truth she had never seen before—a truth that she could not have imagined before. She recognized that her misguided, self-satisfying path had actually been a path of violence. Her path did not, as St. Paul's did, involve violence to others. After all, she had been trying to act exactly the opposite of violent; she had been trying to be good and pleasing. Rather, the violence on Thérèse's path was the violence she was doing to herself by violating her own authenticity—compromising her personal integrity and being untrue to herself.

On this false path, she had allowed her inner freedom to be dominated by the excessive need to please others and thus to be affirmed, supported, and close to people at any cost. On this false path, she had been violent to her true self. She had been trying to be someone other than who she was. She had secretly been unwilling to accept herself as she really was in God's eyes. She had indeed been practicing virtue *in a strange way*—the way of self-violence. Relief and gratitude healed in an instant the brokenness of her heart.

A night of light

Thérèse later recalled that *it was December 25, 1886, that I received the grace of leaving my childhood, in a word, the grace of my complete conversion.* She experienced that grace especially as a night of light and as a blessing of empowerment, making her strong and courageous. She understood further that all was done by Jesus (SS 98).

Her enlightenment about the falseness of her path had been a complete gift; it was not a logical conclusion that she reached after conscious, rational thinking and psychological considerations. Rather, it was a sudden, spontaneous illumination shining into the family pattern and, more specifically, illuminating the depths of her own heart. Thérèse caught a glimpse of the shadowy side of her nature. Her illusion had been shattered; her attempt to live a dark lie, flooded with light. She was gifted with an encompassing insight that required no analysis but only willing receptivity. It was simply enlightenment. The truth was as clear to Thérèse as was the next step on the stairway she was presently walking to put away her hat and coat.

What was also astonishing to Thérèse was that she could take that next step on the stairway and not fall into the dark void or be overwhelmed by the dread of nothingness. She was *strong and courageous* (SS 97). And she did take that next physical step as an expression of her willingness to accept herself and her life honestly. She knew immediately that she could also take the next emotional step required of her, and she did take that step as well. She had received courage at the midnight Eucharist, and she did not reject it. Now she stepped courageously through her feelings and beyond her feelings into the light of faith.

That courage was also sheer grace coming from Jesus. It was the courage to bear the frightful feelings welling up within her without resisting or denying them. Without allowing a sense of intimidation to control her, she bore the feeling of anguish at having lost the approval of her father, of being emotionally separated from her "king." She bore as well the humiliation of knowing that her motivations for practicing virtue had been contaminated, and thus, she had been a complete failure in her efforts to be perfectly good and loving. And further, in all of this, she bore the momentary feeling of terror as her ego identity broke apart and her inner world of illusion crumbled.

The emotional step that she took under the weight of these feelings she would fully share with no one. She would live out the rest of her life secretly nourished by the graces of the enlightenment and the courage of that moment. Almost ten years later, describing the experience, she saw it all so clearly and proclaimed it so gratefully and joyfully: *Jesus, the gentle, little Child of only one hour, changed the night of my soul into rays of light. On that night when He made Himself subject to weakness and suffering for love of me, He made me strong and courageous* (SS 97).

Over the previous years, she had consciously been intending to do all her actions for God alone and as a manifestation of love and virtue. Only when her presumed selfless intentions were challenged by her father's remark did she notice that her intentions might not be totally selfless. In part, perhaps she had been good and loving as a way of acquiring the sense of being close. Perhaps, in part, she had been striving to be the perfect little child to be admired and accepted. Perhaps she had been acting in a loving way toward her family and especially her father partly to be affirmed and supported. Such thoughts never before had really found a home in her mind. Her father's displeasure challenged her dominant personal style of relating and, in a profound way, called into question the core of her motivation. Previously, the sense of the lack of inner peace had warned her that something was not right in the orientation of her desire to love; now she saw clearly and could act courageously in peace.

In retrospect, she was surprised at the light and especially the strength and courage she had found within her heart. She had never experienced such personal clarity and had never felt inner strength quite so powerfully before. On that Christmas Day, she had been able to stand her ground emotionally, take the next step, and not be intimidated by her feelings. That reality had been thrust upon her by grace.

Of course, as a very young child, Thérèse had stood her ground in the sense that she had been stubborn. In fact, her mother described her in the first years of childhood as having a willpower stronger than any of her sisters. At times, her mother actually found Thérèse's stubbornness frightening. But Thérèse's stubbornness as a child did not flow from the enlightenment and the courage of inner freedom. Her childhood stubbornness erupted when feelings of separation and loss intimidated her (cf. EIG 70).

Now, on the stairway as she stepped over the abyss of nothingness and through the feelings of hurt and fear that arose within her, she walked with a new self-awareness and deep inner courage. In an instant, her willful stubbornness was transformed into willingness, embracing the painful graces that arose within her heart from the gift of her father's chance remark.

On that stairway, she experienced a moment of total weakness and a moment of complete empowerment. In that moment, she retired into herself but now as into an inner sanctuary, and there, with willing self-surrender and gratitude, she received the embrace of Jesus. And the grace that came to Thérèse's heart as she triumphed over her weakness she experienced as infinitely superior to the good that had resided in her heart previously. And it had happened all in an instant of grace.

CHAPTER 5

The Grace of Leaving My Childhood

REGAINING HER TRUE CHARACTER

Thérèse's Christmas experience was the *grace of leaving my childhood, in a word, the grace of my complete conversion*. Her response on that stairway, as she took the next physical step with *tears already glistening in my eyes* (SS 98), was to surrender herself into the simple acceptance of the truth of who she really was with all of her weaknesses and inadequacies. And by surrendering herself with faith-filled confidence into this truth of herself, she intuited that she was abandoning herself into the arms of God, into the Spirit of truth.

Thérèse's self-surrender happened in an instant, flowing from a deep inner reserve that she had been fostering in her prayers over the previous ten years. It arose within her just as spontaneously and freely as her tears arose, glistening in her eyes, at the remark of her father. Her self-surrender arose as a creative surge of God's love within her heart. God's love embraced her as she willingly endured the pain of her shattering ego identity and the collapse of her false world.

Thérèse's conversion did not happen by any willful effort on her part. All such effort would have come from the remnants of the false self now disguised once again as a practice of virtue. Thérèse's self-surrender into this moment of God's providence was rather a death to the false self and the blossoming of her true self. Thérèse's false path had suddenly vanished, as the psalmist had assured her that every false path would (Psalm 1:6). This she experienced as a spontaneous gift, *the grace of leaving my childhood, in a word, the grace of my complete conversion*. It was not something that she had accomplished. *The work*, she said, *was done by Jesus in one instant* (SS 98).

And as she continued to take one step at a time on that stairway, she did not blame herself for her failure to please her father. Nor did she condemn herself for her inadequacies to love authentically. To blame or condemn herself would have been a form of self-loathing and, therefore, more self-violence. Her willing self-surrender ended her need to defend herself or to cultivate her false self and thus also ended the violence that she was doing to her true identity.

And her response to her father standing with Céline near the fireplace was not negativity or retaliation against him. She did not blame or condemn her father in an attempt to defend her good intentions. Such blaming and condemning were not part of Thérèse's nature. As a young child, Thérèse *got into the habit of not complaining ever, even when . . . accused unjustly* (SS 30). She had over the years kept her resolve, establishing in prayer a spirit of accepting as best she could all of her experiences as providential gifts. And further, to condemn her father or to complain about his piercing remark would itself have been a subtle form of self-justification. She would not build her self-righteousness on the weakness of her father. But most important, she understood that to condemn her father would have been a kind of retaliatory violence. She knew in the depths of her conscience that violence was not what God was asking of her. She simply continued her steady steps on that stairway of her conversion.

Thérèse was no longer the same; Jesus had changed her heart

Céline, recognizing that Thérèse had overheard her father's critical comment, ran up the stairs to console her. *Céline,* Thérèse later recounted, *knowing how sensitive I was and seeing the tears already glistening in my eyes, wanted to cry too, for she loved me very much and understood my grief.* Céline said softly and sensitively, *"Oh, Thérèse, don't go downstairs; it would cause you too much grief to look at your slippers right now!"* (SS 98). Céline knew, and Thérèse knew also, that it was not a matter of Thérèse looking at her slippers that Céline had arranged by the fireplace. It was rather a matter of how Thérèse was going to respond emotionally to her father, and what the sight of a distressed and weeping Thérèse would do to her "king," so sensitive and now so weary.

But Thérèse did not need Céline's consoling presence and well-intentioned advice. She had contacted an inner strength and power that Céline was not aware of. Thérèse had become strong, and *since that night,* she later wrote, *I have never been defeated in any combat* (SS 97).

Nor did Thérèse need Céline's comforting suggestion to withdraw, to not go downstairs and thus take no initiative. Céline's advice was based on her previous experience of her sister's characteristic style of reacting out of what seemed to be a *weak character,* of making a *big fuss over everything,* and of still being *only a child who appeared to have no will* of her own, or of simply retiring within herself in practiced shyness (SS 91).

For Thérèse to have accepted her sister's well-intentioned suggestion would have confined Thérèse to her old emotional pattern and into automatically following the family pattern of pleasing. If Thérèse had simply followed her sister's advice, she would again have been compulsively trying to accommodate and please Céline as well as her father. Céline's suggestion was a kind of temptation, and at that moment, Céline became a stumbling block for Thérèse. But Thérèse, without stumbling and without resisting, simply let Céline's advice pass away.

Nor did Thérèse need Céline's confirmation of the reality that was unfolding within her. Thérèse was being transformed, and the validation of her conversion came to Thérèse from within her own experience. Her own new sense of inner freedom and her own appreciation of the kinship of the truth of her new self-awareness and self-acceptance were confirmation of the validity of that truth.

To validate her transformation, Thérèse needed no outside affirmation. In her willingness to embrace the truth of herself, she was being confirmed by the Holy Spirit surging within her spirit. *Thérèse was no longer the same; Jesus had changed her heart* (SS 98). In an instant, her identity, security, and self-worth had been established in the embrace of Jesus and of his Holy Spirit, the Spirit of truth and freedom.

As a new person, Thérèse's action could also be new and no longer controlled by her excessive feelings or by the family pattern. She was experiencing a new inner freedom that could express itself in creativity and compassion. Now she could take the initiative, and her initiative could flow spontaneously, peacefully, joyfully, even through glistening tears and from a broken heart. The Truth had taken hold of Thérèse and set her free, and she would respond from the center of her true self, from within the embrace of the Spirit of truth and with the creative love energy of that freedom.

Instead of taking Céline's recommendation, Thérèse recalled, *Forcing back my tears, I descended the stairs rapidly; controlling the poundings of my heart, I took my slippers and placed them in front of Papa, and withdrew all the objects joyfully. I had the happy appearance of a Queen. Having regained his own cheerfulness, Papa was laughing* (SS 98).

Indeed, from the point of view of both Céline and her father, Thérèse appeared to be replaying the family pattern of denying herself, of pleasing at any price, and of playing again the role of the baby that was expected of her. But in reality, Thérèse was no longer doing any of those things. She was not continuing the family Christmas tradition of pretending to believe in Santa Claus. She was rather taking those first steps that would take her *from victory* to victory. She was, as she said, *beginning, so to speak, "to run as a giant"*! [Psalm 19:6] (SS 97). Everything had changed and nothing had changed.

I felt charity enter into my soul

Thérèse opened her little gifts with her usual cheerfulness and expressions of surprise and glee. She was, indeed, performing the family Christmas ritual and taking particular care to please her father. But unlike the previous Christmas performances, she was acting from an inner freedom with a compassionate love for her father that she had not previously possessed. Now she did not need to please him from any sense of compulsion. She did not need to feel connected and virtuous. Her cheerfulness was not masking self-centeredness or codependence. Her attention now was not on herself and her own needs but rather on her father and his needs. She was pleasing him now because from the depths of the inner freedom of her true self, she could act in whatever way was appropriately compassionate and creative within the boundaries of her own weakness and giftedness.

Over the years, Thérèse had become an expert at pleasing people, and in particular, she had become proficient at performing this Christmas ritual. She could perform now but with an entirely new motive, as an entirely new person, with an integrity she had never had before. She could do this in real happiness because she was in touch with the joy of her own spirit. She had regained her *childhood character* at an even more profound depth (SS 98, 34). Thérèse was engaging in performance without pretense.

Thérèse had left her own needy world, where she had been mired in the feelings of the past, to enter the present world of the immediate moment—the world that embraced the needs of her father. She could empathize, accommodate, and support him on his terms. She had moved from her own pattern of self-preoccupation and self-indulgence. It was during the period following this Christmas Day, Thérèse later wrote, that *I felt charity enter into my soul, and the need to forget myself and to please others* (SS 99). She could do this in the authentic love that blossoms from inner freedom into creativity and compassion.

Thérèse's real joy delighted her father, eliminated his tiredness, and brought him back to his true self. He regained his light and happy spirit. Actually, he seemed to have noticed nothing different from prior Christmas rituals except, perhaps, his own previous weariness and irritation, which now, by experiencing the freedom of his little queen, he was happy to know had amounted to nothing. But Céline, participating in the unfolding scene, was amazed.

Céline had seen Thérèse in this Christmas role before; indeed, Céline had orchestrated this ritual in her attempts, as Thérèse noted, *to continue treating me as the baby* (SS 98), and yet Céline had never before experienced Thérèse quite like this. Céline was caught in wonderment. She had had a fleeting glimpse of Thérèse's inner world just minutes before reflected in her little sister's glistening tears. She saw that Thérèse had experienced deep hurt and had tried to advise, console, and protect her, but now she knew that Thérèse had changed profoundly. Thérèse's behavior was not especially different, except perhaps that she was acting more spontaneously and gracefully, but Thérèse herself was different. Thérèse later observed that Céline *believed it was all a dream!* (SS 98).

To run as a giant

Thérèse had lost herself, her true self, after her mother's death. Alone she had tried to pull herself out of the darkness and swamp of melancholy and depression, but she was helpless in the clutches of her excessive feelings. Now the experience of this Christmas Day had transformed her, and therefore everything in her world had changed. She recalled with joy and amazement, *The work I had been unable to do in ten years was done by Jesus, . . . contenting himself with my good will which was never lacking* (SS 98).

Thérèse's *good will which was never lacking* was her willingness to surrender into the truth, into the self-acceptance of her weakness, into God's providential action incarnated through the words of her father. Self-acceptance, self-appreciation, and self-surrender in a spirit of gratitude into God's will, into God's arms, into God's love were to become for Thérèse the preeminent disposition in her developing spirituality.

As she reflected at the end of her life on the spiritual path on which God had led her, she wrote, *I understand so well that it is only love which makes us acceptable to God that this love is the only good I ambition. Jesus deigned to show me the road that leads to this Divine Furnace* [of God's love], *and this road is the surrender of the little child who sleeps without fear in its Father's arms* (SS 188).

Perhaps reflecting specifically on her conversion experience, she explained, *Jesus does not demand great actions from us, but simply surrender and gratitude*

(SS 188). Thérèse's Christmas conversion was the moment in which she was granted a profound glimpse of that road and that childlike surrender. It was also the moment when, feeling the empowerment of grace, she took a decisive step on that path and knew that she was *beginning "to run as a giant"!* [Psalm 19:6] (SS 97).

Thérèse complete conversion, which had enlightened and strengthened her, *had changed her heart*, restoring her *strength of soul* and *childhood character* (SS 98, 34). It did not, however, completely remove those distressing primary feelings of loss, separation, and abandonment, nor did it change her nature. To her final days, Thérèse still had strong feelings of needing to please others, to be close and affirmed. She would also always have the human tendency and gifted capacity to accommodate others.

Given her tender nature, her ability to be empathetic, and her sensitive spirit, Thérèse throughout her life would continue to please people and sometimes make mistakes in her affection. But now, after her conversion, she would have the ability to manage her feelings with more inner freedom. She would never again fall into the mire of pleasing others in a compulsive, self-indulgent way for her own sense of security or closeness or feelings of self-worth. Now she would be able to more often accommodate others on their terms, in a spirit of freedom and creativity and as an expression of real love. She would never again completely violate her own integrity by trying to establish her identity by pleasing others. She was no longer a baby pushed about by every wind of emotion. She would now begin to express the boldness of the transformed Magdalene.

Without paying too much attention to our own faults

Thérèse's diminishing but continuing strong tendency to please others in spite of herself served to make her constantly aware of her tendency to allow herself to be controlled by her feelings and, therefore, of her need for God's mercy. Her feelings of needing to be pleasing and of needing to feel bonded were to resurface again, especially in her relationship with the sisters in the convent she would join in just over a year. In particular, in her relationship with the convent superior, she was vulnerable to the recurring feelings of needing closeness and mothering. The awareness of her weaknesses was the other side of the grace of knowing that God's love in advance had prevented her fall.

Her ongoing weakness, abiding in her from those early experiences of separation from her mother and family, provided God's providence with the stepping-stones of her spiritual path.

By accepting her faults, Thérèse received the grace that took her, like Mary Magdalene, into the arms of her Beloved. *The remembrance of my faults humbles me, draws me never to depend on my strength which is only weakness, but this remembrance speaks to me of mercy and love even more* (GC 1133), she wrote at the end of her life. *It is easy to please Jesus,* she said, *to delight his heart: it is necessary only to love Him, without paying too much attention to our own faults. A glance at Jesus and recognition of our own weaknesses makes all well again* (HF 229).

Even as she lay on her deathbed, Thérèse's feelings of needing to please others almost got the better of her. Thérèse's older sister Pauline, who was in the convent with her and at her side in the final days of her life, recounted the story of Sr. Philomena's nephew who had just been ordained a priest and intended to celebrate his first Mass at Carmel with his aunt.

Sr. Philomena, knowing that Thérèse was near death and regarding her as a holy sister, hoped that Thérèse would honor her by receiving Communion from her nephew's hand. At the time, Thérèse, suffering severe physical and emotional distress, had been regularly vomiting blood and had not been able to receive Communion, a situation that embarrassed some in the community.

But Pauline also wished to please Sr. Philomena and the community and so asked her dying sister to pray to be able to receive Communion. Thérèse answered, *This evening, in spite of my feelings* [of physical and emotional pain], *I was asking God for this favor* [of receiving Communion] *in order to please my little sisters* [including Sr. Philomena and Pauline herself] *and so that the community might not be disappointed.* Then she added, *But in my heart I told Him* [God] *just the contrary; I told Him to do just what He wanted* (HLC 99).

Even as she was dying, Thérèse continued to be sensitive to the feelings of others, but now, content to be a disappointment and an embarrassment, she simply surrendered the matter into God's hands.

Without this change I would have had to remain for years in the world

By her complete conversion on that Christmas Day, Thérèse, as she wrote, *began the third period of my life, the most beautiful and the most filled with graces from heaven* (SS 98). When in her conversion she accepted Jesus' invitation into a deeper relationship of authentic love, her spirit expanded and her life changed. *Since then*, Thérèse noted, *I've been happy* (SS 99). She knew that she *had discovered once again the strength of soul which she had lost at the age of four and a half, and she was to preserve it forever!* (SS 98).

At her young age, Thérèse, of course, did not understand all of the dynamics unfolding within her heart that Christmas Day. But by naming her experience a *"complete conversion,"* she clearly identified that experience as the major turning point in her life (SS 98). She knew clearly that God had given her a great gift. She later referred to that day as *the day of graces among all days*, and for the rest of her life, she contemplated her experience in a spirit of deep gratitude (GC 1016). The profound meaning of her complete conversion, as well as the rich personal implications and challenges, gradually unfolded for Thérèse throughout the remaining ten years of her life and provided a significant foundation for her little way of love.

Thérèse's conversion contributed significantly to her understanding of *the science of love,* and in that experience, she glimpsed at least briefly each of the personal dispositions, the psychological indicators, the heart qualities that would tell her what authentic loving looked and felt like: inner freedom, creativity, compassion, willingness, self-surrender, and gratitude. She was, in addition, granted an insight into the fear, self-defensiveness, and self-centeredness that block love. And she also became aware of a form of violence that had previously been hidden from her: she discovered the self-violence that poisons love in the human heart.

Thérèse experienced her Christmas miracle as the transition from childhood to maturity. *Jesus, who saw fit to make Himself a child out of love for me, saw fit to have me come forth from the swaddling clothes and imperfections of childhood,* she reminisced. *The Lord . . . clothed me in His divine strength* (GC 1016).

No longer the baby she had been, she was now a strong young woman of personal integrity, conviction, and direction. She was certain that she was ready to fulfill the desire that had entered her heart in her earliest years. She was determined to enter the religious vocation to which God was calling her. *The night of Christmas 1886 was, it is true, decisive for my vocation,* she wrote many years later. *On that blessed night, . . . He transformed me in such a way that I no longer recognized myself. Without this change I would have had to remain for years in the world* (GC 1016).

Her complete conversion had transformed her in a way that prepared her to enter the Carmelite community at Lisieux. Her relationship with the members of the convent community was to be her next major experience in knowing more deeply the heart qualities of love, understanding more fully *the science of love,* and walking more confidently the beginning of her little way of love.

Thérèse's Experience of Living in Community

Thérèse at fifteen, photographed with her hair knotted on top of her head, the coiffure she adopted in order to appear older for her visit to Bishop Hugonin in October 1887. This photograph was taken in April 1888, a few days before Thérèse entered Carmel.

CHAPTER 6

I Felt Charity Enter My Heart

ENTERING THE CARMELITE COMMUNITY

Thérèse was convinced that her complete conversion had been God's way of preparing her emotionally and spiritually to respond to her vocation to enter the Carmelite community. Her experience had made her a new person.

At the end of May 1887, on Pentecost Sunday evening and five months after her conversion, Thérèse asked her father for his permission to enter Carmel. He at first objected, suggesting that having just turned fourteen the previous January, she was too young. But in his heart, he knew the spiritual maturity of his little queen, and he also recognized her long-established desire for religious life. He quickly and willingly gave his approval and encouragement.

Thérèse also needed the permission of her Uncle Isidore, and he initially also objected because of her age. However, he, too, quickly came to believe in Thérèse's recent emotional growth, and he never doubted her deep-rooted sincerity. So having established his point of objection, he willingly relinquished his resistance (cf. EIG 141ff.).

Thérèse's next task was to secure the approval of the clerical superior of the convent and of the local bishop. Each initially refused; each also considered Thérèse too young. But Thérèse was determined, and she focused all of her youthful stubbornness on fulfilling what she believed to be God's will.

Thérèse's father had previously arranged to take Thérèse and her sister Céline on a pilgrimage to Rome to celebrate the golden jubilee of Leo XIII's ordination. With the support of her father and Céline, as well as with the encouragement of her sister Pauline, who was already a member of the Carmelite community, Thérèse boldly decided that when she got to Rome, during the papal audience, she would ask the pope himself for permission. No one could resist the pope's approval, not even the local bishop.

After several weeks of sightseeing, the pilgrims finally came to the reason for their pilgrimage. They were ushered into the immense and splendid hall in which the pope would receive their congratulatory respects individually. When Thérèse's turn came to approach the Holy Father, she was like Magdalene whom Thérèse would have imaged approaching Jesus to wash his feet; she gave little attention to the solemnity of the occasion or the grandeur of the surroundings. Intimidated neither by the gravity of the ceremonies nor the piety of the onlookers, she disregarded the awe-inspiring procedures. She even ignored the specific directives forbidding any of the pilgrims from speaking to the ailing pope.

Breaking the rules of formality and protocol, Thérèse, in her turn, knelt before the pope, who was seated on an ornate chair on a raised platform. She kissed his foot as the required sign of respect; then she audaciously joined her hands on his knees, clutching his robe. In a nervous but firm voice, Thérèse asked the Holy Father to grant her permission to enter Carmel. Thérèse's way was not unlike *the conduct of Magdalene* that Thérèse had so admired; *her astonishing or rather her loving audacity which charms the Heart of Jesus* [and] *also attracts my own* (SS 258–59).

The papal guards were shocked. The local dignitaries leading the pilgrimage were at first dumbfounded, then embarrassed. The pope was taken aback and confused. Then he replied to Thérèse in a noncommitted way: "*Go . . . go . . . You will enter if God wills it*" (SS 135). He did not wish to get involved and kindly dismissed the idealistic young girl.

I was crushed, Thérèse wrote that night to her sister Pauline as she recalled the scene with tears in her eyes. *I felt I was abandoned* (GC 353). *Two guards touched me politely to make me rise. As this was not enough they took me by the arms. . . . It was with force they dragged me from his feet* (SS 135; cf. GC 354, note 5).

The pope must have been quite astonished at the boldness of this teenager, and Thérèse herself may have been surprised at her own daring. But she had proven her courage and determination, and that would be reported back to the local bishop by his observant dignitaries, who were in fact secretly impressed. The incident that had disrupted the traditional protocol, so unusual at a papal audience, was also reported four days later in the newspaper available in Lisieux (HLTT 89; cf. EIG 152ff.).

The local bishop was also impressed when he learned of Thérèse's strength and resolve in her approach to the Holy Father and of her mature religious demeanor during the entire pilgrimage. He changed his mind and withdrew his objections. Within a month, by the beginning of the new year, he had informed the Carmelite community of his willingness to permit the fourteen-year-old to join the convent. His permission negated the continued objections of the clerical superior of the convent.

One final obstacle now arose, however. This time the resistance came from within the convent itself, and it originated with Pauline, who had now changed her mind as well.

Pauline was aware that if Thérèse were to enter the convent in early January, she would be required to observe the community's rigorous Lenten austerities beginning shortly after the first weeks of the new year. Concerned about Thérèse's generally weak health, Pauline wished to spare her little sister the pain of the fasting and other observances. She also thought it wise to respect the continuing objection of the clerical superior of the convent. Her arguments had convinced the mother superior and the community.

Pauline's concern about Thérèse's welfare required another delay of three months. It was not, therefore, until the end of Lent, on April 9, 1888, that Thérèse, now fifteen years old, was received into the Carmelite community at Lisieux (cf. EIG 161ff.).

Finally behind the cloistered convent walls of Carmel, Thérèse was about to enter her second formative experience deepening her understanding of the path of love.

During the next nine years, until her death, she needed the light and courage of her complete conversion, especially in her difficult interactions with the sisters of the community. In these interactions, Thérèse read another chapter of *the book of life wherein is contained the science of Love* (SS 187).

Love cannot remain inactive

Within the confined lifestyle of the Carmelite community, Thérèse experienced Jesus leading her along the path of love, frequently in some emotional and physical pain, but always in peace. She came to know more deeply the heart qualities that she had glimpsed in her complete conversion, which alerted her that she was on the path of love, and she became sensitive to the negative feelings warning her that love was being poisoned in her heart.

Along this path she was to learn from her own experience and from the confidences that other sisters shared with her the difference between liking and loving, between infatuation and true love, between counterfeit love in its many guises and authentic love in its complete inclusivity. She learned that loving had little to do with feelings and much to do with faith; that it had little also to do with liking and much to do with respecting, deciding, and acting. She began to understand that love is about detachment from feelings and preferences, especially detachment from favorites associated with self-centeredness.

She learned how to be firm in loving and how to be creatively flexible in loving; how to love by withdrawing momentarily from a relationship and how to love by pressing closer; how to love by a compassionate smile, by responsibly correcting a fault, and by overlooking a mistake. She learned that a heart *burning with love cannot remain inactive* (SS 257–58). She learned to express love in quiet prayer and in creative action, all in a spirit of self-surrender and gratitude.

She learned that loving herself and selfishness were two different things and that loving God and loving others were not two different things. She learned that loving herself, loving others, and loving God were really one act of love: the Holy Spirit of God's love acting in her.

She learned that God's love is completely gratuitous but not overpowering and that she could block God's love by allowing herself to be overwhelmed by her feelings of defensiveness and self-centeredness.

She learned that love radiated from the uniqueness of the loving person and was founded on the person's spiritual and psychological maturity as well as the person's natural gifts and weaknesses. Thérèse discovered that the form of love is different for each person, and for the same person, expressions of love change over the years. She learned that there can be no comparisons in *the science of love*, that the ways of love are always creative and emerge spontaneously from the true self living in Christ.

She learned that because human love is always unique and original, there is always a sense of surprise and mystery about human love, making it difficult, even for St. Paul, to describe love in more specific positive qualities than those of patience and kindness (1 Corinthians 13:4-6). She also learned that God's love, always infinitely creative, is ever shrouded in mystery.

During the nine years of convent life, Thérèse discovered particularly what love is not and how subtle forms of hostility can overwhelm the human heart. She discovered how hurt, resentment, and antagonistic feelings can contaminate love in human relationships. She noticed that excessive and negative feelings poisoned the best intentions of some pious members of the convent community. More important, she came to the humiliating and purifying self-awareness that excessive feelings continued to taint even her own motivations and that she herself had momentary hostile, even violent feelings toward some of the religious sisters she lived with. Above all, she learned that loving required not only honest attention and accommodation to her own weaknesses and needs but also to the limitations and needs of others, and that therefore loving would be filled with self-surrender, self-sacrifice, and emotional suffering.

Her sense of peace would continue to assure her that she was on the right path of authentic love, especially in her relationships, but she needed to refine her awareness of the difference between that God-given peace and her self-centered feelings of comfort and contentment.

Suffering opened wide its arms to me

On her first day in the convent, as she expectantly followed the superior of the community, Mother Gonzague, through the convent's inner rooms and dim passages, Thérèse's dominant feeling was a sense of sweet, *deep peace impossible to express,* confirming her Carmelite vocation (SS 148; cf. HLTT 125ff.; EIG 166ff.). Thérèse had finally attained her great desire of giving herself completely to Jesus in the religious lifestyle of Carmel. Peace was God's precious gift to Thérèse. For the remainder of her life, even in the midst of the greatest physical and emotional sufferings, that peace never left her.

At the same time, however, she acknowledged that by entering Carmel, she was also being welcomed by God into a state of suffering. *Suffering opened wide its arms to me and I threw myself into them with love,* she observed (SS 149). She discovered that the peace that Jesus promised was compatible with suffering, and she later wrote to Céline, *Let us suffer in peace! . . .* [But] *the one who says peace is not saying joy, or at least, felt joy. To suffer in peace it is enough to will all that Jesus wills* (GC 553).

Her life, she noted in her final years, had been a *crucible of suffering* for which she was, nonetheless, grateful to God (SS 277). Her attitude of embracing suffering gratefully was not masochistic. It was, rather, the spirit of willingness to bear in peace the suffering inevitable in a life of love, lived for the rest of her days with unchosen companions with whom she had little in common within a confined, limited physical space and in a situation of mutual physical and emotional poverty.

She embraced suffering in a spirit of availability to Jesus crucified and risen. By suffering willingly and by positioning herself at the foot of the cross during the weeks immediately following her conversion, Thérèse was expressing her complete availability to receiving the outpouring of Jesus' love (SS 99). She was willing to receive and share Jesus' love as her participation in Jesus' paschal mystery. With love she threw herself into the arms of the suffering Jesus and into the arms of the sufferings of Jesus as well. *I am . . . very happy, happy to suffer what Jesus wants me to suffer,* she wrote during her private retreat nine months after entering Carmel (GC 500). And later, possibly reflecting on the image of the Holy Face of Jesus, an image based on the shroud of Turin and a devotion that became the foundation of her spirituality, she wrote, *To be the spouse of Jesus we must resemble Jesus, and Jesus is all bloody. He is crowned with thorns!* (GC 553).

As Thérèse stood at the foot of the cross, she who was so inclined to self-consciousness, self-centeredness, and codependency was intuitively aware that her suffering would inevitably be the hidden suffering of self-surrender to God's will. Her suffering would be inconspicuous and would not even be known by the sisters under whose watchful eyes she lived the rest of her life.

The cry of Jesus on the Cross sounded continually in my heart: "I thirst"

It had been only a short time after Thérèse's conversion and even before she had entered the convent that a holy picture of the image of Jesus crucified fell from her missal during her prayer. She had gazed upon that image many times before, but on this occasion, her heart was touched in a completely different way. She suddenly realized that Jesus' blood had fallen on the barren ground and that his love was not being reverenced. Jesus' love was not being appreciated or reciprocated; it was falling on unreceptive hearts.

Immediately, she had an insight into her role in God's redemptive act. *I was resolved,* she wrote, *to remain in spirit at the foot of the Cross and to receive the divine dew. I understood I was then to pour it out upon souls. The cry of Jesus on the Cross sounded continually in my heart: "I thirst!" . . . I wanted to give my Beloved to drink and I felt myself consumed with a thirst for souls* (SS 99; cf. GC 643, note 5). By participating with Jesus in thirsting for souls, Thérèse became aware of the foundation of her missionary vocation that would unfold during her years in Carmel. At this time of her youth, she understood that *He made me a fisher of souls. I experienced a great desire to work for the conversion of sinners, a desire I hadn't felt so intensely before* (SS 99).

During this same time, there came to Thérèse's attention news of a vicious murderer who was about to be executed. Henri Pranzini was a great sinner in the eyes of all who had heard of him. But despite his denunciation by the secular and religious press as well as the courts, the teenage Thérèse refused to become involved in the condemning gossip circulating even in her family. She was concerned about Pranzini's welfare in his present distress and in his eternal destiny. She simply prayed for his conversion. Referring to her private prayers, her acts of self-discipline, and her secret request to have a Mass said for him, she later wrote, *I employed* [for his conversion] *every means imaginable.* When she learned that after he had mounted the scaffold, Pranzini kissed the crucifix as a sign of repentance, she was convinced that he was her *first child* whom she had birthed into heaven (SS 99–100; cf. EIG 136ff.).

Pranzini was her *first child,* and at the time of her entry into Carmel. Thérèse's love and *thirst for souls* was beginning to expand beyond her family and her sisters in community until her love would slowly become all inclusive, sharing in Jesus' universal love. The singular grace of her conversion had expanded her heart, and she later wrote, *God was able in a very short time to extricate me from the very narrow circle in which I was turning without knowing how to come out* (SS 101).

This happiness was not passing

Now, Thérèse was in a "small and poor" convent, as Thérèse's eldest sister, Marie, had described it when she entered the convent just less than two years before (cf. HLTT 95ff.). The daily schedule, which included extensive physical work, long hours in prayer, and minimal hours of recreation and rest, was unrelenting in its routine and rigor (cf. HLTT 131). The lifestyle was completely devoid of anything a teenager might consider fun. Thérèse, young, barely out of childhood, and coming from a home situation in which she had been pampered as the little queen, endured as best she could this complete lack of creature comforts as a kind of self-offering to God (cf. EIG 166ff.).

Each sister was assigned a small unheated room in which to rest and work. It contained little more than a bed and chair. The convent building, except for a fireplace in the common gathering room, was without heat against the often severe cold of Normandy winters. The food, of poor quality and meager portions, would become another suffering for Thérèse, but from the winter cold she would suffer physically more than from anything else in her life (cf. TLMT 98).

With the food as with the cold and other inconveniences, she followed her childhood resolution of never complaining. Thérèse wrote in retrospect: *Everything thrilled me; I felt as though I was transported into a desert* [of joy]. *. . . The joy I was experiencing was calm. . . . Ah! I was fully recompensed for all my trials* [the difficulties she had encountered trying to enter Carmel]. *. . . This happiness was not passing* (SS 148–49). Thérèse was willing to rest in the open arms of the suffering Jesus with a deep sense of peace and joy.

Having often been on the edge of poor health, Thérèse now suffered considerably from the lack of physical comforts and was exhausted at day's end. She suffered also from feelings of embarrassment and inadequacy as she tried to adjust to the daily routine and to accomplish successfully the physical domestic tasks assigned to her. Her greatest internal pain, however, came in the area of her personal strength, her capacity to establish relationships and to be close to others. From the first days in the community, she experienced her failure to sufficiently accommodate and appropriately please the other sisters and was distressed by her inability to bond immediately and deeply.

During her younger years, when she had visited Pauline and Marie after they had entered the convent, Thérèse had often received signs of affection from the same sisters with whom she was now living. She had really expected to be welcomed with appreciation into the community. But the welcome she received, like the pervading atmosphere of the convent itself, was more formal, rigorous, and austere. Thérèse's sensitive and open heart was confused and hurt.

During the next years within the crucible of community relationships, Thérèse's love was purified. And in no relationship was she to learn more about herself and the heart qualities of love, and in no relationship was her purification to be more painful, than in her interaction with the superior, Mother Gonzague.

CHAPTER 7

I Know That She Loved Me Very Much

RELATING TO MOTHER GONZAGUE

At the time of her mother's death, the child Thérèse had immediately embraced her sister Pauline as her second mother (cf. GC 839). Then a little more than four years later, and less than a year after Thérèse had entered her stressful situation at the Benedictine Abbey school, Pauline left her to enter the Carmelite convent. Thérèse again felt an upsurge of those distressing primal feelings of separation, mother loss, and abandonment. She shed bitter tears at the loss of Pauline. *It was as if a sword were buried in my heart,* she remembered sadly. *In one instant, I understood what life was; until then, I had never seen it so sad; . . . I saw it was nothing but a continual suffering and separation. I shed bitter tears* (SS 58; cf. EIG 72ff.).

But losing Pauline aroused in Thérèse a clearer sense that she, too, was called to Carmel. She wrote, *I felt that Carmel was the desert* [the place of both intimacy and solitude] *where God wanted me to go also to hide myself. I felt this with so much force,* Thérèse later recounted, *that there wasn't the least doubt in my heart; it was not the dream of a child led astray but the certitude of a divine call; I wanted to go to Carmel not for Pauline's sake but for Jesus alone* (SS 58).

Thérèse believed that she had entered the convent to fulfill God's will, but she never lost her deep fondness for Pauline or for Marie, her older sister with whom she was reunited, for Marie, too, had joined the Carmelite community. Although Pauline and Marie welcomed their little sister with a clear desire to rekindle the bonding affection of their home life, Thérèse in her maturity resisted any such tendency. Having known from her school days that her heart *would have easily surrendered* and been *taken,* Thérèse accepted the suffering of detachment from the emotional bonding with her blood sisters as a self-discipline of authentic love (SS 82–83).

She delighted in the love of Pauline and Marie and she continued to please them, but now she related to them with the inner freedom of love that she had recently discovered in her conversion experience. *I didn't come to Carmel to live with my* [blood] *sisters but to answer Jesus' call,* she wrote at the end of her life. *Ah! I really felt in advance that this living with one's own sisters had to be the cause of continual suffering when one wishes to grant nothing to one's natural inclinations* (SS 216). From the earliest days in Carmel, Thérèse with delicate tact and finesse withdrew from Pauline and Marie without offending them and related to them as she did with the other sisters.

In her relationship with Mother Gonzague, however, Thérèse at first experienced no such ability to detach herself and sometimes lost her emotional balance.

The science of love

Thérèse had first met Mother Gonzague when Pauline entered Carmel. The superior immediately expressed a maternal affection for this beautiful, intelligent, pleasing, and promising nine-year-old who visited her sister in the convent. Mother Gonzague's natural charm captured Thérèse's heart by taking seriously her desire to join the community. When Mother Gonzague suggested that "Thérèse of the Child Jesus" would be her religious name when Thérèse became a Carmelite, the young girl was completely enthralled. Thérèse felt respected and validated, because that very morning she herself had thought of that very name as *I was thinking things over in my bed* in meditation (SS 71). Thérèse was fascinated by Mother Gonzague.

Through these visits and subsequent correspondence, Mother Gonzague and Thérèse quickly established a deepening mutual fondness. The bonds of trust and affection grew over the years as Thérèse took steps to enter Carmel. Thérèse believed without hesitation that she was doing God's will by entering, but Carmel was also a place where she would find a secure home and a maternal embrace.

When the teenage Thérèse joined the community, Mother Gonzague initially expressed her affection for the newly arrived candidate, but gradually over the next months and years, the superior's attitude became more sober and began to fluctuate. Mother Gonzague became more withdrawn from Thérèse and more critical. Thérèse's expectation and her human need for a warm, especially maternal relationship that would have been so supportive and comforting were slowly thwarted. In the daily interactions of convent living, Thérèse experienced Mother Gonzague acting quite ambivalently toward her, at times extending her the most tender affection; at other times, an excessive harshness.

The newly arrived Thérèse had to learn and conform to all the community customs and expectations and to the way things had always been done. She had to discover the assigned place for every item; the correct gesture at the precise time during every chapel service and community gathering; the proper way of standing, walking, and sitting for every occasion; and the appropriate manner of interacting with each unique community member (cf. HLTT 101ff.). Every sister, every thing, every place, every situation in the community had a hidden but correct way of being engaged—that perfect way Thérèse learned mostly by trial and error, reinforced by reprimands and punishments.

Even with all of her goodwill, Thérèse at first could do nothing quite right. She did not always walk with proper posture, gravity, and decorum; neither did she correctly sweep the floor or adequately dust the steps or properly cut the bread or competently kill the terrifying spiders hiding under the steps in the place where the bread was kept. Having never done even simple house-work at home, Thérèse brought no reserve of common knowledge to the daily chores of convent life. Her incompetence quickly became apparent, and Mother Gonzague let few of her mistakes go unnoticed or uncorrected. The superior often criticized and humiliated her, both privately and publicly.

In the daily presence of Mother Gonzague and under her increasingly critical eye, Thérèse was confused by strong conflicting feelings. She felt inadequate, embarrassed, and isolated. She especially experienced rejection, a kind of betrayal, and a feeling of having been abandoned. Yet she also felt more and more drawn by the powerful personal magnetism of the superior. It was in the interplay of these feelings, in her successes and failures to maintain her emotional balance, that Thérèse was to learn much about *the science of love*.

Violent temptations to satisfy myself

Some years later, reflecting on her early compulsive need to be near Mother Gonzague, Thérèse admitted that she had felt a powerful desire to simply be in the presence of the superior, to be consoled and affirmed during the confusion, the hurt, and the humiliations of her first months of convent life (GC 426, note 2; 501–2, note 3). Thérèse acknowledged how deeply she had longed to be accepted and appreciated by a maternal figure. She confessed that she had had *violent temptations to satisfy myself and to find a few crumbs of pleasure* [of being close to Mother Gonzague] (SS 237). That Thérèse identified her feelings as both *violent* and as *temptations* reveals not only the power of her attraction to Mother Gonzague but also her awareness that these feelings could not be harbored in peace and were not indications of authentic love.

Prior to her conversion, Thérèse had experienced similar strong feelings of desiring closeness and acceptance, but now she suffered the embarrassment of sensing the completely inappropriate nature of such a relationship with a mother figure in the convent setting. Thérèse was also more aware that her powerful feelings were doing violence to herself, victimizing her, dragging her into the darkness of infatuation, and now once again ensnaring her in the neediness of codependency. She was sensing that she was *allowing myself to be taken and my wings to be clipped* (SS 83), a weakness she had noticed many years before that could taint her relationships. Her feelings, in spite of her emerging awareness, were igniting her neediness to grasp *a few crumbs of pleasure*, even as she did violence to herself. She knew that she was not on the path of love.

Writing in the autobiographical manuscript that Mother Gonzague had requested, Thérèse acknowledged to the superior that *I was obliged to walk rapidly by your door and to cling firmly to the banister of the staircase in order not to turn back* [to be with you]. *There came into my mind a crowd of permissions to seek* [to have the opportunity to talk with you]. . . . *I found a thousand reasons for pleasing my nature* [my compulsion to be close to you] (SS 237).

Thérèse had been momentarily driven into a tangle of deceit and self-compromise, and as had happened at the time of her conversion when she took the next physical step to her room, now she also needed a physical expression of her determination to walk through her feelings and not be held in bondage. This time, besides walking rapidly by the superior's door, she clung *firmly to the banister of the staircase.*

My last plank of salvation was in flight

Even though her self-awareness increased, Thérèse's infatuation toward Mother Gonzague did not completely disappear. On one specific occasion about a year after her entrance, Thérèse had a good reason to visit Mother Gonzague. Thérèse tells this story in the same manuscript written to the superior, revealing the inner struggles she experienced to maintain her inner freedom under the power of her feelings. In her writings, Thérèse again directly addresses Mother Gonzague, and with the calm of hindsight, she writes in an amusing manner: *I wish, Mother, to give you an example which I believe will make you smile. During one of your bronchial attacks, I came to your cell very quietly one morning to return the keys of the Communion grating since I was sacristan. I wasn't too displeased at having this opportunity to see you; I was very much pleased.* Then Thérèse adds these self-revealing words: *But I didn't dare to show it* (SS 223).

Thérèse knew at some level in her heart that her desire to be in contact with the superior was not an expression of authentic love but was self-indulgent. She had a good reason to enter the superior's room, it was true, but she knew that she was rationalizing her action and trying to distract herself momentarily from the deeper reality of the inappropriateness of her feelings. She knew she was being driven by her excessive feelings and that they were in conflict with her true self, but she tried to hide this reality even from herself. She disguised her real need, which was not simply to fulfill her duty, as she alleged to the sister who now confronted her.

A Sister, Thérèse continued in a light style, *animated with a holy zeal, and one who loved me very much, believed I was going to awaken you when she saw me enter your quarters; she wanted to take the keys from me. I was too stubborn to give them to her and to cede my rights. As politely as I could, I told her that it was my duty to return the keys. I understand now that it would have been more perfect to cede to this Sister, young, it is true, but still older than I. I did not understand it at the time* (SS 223).

The power of Thérèse's *violent temptations to satisfy myself* darkened her understanding that the *more perfect* thing she could have done, as she recognized only in retrospect, would have been to admit to herself her real motivation, accept her weakness, renounce her stubbornness, and *cede to this Sister*. She acknowledged as much by noting immediately, *I wanted absolutely to enter in spite of the fact that she was pushing the door to prevent me* (SS 223–24). In retrospect, Thérèse saw clearly that her desire *absolutely to enter* was an expression of an attitude of willfulness, a kind of compulsivity. She was at war with herself, victimized by her feelings. Her true self was being violated.

Thérèse continued her story, adding with humor at the ridiculousness of the situation and the foolishness of her own weakness, that

> *very soon the thing we feared most happened: the racket we were making made you open your eyes. Then, Mother, everything tumbled upon me. The poor Sister whom I had resisted began to deliver a whole discourse, the gist of which was: It's Sister Thérèse of the Child Jesus who made the noise; my God, how disagreeable she is, etc. I, who felt just*

the contrary, had a great desire to defend myself. Happily there came a bright idea into my mind, and I told myself that if I began to justify myself I would not be able to retain my peace of soul. I felt, too, that I did not have enough virtue to permit myself to be accused without saying a word. My last plank of salvation was in flight. No sooner thought than done. I left without fuss, allowing the Sister to continue her discourse which resembled the imprecations of Camillus against the city of Rome. My heart was beating so rapidly that it was impossible for me to go far, and I sat down on the stairs in order to savor the fruits of my victory. There was no bravery there, Mother; however, I believe it was much better for me not to expose myself to combat when there was certain defeat facing me. (SS 223–24)

I did not have enough virtue

With almost seven years of faith perspective, Thérèse was able to see some lightness as she wrote about the situation of Mother Gonzague and the keys, but at the time, she had lost her inner freedom and had momentarily failed. *My last plank of salvation was in flight,* she acknowledged, and flight would be her frequent recourse as she continued to grow in her awareness that *I did not have enough virtue to permit myself to be accused without saying a word* [of self-defense or retaliation]. Such a word, she knew instinctively, would have been an expression of hostility and violence and not an expression of authentic love.

Flight gave Thérèse time and distance to move from self-deception to the truth of her own limitations. Flight allowed her the inner space to calm the war within herself, reclaim her inner freedom, and *savor the fruits of victory.* It provided the faith perspective that allowed her to regain the heart qualities that she needed to stay on the path of authentic love.

This experience alerted Thérèse that she was experiencing the same dangerous magnetism of a schoolgirl crush toward the superior that she had experienced at the Benedictine Abbey school in her relationships with some of the teachers and, more specifically, in the dangerous feelings of attachment that she had toward her one classmate friend. Actually, in that peer relationship, she had been spared emotional attachment not so much by her own self-control as by the unresponsiveness of her classmate. Now, as these similar *violent temptations* [of attachment] *to satisfy myself and to find a few crumbs of pleasure* surfaced toward Mother Gonzague, Thérèse was again saved, not by her own doing, but by the embarrassing racket that woke the superior. She was also saved by her sudden awareness that she was losing *my peace of soul*, the very same warning sign that she had recognized prior to her complete conversion.

Over the years, Thérèse noticed that other sisters were also attracted to Mother Gonzague, and some, Pauline and Marie among them, related to her quite appropriately. But Thérèse knew in the light and courage of her conversion experience that she could not honestly regard her own natural fondness as a sign of authentic love (GC 426, note 2).

For her part, Mother Gonzague needed all of her self-discipline and insight into the nature of Thérèse to remain detached from Thérèse's infatuation and clinging. Sensing Thérèse's dark need for maternal affection and her desire for some consolation, Mother Gonzague seems to have had her own wisdom in her early overly strict and cautious manner. Mother Gonzague recognized Thérèse's personal and spiritual potential. Had the superior not personally distanced herself but allowed Thérèse to become the favorite, the pampered one of the community, Thérèse could easily have squandered her personal gifts chasing after human consolations. She could have wandered far on the codependent side path of self-indulgence and never attained the degree of authentic love that she finally reached.

What would have become of me if I had been the "pet" of the community?

In her maturity, Thérèse had wondered, as she mentioned to her sister Pauline, *how you were able to raise me* [through my childhood years] *with so much love and tenderness without spoiling me* (SS 44). When Thérèse later reflected on her relationship with Mother Gonzague, she also wondered: *What would have become of me if I had been the "pet" of the community as some of the Sisters believed? Perhaps, instead of seeing Our Lord in my Superiors, I would have looked upon them as ordinary persons only and my heart, so well guarded while I was in the world, would have become humanly attached in the cloister. Happily I was preserved from this misfortune* (SS 150–51).

Mother Gonzague did not have the innate tenderness of Pauline, but in her own sometimes clumsy and capricious way, the superior seems to have respected Thérèse and feared spoiling her. Without Mother Gonzague's firm hand, Thérèse's great potential for spiritual growth may never have been actualized. She may never have reached the degree of holiness, *the degree of glory You have prepared for me in Your Kingdom,* that she later prayed for (SS 276; PST 53ff.).

At a deep personal and spiritual level, Mother Gonzague had always revered and loved Thérèse. The superior seems to have actually admired her more than any other member of the community, especially appreciating her common sense and sound judgment (GC 430, note 4; GC 678). She valued Thérèse's wisdom and interpersonal skills, particularly as Thérèse assisted her in the guidance of the newer candidates in the community. Later referring to Thérèse's holiness and spirituality, the superior wrote to one of the priests whom Thérèse was mentoring: "You have a very fervent helper who will neglect nothing for the salvation of souls. The dear little thing is all for God!" (GC 980, note 13).

Years later, Mother Gonzague told one of the sisters in confidence that "if a prioress were to be chosen from the whole community, I would unhesitatingly choose Sister Thérèse of the Child Jesus in spite of her young age. She is perfect in everything" (STL 253; TLMT 115).

Thérèse later acknowledged, *I know that she* [Mother Gonzague] *loved me very much and said everything good about me that was possible, nevertheless, God permitted that she was VERY SEVERE without her even being aware of it* (SS 150).

Having grown psychologically and spiritually, her heart having been purified, Thérèse at the end of her life could say, *I loved Mother Prioress very much, but it was a pure affection* (SS 151). Thérèse could have added that her relationship with Mother Gonzague had cleansed her heart, had prompted her to run swiftly along the path of love, and had helped her to deepen significantly her wisdom of *the science of love.*

Thérèse as a novice, January 1889

CHAPTER 8

There Is Something, I Don't Know What, That Repels Me!

LIVING COMMUNITY LIFE

During her early months in community, Thérèse had made a favorable impression on most of the sisters. Her novice mistress noted that "in her bearing she was marked by a kind of majesty that one was far from expecting in a child of fifteen" (cf. GC 414). Yet a small minority of the sisters, following Mother Gonzague's lead of correcting Thérèse's mistakes, now more confidently assumed a maternal role, but it was the role of a critical mother. They became quick and constant in their reprimands of Thérèse, and some even began to harbor a more general negative attitude toward her.

As a child in the convent parlor visiting her sisters Pauline and then Marie, Thérèse seemed to all the community members to be the charming, attractive child with a Carmelite vocation to whom they freely expressed their maternal concern. But now a few of the sisters saw Thérèse as the needy teenager who had received the special privilege of admission to their convent before the proper age and who had two blood sisters welcoming her as the "queen," eager to provide special attention (cf. GC 433).

I cannot give you any explanation

All the sisters forming the community were, of course, older than Thérèse; many were old enough to be her mother, and some could have been her grandmother. The average age of the twenty-six members of the community was almost forty-seven.

Having been a pleasing presence at home, Thérèse had had extensive practice in being gracious in every circumstance. Now, in spite of her difficulties in adjusting to community life, Thérèse easily fell into the role of trying to be the very pleasant, pleasing young candidate. Yet over the months, as her natural sensitivity began to flower into empathy and her capacity to please blossomed into self-forgetfulness and generosity, she continued to arouse distressful and ambiguous feelings in some of the sisters. The fondness of motherliness as well as the burden of celibacy, the attraction of sisterly feelings as well as the embarrassment of jealousy, the alluring beauty of innocence as well as the bitter pain of their own failed perfectionism—these were among the confusing feelings that seemed to have distressed some of the sisters in the presence of this innocent and lovely young community member.

To satisfy their own feelings or simply to express their own cantankerous temperaments, some sisters resisted Thérèse, allowing her youth and awkwardness no special considerations. One sister mocked Thérèse's inability to do domestic duties well. She thoughtlessly and hurtfully nicknamed Thérèse "the big kid goat" (HLTT 117; cf. GC 505, note 1).

Any exceptions given to Thérèse would have offended the sisters personally and disrupted the properly established routine of convent life. Special treatment to this novice would have also undermined whatever status and privileges the sisters had established among themselves. Some sisters believed that for their own good, for the good order of the community, and even for her own good, Thérèse needed the strict discipline of an unforgiving environment.

Reflecting later on the corrections that she received as a young sister, Thérèse knew that the harsh reprimands did alert her to changes necessary in her outward behavior. But she could not deny that the corrections were also a source of hurt, resurrecting in her the same feelings of separation and abandonment that had plagued her from her very earliest years. The scolding also evoked spontaneous hostility and defensiveness. Within nine months of her entering Carmel, Thérèse acknowledged that *those who surround me are very good,* but she also noticed that *there is something, I don't know what, that repels me! I cannot give you any explanation* (GC 499–500).

At the time, Thérèse could not give any explanation for her negative thoughts and feelings because they were ushering her into a new experience. Until her entry into the convent, except for the boisterous and mean classmates at the Benedictine school, she had never been confronted with personalities that were so bothersome to her. The convent community was Thérèse's first close-up experience of being with adults who were not well integrated, sensitive, and caring.

Thérèse's childhood in a loving family and with loving relatives had been a great blessing in her life. Now the other side of that blessing was being revealed to her. Her early years had conditioned her into assuming that adults were loving and emotionally well-balanced. She had not noticed the expectations flowing from her early experiences until those expectations were not met. In her unawareness, Thérèse had become vulnerable to the cravings of her hidden assumptions and expectations. She was, therefore, thrown off balance when those cravings surfaced as her own negative thoughts and feelings. Thérèse wanted to believe that the sisters of the community were *very good*, and clearly, they were women striving to live a life of love. But they were not perfect, and their weaknesses clutched onto Thérèse's own weakness and vulnerability. Thérèse was becoming more clearly aware that she was not perfect either. Her personal interactions in community were becoming seeds of growth in her self-knowledge.

Her failed expectations were starting to make Thérèse aware of a dark, weak area of herself. She was becoming enlightened to the fact that she had not only the external faults of doing her community duties imperfectly but also that she was not exempt from the natural but unholy feelings of repulsion, hostility, and retaliation when her expectations were not met. A corrective to her tendency to self-righteousness, this awareness was another providential stepping-stone on Thérèse's discovery of *the science of love*.

Her willingness to embrace the truth of herself in her weakness would be part of her continuing *suffering that had opened wide its arms* to her (SS 149). Her self-surrender into the reality of her participation in the human condition, as well as her continued gratitude for God's blessings, allowed her to walk her spiritual journey in peace.

Everything seems very disagreeable to me

As she matured through the next years and gained the confidence of the community, she also noticed that a few of the sisters not only evoked these difficult feelings within her own heart but aroused similar toxic feelings among themselves. Then she tried more consciously with her empathy to bridge some of the troubled waters that churned throughout the community. Her simplicity and humility created a nonthreatening atmosphere; her peace and joy, a calming comfort, especially to the oldest sisters and the infirmed. Over the years, as she became more skilled at befriending and managing her feelings of repugnance, she took it upon herself to companion the sisters who were particularly difficult and disturbing.

Some of the sisters who had thorny personalities, Thérèse noticed, were living in chronic physical pain. Some were perfectionists living with a sense of frustration, continually correcting her but also constantly and unsuccessfully attempting to correct themselves into a state of perfection. Others were suffering from their own strong feelings of inadequacy and isolation, troubled with thoughts of being spiritual failures and plagued with feelings of loss and sadness as their own lives, like their tattered garments, simply wore out without a trace. And Thérèse pleased them all as best she could, interacting creatively and compassionately with a smile, an empathetic glance, or a kind word.

Burdened, however, with her own sensitivities and her continual need for closeness, Thérèse's pleasant ways were not always easy for her. The behaviors of a few of the sisters never ceased to arouse feelings of hostility in her, and toward at least one sister she simply felt total personal repugnance. Thérèse tells several stories at the end of her autobiography that capture the details of her exchanges with some of the difficult sisters and of her personal feelings that continued from her early years in the community.

One particular sister needed help walking, and Thérèse escorted her as gently as she could into the dining room every day. Later she wrote, *When I was guiding Sister St. Pierre, I did it with so much love that I could not possibly have done better had I been guiding Jesus Himself* (SS 249). The sister's inflexible style of animosity became an unspoken and constant thorn to Thérèse's sense of personal adequacy and need to please.

One sister positioned herself beside Thérèse as they did the laundry together and thoughtlessly splashed Thérèse with the dirty water. Another sister with whom Thérèse shared the dinner table would more often than not drink all the cider in the pitcher without noticing Thérèse's needs (HLTT 107). Another sister sat behind Thérèse during the community prayers and made a continuous clicking sound with her teeth that was extremely irritating to Thérèse. And then there was the sister who, Thérèse simply wrote, *has the faculty of displeasing me in everything, in her ways, her words, her character, everything seems very disagreeable to me* (SS 222).

In recounting these incidents in her memoirs, Thérèse was describing the ordinary, everyday experiences of group living, even among those trying to live holy lives. The incidents do not represent extraordinary exchanges; they are simply common human interactions. Because of her sensitivities, however, they aroused strong feelings in Thérèse—feelings of impatience, hostility, and animosity, of being inadequate and not respected, of being taken for granted and used, of being intimidated and threatened. These were the feelings of being a victim, of being helpless, with no personal power or control. They were the feelings of being in the presence of "the enemy."

These difficult, spontaneous feelings sometimes caught Thérèse off guard, and then she felt a war beginning in her heart. These were not the feelings of love that she wished to have. These negative feelings did not express the deepest desire of her true self. The difficult feelings themselves were becoming "the enemy" inside herself. At such times, Thérèse found herself in a dilemma: what to do in the presence of the adversary, the troublesome sister, but also what to do in the presence of her own distressing feelings, "the enemy" within.

The community at recreation in the chestnut walk, February 1895, with Thérèse at upper left

CHAPTER 9

We Don't Have Any Enemies in Carmel but There Are Feelings

RESPONDING TO DIFFICULT SISTERS

As Thérèse contemplated Jesus' words in the Gospel to "love your enemies" (Matthew 5:44; Luke 6:27), she wondered at first how they might apply to her living in this Carmelite convent among women committed to a life of prayer and charity. Recognizing that the supernatural love among the community members could not be questioned, Thérèse said, *No doubt we don't have any enemies in Carmel* (SS 225). No doubt what Thérèse said was true at the level of intention. None of the sisters intentionally saw anyone else as an enemy, nor did anyone see herself as being an opponent to anyone. But on the level of feelings, Thérèse experienced some of the sisters as being difficult and contentious.

Thérèse could not deny that with some sisters, she felt as if she were in the presence of an enemy. Moreover, she was also becoming aware that the sisters were arousing the same hostile feelings among themselves. To her reflection that *we don't have any enemies in Carmel*, she quickly added another truth with disarming honesty: *but there are feelings* (SS 225).

The feelings of hostility were spontaneous and often only momentary. They were among those *natural feelings* that if freely prolonged and cultivated, however, could drip poison into a loving heart. Thérèse referred to them when she noted, *Ah! what peace floods the soul when she rises above natural feelings.* From the experiences surrounding her conversion, Thérèse knew the interplay between the disturbances of excessive natural feelings and the peace that arose when these feelings were simply let go of in a spirit of detachment, in a spirit of inner poverty. *No, there is no joy comparable to that which the truly poor in spirit experience*, she wrote at the end of her life (SS 226).

The most holy souls will be perfect only in heaven

Thérèse was also noticing another important truth. By remarking that *we don't have any enemies, but there are feelings,* Thérèse was also pointing to the fact that natural feelings do not only identify "the enemy," but they also actually invent "the enemy."

"The enemy," Thérèse began to understand, was the label placed on any person who aroused the natural feelings of repugnance, hostility, or threat— or any such feelings of being a victim. She was beginning to recognize that her negative feelings and thoughts made her believe that the offending sister was to be treated as an adversary and resisted or avoided. *One feels attracted to* [one] *Sister,* she wrote knowingly, *whereas with regard to another, one would make a long detour in order to avoid meeting her. And so, without even knowing it, she becomes the subject of persecution* (SS 225).

The *subject of persecution* was the sister who was silently labeled "the enemy." And the form that the persecution took was not, of course, physical or even external in most cases. Thérèse and all the sisters were too personally and spiritually controlled and mature for the persecution to often take even the form of cruel words, and feelings of animosity were never expressed in physical violence. Rather, the persecutions took the form of harbored thoughts and feelings of repugnance, unkind avoidance, and being "prone to anger" and the "brooding over injury" that St. Paul spoke of as being contrary to love (cf. 1 Corinthians 13:5). These, however, were reactions that Thérèse also found lingering at times in her own heart.

Moreover, when she became responsible for guiding the newer members of the community, their disclosures confirmed that the feelings of being a victim, the feelings of hostility and retaliation, were provoking some of the discontent and gossip circulating throughout the community. Such feelings were also causing some of the unholy bonding among groups of sisters. Many sisters had, of course, their favorite community friends, but they also had their own secret sister enemies as well. The preferences were naturally based on likability and formed some of the community factions and conflicts.

I have noticed, Thérèse wrote, describing some of the interactions among the sisters, *that the most saintly Sisters are the most loved. We seek their company; we render them services without their asking; . . .* [But] *imperfect souls are not sought out. No doubt we remain within the limits of religious politeness in their regard, but we generally avoid them, fearing lest we say something which isn't too amiable* (SS 245–46).

To *say something which isn't too amiable* was to speak harshly, and that would have violated *the limits of religious politeness.* More significant, perhaps, cruel words would have exposed the violence within the heart of the speaker, and that would be deeply humiliating to the sister seeking holiness and believing herself to be loving toward others. It was simpler and more effective to give the *imperfect souls* the silent treatment—to *avoid them.*

When I speak of imperfect souls, Thérèse clarified her thought further, *I don't want to speak of spiritual imperfections since the most holy souls will be perfect only in heaven.* Rather, Thérèse was referring to those sisters who were humanly irritating and repulsive here on earth. She experienced them as having *a lack of judgment, good manners, touchiness; . . . all these things which don't make life very agreeable. I know very well that these moral infirmities are chronic, that there is no hope of a cure* (SS 246).

Thérèse found several such sisters in the community. Walking the path of love in their company was one of her major and continuing challenges. To live peacefully in a community of difficult persons became for Thérèse an important formative experience in her understanding *the science of love* and in identifying important aspects of the heart qualities of love.

This Sister must be loved even if I believe that she doesn't love me

Thérèse was noticing that the convent was divided into "friends" and "enemies," according to a sister's own preferences. The subjectivity of these labels struck Thérèse most forcefully when she became aware that her own blood sister Pauline, whom she loved so deeply, was not liked by all the other sisters.

Pauline had been elected superior five years after Thérèse had entered the convent. Since Pauline was so lovable in Thérèse's eyes, Thérèse found hostility toward her as the superior difficult to understand. When Pauline failed to win reelection, Thérèse was stunned. How could anyone not appreciate Pauline as a person or not value her as the talented leader of the community? How could anyone think of Pauline as an adversary, as some of the sisters did?

What Thérèse noticed firsthand clearly confirmed her insight that the enemy was an invention of thoughts and feelings. The one labeled "the enemy" was simply the one who did not fulfill preferences and expectations and who aroused opposition. The label had nothing to do with whether the person was lovable, good, or effective. One sister's adversary could be another sister's best friend.

Thérèse's own early behavior had openly disturbed some of the sisters, and now she wondered if some might still be secretly harboring feelings of animosity toward her, as they had toward Pauline. Even so, she did not need to *give in to* any *natural antipathy* in return (SS 222). She meditated on these words of Jesus: "If you love those who love you, what credit is that to you? Even sinners love those who love them" (Luke 6:32). Jesus' words were telling her *that it is this* [enemy] *Sister who must be loved, she must be prayed for even though her conduct would lead me to believe that she doesn't love me* (SS 225).

If Thérèse herself would not "brood over injuries," nor foster any of her spontaneous, natural adversarial feelings, then she could have creative compassion toward all the sisters. She would not feel that any of the sisters were her enemy. She herself would simply have no enemies. Her love would become inclusive.

Thérèse saw that by simply not submitting to her natural feelings of repugnance but by praying for the sister, she was taking the first step toward responding to Jesus' command to love everyone, particularly to "love your enemies" (Matthew 5:44). A heart quality of love, she noticed, was the willingness to hold on to her hope and inner freedom and to let go of her preferences and expectations. Without being attached to her likes and dislikes and without indulging her feelings of animosity, she would not think of anyone as an enemy.

Feelings of love, even feelings of liking, were not necessary to walk the path of authentic love. What was necessary was to let go of thoughts and natural feelings of antipathy. This, Thérèse was to discover, required much patience and the ability to bear serenely her own inner disturbance. She needed to find refuge in a deeper relationship with God.

Charity must not consist in feelings but in works

She prayed, bringing her negative thoughts and feelings to God: *I understood above all that charity must not remain hidden in the bottom of the heart. Jesus has said: "No one lights a lamp and puts it under a bushel basket, but upon the lamp-stand, so as to give light to ALL in the house"* [Matthew 5:15]. *It seems to me,* she pondered, *that this lamp represents charity which must enlighten and rejoice not only those who are dearest to us but "ALL who are in the house" without distinction* (SS 220). *I want to be friendly with everybody,* she wrote, struggling interiorly to let go of her preferences (SS 246).

Thérèse understood that she was called to inclusive love, and she was recognizing an important way of allowing that to happen. *I told myself that charity must not consist in* [just good] *feelings* [or thoughts only] *but in works* (SS 222). By understanding that love *must consist in works*, Thérèse was also beginning to recognize another deep truth in *the science of love*: the truth that creative, loving acts themselves, regardless of her feelings, helped her on the path of authentic and inclusive love.

She had seen that the sense of being a victim contributed to the feelings of being in the presence of an adversary. By taking some control and initiating *works* of love, she identified an important way of letting go of the feeling of being a victim. If in the presence of feelings of animosity she could detach herself, standing her ground emotionally as she had done on the stairway that Christmas bearing the pain of her father's remark, then she could take the next step. Then, bearing the pain of feeling like a victim, she could take the step of initiating a creative expression of love *in works*. She could step through the feelings of being a victim into the truth, embracing her real desire to love her sisters, *to be friendly with everybody*.

Thérèse sought out in recreation, on free days, *the company of the Sisters who are the least agreeable to me, in order to carry out with regard to these wounded souls the office of the Good Samaritan. A word, an amiable smile, often suffices to make a sad soul bloom; but it is not principally to attain this end that I wish to practice charity, for I know I would soon become discouraged; a word I shall say with the best intention will perhaps be interpreted wrongly* (SS 246).

Thérèse saw that perhaps an act of kindness would not be received in kindness. If that happened, she knew, then more awareness and creativity needed to be brought to the next act of kindness so that it would meet the terms of the other person; but what mattered deeply was that Jesus' inclusive love, even the love of enemies, find expression through her kindness.

She developed the practice of noticing the needs of the sisters and then creatively responding, not only in prayer, but in acts of patience and accommodation. She recounted her interaction with one sister whom she must have found among the *least agreeable*, one whose *moral infirmities are chronic*, with *no hope of a cure* (SS 246), an "enemy" who happened to have the place behind her in the chapel.

A Sister who had a strange habit

Thérèse told the story of the sister who made a continuous clicking sound with her teeth. *For a long time at evening meditation,* Thérèse recounted, *I was placed in front of a Sister who had a strange habit and I think many lights* [inspirations] *because she rarely used a book during meditation. This is what I noticed: as soon as this Sister arrived* [in the chapel for meditation], *she began making a strange little noise which resembled the noise one would make when rubbing two shells, one against the other. I was the only one to notice it because I had extremely sensitive hearing (too much so at times)* (SS 249).

Thérèse became deeply agitated: *It would be impossible for me to tell you how much this little noise wearied me.* In her natural feelings of annoyance, Thérèse spontaneously felt the urge to strike back against this sister. *I had a great desire to turn my head,* Thérèse continued, *and stare at the culprit who was very certainly unaware of her "click"* (SS 249).

Feeling a lack of respect and victimized, Thérèse had met the enemy, *the culprit.* She was provoked to retaliate, not of course physically, nor even with a sharp word. Either of these would have been too offensive to Thérèse's self-image and too blatantly an unholy act and a sign of potential violence in her own heart. But a severe stare Thérèse did momentarily consider. *This would be the only way of enlightening her,* Thérèse noted (SS 249).

A stare, it is true, would have alerted the sister to the distracting nature of her behavior and stopped it. But Thérèse knew that there was a falseness in thinking this way. Instead, she needed to reject the poison beginning to drip contamination into her heart's desire to love. Thérèse quickly acknowledged the danger: *However, in the bottom of my heart I felt it was much better to suffer this out of love for God and not to cause the Sister any pain* (SS 249).

Thérèse could not, with love, *stare at the culprit* in a reprimanding way. A stare may have been enlightening for the sister but would not have been a loving act for Thérèse. For Thérèse, it would have been more of a way to even the score with the sister and shame her. With an agitated turn of the head and a severe stare, Thérèse could have ended *the culprit's* disturbing behavior, but in compassion and charity, with her natural gifts and limitations, she could not make such a harsh and self-righteous gesture.

Thérèse could not act at the same time with both love and agitation. If in retaliation she were to step off the path of love to relieve her own distress, then her agitated feelings themselves would become a second adversary, opposing her desire to love and arousing a war in her heart. To remain at peace with her true self, to resist being controlled by her feelings, and to hold to her desire to walk the path of love, Thérèse would have to respond in another way.

Thérèse instinctively knew that if she were to act in love toward *the culprit* on the outside, on the inside she would first have to deal with her own angry feelings of hostility and bring peace to her own distress. She needed to regain her balance and maintain her inner freedom. Only by being patient with herself, befriending her feelings, and not letting them become the enemy inside could she respond with love and without violence to *the culprit* outside.

I was obliged simply to make a prayer of suffering

Thérèse revealed her inner state as she continued her story: *I was the only one to notice it* [the clicking noise] *because I had extremely sensitive hearing (too much so at times)*. The core of the issue, of course, was not in her *extremely sensitive hearing* but, rather, in her extremely sensitive nature. Thérèse's inner disturbance, aroused by the clicking sound, was coming from the feeling of being disregarded. She was aggrieved by the violation being done to her natural sensitivities and to her assumptions and expectations regarding the normal habits of personal refinement, especially in the chapel, a place of reverence.

These sensitivities and expectations Thérèse had simply taken for granted. Another sister not sensitive in the same way and with different expectations may not have even noticed the noise or, noticing it, may not have become so agitated. Another sister may even have simply disregarded the clicking noise, not because her hearing would have been less sensitive, but because her nature may not have been so refined. She may not have been so vulnerable to being personally disregarded. Yet another sister may have been able to correct the clicking sister peacefully or may have even found the clicking sound amusing in this place of solemnity.

Gathering what were, perhaps, the experiences of many occasions into this single description, Thérèse continued to tell her story of how she finally creatively befriended her feelings. *I remained calm, therefore, and tried to unite myself to God and to forget the little noise* (SS 249).

By this first response, Thérèse refused to step from the path of love onto the path of violence toward the sister or onto the path of self-righteousness.

Yet this initial attempt to pray was a reaction that verged on denial of the situation. Furthermore, she was reaching the point of being violent to herself because she was disregarding her feelings. Perhaps with a willful, forced focus, Thérèse could have concentrated her mind, *remained calm,* and blocked the noise, but that would not have been authentic prayer. She immediately became more realistic and noted honestly that *everything was useless. I felt the perspiration inundate me* (SS 249).

Thérèse admitted the fruitlessness of attempting to go against the reality she was facing. She also did not enter the self-condemning path of becoming annoyed at herself for being annoyed at the sister or disturbed at herself for not being more capable of praying. Rather, in a spirit of self-surrender to what she could not change—either the annoyance within herself or the clicking sound outside of herself—she again united herself to God, but this time with the full awareness of the painful irritation of the noise. Her prayer was different; it was not denial. *I was obliged simply to make a prayer of suffering,* Thérèse acknowledged with simplicity.

For Thérèse, this suffering would not be a form of violence to herself. Authentic prayer would consist in her bearing the situation with Jesus in a spirit of willing self-surrender to God's providence in the present moment. And this she did. With further awareness and in self-respect, Thérèse noted that *while suffering, I searched for a way of doing it without annoyance and with peace and joy, at least in the interior of my soul. I tried to love the little noise which was so displeasing,* she wrote, describing her willingness to be patient with herself and with the sister (SS 249).

She could take no realistic control over the outside situation, so by her willingness to bear it serenely, she took control of what it was doing to her. This initiative, which was an inner act of charity, a good work to herself that was also a good work to the sister, and a step toward reconciliation, helped her to prayerfully release feelings of being a victim and allowed her to walk the path of love.

My prayer was spent in offering this concert to Jesus

With a light heart coming from years of reflecting on this experience, Thérèse continued her story. *Instead of trying not to hear it (impossible), I paid close attention so as to hear it well, as though it were a delightful concert, and my prayer (which was not the Prayer of Quiet) was spent in offering this concert to Jesus* (SS 249–50). Her two sets of parentheses expressed her amusement as she reminisced years later. By then, she was able to see some humor in one of the little problems of life.

As Thérèse reflected on and wrote about this incident, her faith perspective may have been enhanced by her consideration of some real distresses that ordinary people have to endure daily and patiently in their family and work. She may have thought about all the upsetting things her mother had to put up with in raising her five daughters with all their idiosyncrasies. She may have even considered all the personal distress her parents had tolerated as they coped with her stubbornness. She may have also reflected on the daily suffering her mother had serenely endured for years with her cancerous condition. She may have thought of her father patiently bearing the burdens of his physical and mental deterioration during the last years of his life. In the grand scheme of things, what did the annoyance of a little clicking sound really matter?

Little things can prompt enormous emotional reactions in sensitive hearts, and little things were the usual things in the confined situation of convent life. When Thérèse could detach herself from all the emotional fuss, she saw the comical in the clicking and in her feelings. But at the time, her sufferings were real, and she *felt the perspiration inundate me.*

The clicking sound of *the culprit* outside she made part of the *delightful concert* of prayer. The natural feelings of anger and hostility—the enemy inside— she also befriended. In her authentic prayer, Thérèse calmed her distress and animosity and discovered a creative way to be patient with herself as well as loving to *the culprit.* While *not the Prayer of Quiet* that she had intended to offer during her meditation, this realistic prayer of her experience in the present moment became her moment of self-surrender, her offering of self.

In offering this concert to Jesus, she offered an incarnational prayer of compassion and forgiveness for the sister in the sister's weakness. She also offered a prayer for herself in her own weaknesses—her ongoing excessive sensitivities, her present state of vulnerability, her feelings of agitation, and her awareness of her limitations to love. In abandonment into God's providence unfolding in the situation and by accepting the reality of her own humanness, Thérèse understood more clearly another dimension of *the science of love* and experienced more fully the heart quality of self-surrender telling her that she was on the path of love.

The community gathered at the laundry, 1895, with Thérèse second from left

CHAPTER 10

I Would Be Very Foolish to Refuse These Treasures

EXPRESSING THE SPIRIT OF LOVE

Thérèse told other stories of interactions with the sisters that irritated her. She was particularly disturbed by some sisters who expressed a *lack of judgment* and *good manners* (SS 246). There was, for example, the occasion when Thérèse was doing the laundry with a group of sisters. One sister inadvertently but continuously splashed water on Thérèse's face. Probably including memories of more than one such occasion, Thérèse described what loving a difficult sister might look like in the ordinary day-to-day experiences of life. She also identified some dispositions, some heart qualities of love.

These moral infirmities are chronic; there is no hope of a cure

The sister doing the splashing did not notice the inconvenience she was causing Thérèse and had no intention of being unpleasant. She was one of the several community sisters Thérèse was probably describing as having *all these things which don't make life very agreeable*. But Thérèse also understood that often enough, *these moral infirmities are chronic, that there is no hope of a cure* (SS 246). So although Thérèse knew that she could have expressed her irritation and embarrassed this thoughtless sister into changing her behavior, instead, as she had done with the sister in the chapel, she remained patient and did not overreact.

If Thérèse had other natural gifts or if she had not experienced the sister's thoughtlessness as *chronic*, she may have been able to directly and lovingly challenge the offending sister. But respecting her own limitations of resistance to confront others and grappling with the question of what love might feel like and look like for her in such a situation, Thérèse quickly recognized an opportunity to profit from the sister's actions.

Again with awareness and a sense of humor, she describes how she managed her own feelings. *My first reaction*, she wrote, *was to draw back and wipe my face to show the Sister who was sprinkling me that she would do me a favor to be more careful. But I immediately thought I would be very foolish to refuse these treasures which were being given to me so generously, and I took care not to show my struggle. I put forth all my efforts to desire receiving very much of this dirty water, and was so successful that in the end I had really taken a liking to this kind of aspersion* (SS 250).

By acknowledging her disturbance but by taking *care not to show my struggle*, Thérèse refused to parade the self-indulgent attitude of being a victim or to react self-righteously to the sister's *lack of judgment* and *good manners* (SS 246). By not refusing *these treasures which were being given*, Thérèse took creative initiative and willingly welcomed the providence of God's love in the present moment. In faith, self-control, and in patience for herself, Thérèse continued to walk the path of love. She avoided losing her inner freedom and did not allow her spontaneous hostile feelings to control her or drive her to overreact. She refused to become an enemy to herself. At the same time, while not denying that the sister's action was inconsiderate, Thérèse avoided the retaliation implicit in her first impulse to *draw back . . . to show the Sister . . . to be more careful.* She refused also to become an enemy to the sister.

None of the other sisters at the laundry noticed the situation. Like her Christmas conversion, it was a drama unfolding within Thérèse herself. It was another common interaction of ordinary life in which hostility was avoided and love expressed inconspicuously. It was another example of Thérèse being in the presence of the enemy, but quickly putting the situation into a faith perspective and into the perspective of ordinary difficult human interactions that need not elicit overreactions. In this trivial experience—what does splashing really mean in the bigger scheme of things—and in receiving *treasures* from other *small sacrifices carried out in the shadows*, or other such *nothings*, as Thérèse referred to them (SS 125, 144; cf. GC 504, 801), she embraced the grace of her vocation to love and read *the book of life wherein is contained the science of Love* (SS 187).

I used to run away like a deserter whenever my struggles became too violent

Thérèse also elaborated on the story about the *Sister who has the faculty of displeasing me in everything, in her ways, her words, her character, everything seems very disagreeable to me* (SS 222; HLTT 111). This sister was a prime candidate for Thérèse to label "the enemy." Yet Thérèse recognized in faith that *she is a holy religious and . . . must be very pleasing to God* (SS 222). In particular, Thérèse understood that the problem she had with this sister came from her own natural antipathy and was mostly a case of her own weakness and vulnerability.

This sister must have been one of the sisters to whom Thérèse was referring when she wrote to Pauline less than a year after she had joined the community: [Jesus] *is so gentle! . . . But creatures! . . . Those who surround me are very good, but there is something, I don't know what, that repels me! . . . I am, however, very happy, happy to suffer what Jesus wants me to suffer* (GC 499–500).

Knowing that she herself could not love this woman on the level of her natural feelings, Thérèse accepted the spiritual challenge to bear serenely her own feelings of repugnance and moved her attention to the level of action in faith: *Each time I met her I prayed to God for her, offering Him all her virtues and merits* (SS 222). Interiorly in prayer, Thérèse held this sister in a spirit of appreciation. But how, in the actual everyday human encounters with this sister, was Thérèse to carry out the important insight that she had gained previously in her prayer: *that charity must . . . consist in works* (SS 222)?

By praying for this sister, Thérèse was performing an inner work of love, but she did more. *I wasn't content simply with praying very much for this Sister who gave me so many struggles*, Thérèse wrote, *but I took care to render her all the services possible, and when I was tempted to answer her back in a disagreeable manner, I was content with giving her my most friendly smile, and with changing the subject of the conversation* (SS 222–23).

While Thérèse prayed for this sister and offered her *all the services possible*, Thérèse also acknowledged that she had feelings of retaliation and was prone to *answer her back*. The prayers, *the services*, and especially the *most friendly smile* were creative initiatives—the *works* of charity—that helped Thérèse let go of her feelings of being a victim in the sister's presence, avoid overreacting, regain her inner freedom, and resist her spontaneous feelings of retaliating. But then Thérèse added still another *work* of charity for this sister. While other members of the community sometimes avoided this difficult sister, Thérèse volunteered to help her with her community responsibilities.

By volunteering to work with this sister, however, Thérèse may have unknowingly fallen victim to a certain arrogance by thinking she was capable of working peaceably with anyone. Thérèse rather quickly learned that she was more weak and vulnerable than she had believed.

At times when the two were working together, Thérèse felt her natural antipathy surface. In the presence of the sister's disturbing behavior, Thérèse experienced the painful feelings to which she was prone: feelings of not being pleasing, of separation, and of self-righteousness. Thérèse also experienced the hostile, retaliatory feelings of being *tempted to answer her back in a disagreeable manner.* If Thérèse cultivated any of these feelings, they would become an obstacle to the love desire of her true self.

Even though the sister apparently did not intend to be disagreeable, Thérèse became intimidated, defensive, and angry. Sometimes Thérèse could maintain her balance and *was content with giving her my most friendly smile, and with changing the subject of the conversation.* But *frequently, when I . . . had occasion to work with this sister,* Thérèse wrote, revealing the inner workings of her heart, *I used to run away like a deserter whenever my struggles became too violent* (SS 223).

In sensing the violence of her own inner struggles, Thérèse knew that she could not for the moment bear in peace her own difficult feelings. Thérèse was disturbed, not only by the sister's contentious behavior, but also by her own overreaction.

Thérèse also knew that she had to respect her own sensitivity and weaknesses in dealing with the situation. She could not let her hurt and hostile feelings run roughshod over her own limitations in an otherworldly attempt to be pleasing to this sister. Thérèse had a *natural antipathy* against this sister, and she had to be realistic about the limits to her adaptability and patience.

This was another occasion when Thérèse had feelings of being in the presence of an enemy, and she was disturbed by her own toxic feelings of animosity and shame that were about to war with her true self. Thérèse's only prudent and humble course of action was *to run away. My last means of not being defeated in combats,* she says with humble honesty, *is desertion* (SS 223). She calmed her own inner struggle by flight.

I was smiling because I was happy to see her

When Thérèse *used to run away* in hurt, fear, and embarrassment, she may have experienced self-diminishing feelings of being *a deserter,* abandoning her desire to love. Actually, however, her love for herself and her love for the sister at that moment required her to reclaim her true self. She could not allow herself to continue to be subjected to the offensive behavior of the sister, and she could not permit herself to be violated by her own negative feelings. Nor could she, out of a sense of self-defense or self-righteousness, allow herself to do violence to the sister by retaliating. Desertion was not cowardliness for Thérèse at that moment. It was a realistic acknowledgment of the sister's inappropriate behavior, of Thérèse's own weaknesses, and of her only honest way to avoid violence to herself or to the sister.

By leaving the sister's presence, Thérèse established a kind of boundary to the offensive ways of the sister as well as to her own feelings. While fleeing externally, internally Thérèse was trying to stand her ground emotionally and not allow her feelings to control her. In that way, Thérèse took some initiative and took control of her own inner experience of turmoil. Then having regained her true self, she returned to the sister with more emotional protection and with more patience and acceptance of her own limitations. She befriended her hostile feelings and interacted more lovingly with the outer enemy as well.

Thérèse recounted further details about this relationship. Again with humor, she wrote in retrospect, *As she was absolutely unaware of my feelings for her, never did she suspect the motives for my conduct and she remained convinced that her character was very pleasing to me* (SS 223). Thérèse interacted with this sister with such creativity and compassion that even though they lived together for nine years, this sister never experienced herself as being difficult for Thérèse. In fact, this sister really had a deep affection for Thérèse and thought that she was one of Thérèse's favorite companions.

One day at recreation, Thérèse wrote, the sister asked her in *almost these words: "Would you tell me, Sister Thérèse of the Child Jesus, what attracts you so much towards me; every time you look at me, I see you smile?" Ah! what attracted me was Jesus hidden in the depths of her soul. . . . I answered that I was smiling because I was happy to see her.* Thérèse then adds playfully in parentheses: *(it is understood that I did not add that this was from a spiritual standpoint)* (SS 223; GC 790, note 1).

It was, however, only *from a spiritual standpoint* of faith that Thérèse was able to survive the emotional onslaught of her own sensitivities and *natural antipathy*. And only after much prayer that put the interaction into a faith perspective did she find anything humorous in the relationship.

A further dimension to this story developed when Thérèse's blood sister Marie, seeing how Thérèse treated this sister so graciously with her words and personal written notes of encouragement, became jealous of the relationship. Marie was aware that Thérèse had composed her first poem at the request of this sister (CP 5), and over the years she became convinced that Thérèse loved this sister more than Thérèse loved her. When Marie complained that Thérèse's love for this sister was not fair to her, Thérèse realized that she had a new relational problem to solve and responded again with humor. She smiled a mischievous smile and then laughed good-naturedly (STL 97–98). But she did not explain or justify herself.

Perhaps Thérèse could not explain herself since at the time, she may not have fully understood what was happening within her. Thérèse was actually walking intuitively on the path of love, taking missteps and regaining herself. She was learning, however, from her experiences in prayer that regardless of what the behavior or intention of the other sister was, when she herself experienced the embarrassment of spontaneous negative, hostile feelings, she needed to know that she was on the edge of doing violence to herself or to others. To continue to walk the path of love, she needed to respond without violence.

To maintain her true self and to not allow her natural feelings to control her, Thérèse sometimes could detach herself internally while remaining physically present, as she had done with the sisters in the chapel and in the laundry. But sometimes she needed to flee externally to give herself time and space to reestablish her inner freedom. Always it was true that if she did not harbor or cultivate these spontaneous hostile feelings, they were not an obstacle to love. If the hostile feelings could be borne in a spirit of faith and patient prayer, they would not erupt in a war within herself but could actually assist her on the path of love by moving her closer to the source of love.

I gave her my most beautiful smile

Thérèse also described in detail her interactions with an older sister, Sr. St. Pierre. This sister Thérèse must have also numbered among the *least agreeable* to her in the community, one whose *moral infirmities were chronic,* with *no hope of a cure* (SS 246). For Thérèse, then still a novice, these interactions were particularly irritating and demanding. Because this sister was so critical, Thérèse's natural feelings were fear, inadequacy, and hostility. However, not given to being passively aggressive, Thérèse again courageously initiated a work of love by serving the sister.

In telling the story of her interactions with this sister, Thérèse acknowledged her negative feelings.

Each evening when I saw . . . [her] shake her hour-glass I knew this meant: Let's go! It is incredible how difficult it was for me to get up, especially at the beginning; however, I did it immediately, and then a ritual was set in motion. I had to remove and carry her little bench in a certain way, above all I was not to hurry, and then the walk took place. It was a question of following the poor invalid by holding her cincture; I did this with as much gentleness as possible. But if by mistake she took a false step, immediately it appeared to her that I was holding her incorrectly and that she was about to fall. "Ah! my God! You are going too fast; I'm going to break something." If I tried to go more slowly: "Well, come on! I don't feel your hand; you've let me go and I'm going to fall! Ah! I was right when I said you were too young to help me." (SS 247–48)

Thérèse had feelings of being a victim in reaction to the sister's cantankerous, demeaning attitude, but she bore these feelings as peacefully as she could. She did not take the sister's behavior personally and did not allow her feelings to control her. She continued to inconspicuously assist the sister.

Finally, we reached the refectory without mishap; and here other difficulties arose. I had to seat Sister St. Pierre and I had to act skillfully in order not to hurt her; then I had to turn back her sleeves (again in a certain way), and afterward I was free to leave. With her poor crippled hands she was trying to manage with her bread as well as she could. I soon noticed this, and, each evening, I did not leave her until after I had rendered her this little service. As she had not asked for this, she was very much touched by my attention, and it was by this means that I gained her entire good graces, and this especially (I learned this later) because, after cutting her bread for her, I gave her my most beautiful smile before leaving her all alone. (SS 247–48)

Thérèse never denied the spontaneous hostile feelings that arose within her, but she did not cultivate these feelings. By simply putting charity to work helping this sister *turn back her sleeves* and in particular by rendering *her this little* unasked *service of managing her bread*, Thérèse deliberately took some creative initiative. By this courteous gesture, Thérèse stepped through her feelings of being a victim. She regained her confidence of having something to contribute, and she acted in love.

The entire cluster of negative feelings toward the sister that had momentarily arisen in Thérèse's heart began to change. Instead of this difficult potential adversary, she saw a lonely, suffering, and lovely sister *with her poor crippled hands*. Sr. St. Pierre herself, experiencing the genuine kindness of someone to whom she had been harshly demanding, was deeply touched. Thérèse's love had transformed her own antagonistic feelings and had calmed the distress in the heart of Sr. St. Pierre as well. In the presence of authentic love creatively expressed, even the lifelong negative feelings within this wounded sister began to dissolve.

Speak with detachment of heart

Although Thérèse herself was not argumentative, she did see some of the sisters who had good intentions scolding, arguing, holding grudges, and gossiping among themselves. They were unaware of the seeds of violence they were sowing in themselves and in their community. Later she advised Céline, her blood sister who entered the community six years after Thérèse, not to let the power of her hostile feelings against another sister move her to justify herself or to retaliate, even when she was wronged or had reason to argue.

When you tell someone, even Mother Prioress, about some argument, she warned Céline, *never do it to have the sister who caused it corrected or so that the thing you're complaining about might stop; rather, speak with detachment of heart. When you don't feel that detachment, if there is still even a spark of emotion in your heart, it is more perfect to keep quiet and wait . . . because talking about it often only aggravates it* (FGM 188). Later she would remark further to Pauline, *It does us so much good and it gives us so much strength not to speak of our troubles* (HLC 135).

Thérèse was speaking from her own experience. That *detachment of heart*, not taking the behavior of others personally, gave her the strength to maintain the inner freedom that she needed to do the work of love with the sister's best interest at heart. The *spark of emotion* told her that she was under the control of her feelings and was on the edge of losing her balance. Then, any act that followed would be not only an act of impatience with herself but also a reaction of egotistical self-protection. It would not be an act of God's love in her for the good of the other. Sharing this hard-earned advice with Céline, Thérèse was offering her soul mate a tender act of love, pointing out the path of love through a minefield of self-serving temptations.

She also shared with Céline another important truth. *How easy it is to please Jesus, to delight His Heart,* she revealed to her sister. *One has only to love Him, without looking at one's self, without examining one's faults too much.* Thérèse had come to understand that her spontaneous negative feelings could become faults if harbored or cultivated, but more important, she recognized that her feelings were drawing her to rely even more on Jesus. *Jesus is teaching* [me] she wrote, *to learn "to draw profit from everything, from the good and the bad she finds in herself"* [reference to St. John of the Cross] (GC 795; cf. SS 179; HF 339).

Thérèse saw that her natural feelings and faults were not incompatible with her love of God or with her deep desire to love her sisters. She could pray, forgiving the sisters who displeased her as well as forgiving herself for any tendency to cultivate the negative feelings that were at war with her true self. Her prayer became a way of loving the enemy.

She could love her sisters without actually liking them, and she could love herself in her vulnerability, her weaknesses, and her faults. At the end of her life, Thérèse shared with Céline yet another insight into *the science of love. Charity,* she said simply, *consists in bearing with those who are unbearable* (MSST 229).

By contemplating her own experiences of these ordinary interactions with the difficult sisters and by meditating on Jesus' life and words, Thérèse came to understand that Jesus' command to "love your enemies" was not really a command at all. Love cannot be commanded. Love of its nature must be free and willing. Rather, Jesus' words are really more of a description of the human heart's deepest longings that arise when not poisoned by fear and self-centeredness. The human heart, created in God's image and united to God's love, is not meant to be adversarial to oneself or to anyone.

Thérèse knew from her experience that the wounded human heart, "brooding over injuries," would create enemies to defend its own egotistical dark side of self-indulgence and self-righteousness. But she gradually saw that when she allowed herself to be embraced by God's providence at each moment, she was able to love herself and the difficult sisters. Then she could walk the path of love and fulfill God's *measureless desires* (SS 197) within her. Sr. Marie of the Angels, who had been Thérèse's novice mistress, described Thérèse as she matured on her path: "She was an angel of peace for everybody" (STL 207).

The difficult toxic feelings that Thérèse spontaneously experienced subsided over the years, but even her prayer-filled desire to love never completely eliminated them. Believing that the arms of suffering that had opened wide to her when she entered the community were the arms of the crucified Jesus inviting her to accompany him in his paschal mystery, she saw that the path of love would lead specifically through the disquiet of loving her sisters in their very human weaknesses. That path would also move through the humiliating distress of accepting her own frailties and limitations. These insights became important lessons as Thérèse grew in *the science of love*.

CHAPTER 11

We Should Never Allow Kindness to Degenerate into Weakness

SHARING LOVE IN SPECIAL WAYS

Thérèse saw that there were multiple dimensions to loving both friend and enemy. She wondered how to handle a situation in which her sister companions were not just thoughtless or inconsiderate but, with more direct intent, were actually doing something wrong, acting not in their own best interest or not in the best interest of the community. Would it be an expression of love for her simply to bear the situation or totally ignore it? Was she not rather called to correct it? In this regard, Thérèse's first concern was her degree of responsibility. Her love was to be for all the sisters without exception, but was the degree of love's responsibility to correct others without exception? Was she responsible to right every wrong? Thérèse did not think so.

Further, Thérèse had learned that she needed to maintain her inner freedom and peace within the bounds of her own limitations and gifts. She also needed to discern, not only how best to correct a wrong, but how to address the offending person on that person's own terms. These considerations needed to be joined to recognizing what was in the person's best interests as well as the community's. Love, Thérèse understood, had to be eminently creative and compassionate and could not issue from a sense of domination, grudges, or retaliation. Love, especially corrective love, could not be expressed in an adversarial or self-righteous attitude.

Thérèse needed all this awareness as she grew to interact more responsibly with Mother Gonzague and particularly as she fulfilled her obligations in her role of guiding the newer members of the community.

There are some trials that should not be given

Although her nature was not aggressive or domineering, Thérèse was capable of being quite assertive and unyielding when she was convinced that God was asking her to act with integrity. She brought to her religious convictions the force of her will, which had erupted in stubbornness in childhood but which now resided in the calm power and passion of her desire for God's will.

As she matured emotionally, Thérèse's strong will turned to quiet resolve and determination. When as a teenager she was convinced that God was asking her to enter Carmel, she had been determined to do everything she could to follow her vocation. At that time, she acted with courageous purpose to gain the required permissions, and with surprising boldness, she had spoken directly to the pope himself.

Forceful and determined behavior was required of Thérèse also after she entered the convent. But most often, her willpower was directed internally in her own steadfastness to continue on her path of love. In particular, several times she needed to be especially vigilant and resolute when she was disturbed with the authoritative stance of Mother Gonzague.

On one occasion, Mother Gonzague commanded Thérèse—contrary to the usual community customs— to make some inappropriate preparations of hospitality for the superior's own relatives. Thérèse experienced a violent internal struggle with her feelings of resistance. She became unnerved by the superior's constant erratic and dominating use of authority that sometimes violated the good order and common regulations of the convent. Thérèse recounted much later to Pauline that in this instance, she had to struggle mightily against the upsurge of hostile feelings that she had against the superior. She was able to fulfill Mother Gonzague's orders only after she had calmed her violent feelings with a prayerful spirit of faith (HLC 90).

She also disagreed with Mother Gonzague's use of power when the superior did not permit the sisters to receive Communion frequently (cf. STL 39). Acknowledging that the superior had legitimate authority to legislate in this way, Thérèse nevertheless was convinced that Jesus had instituted the Eucharist *not to remain in a golden ciborium* [but] . . . *He comes down to us each day from heaven . . . to find another heaven, infinitely more dear to Him than the first: the heaven of our soul, made to His image, the living temple of the adorable Trinity!* (SS 104). She believed that by receiving Communion, she and all the sisters fulfilled their deepest desire, that their Beloved would *come and take possession of . . .* [their] *soul* (SS 276; PST 53ff.).

She once asserted to the superior, *Mother, when I'm in heaven, I'll make you change your opinion* (HLC 262). After Thérèse's death, Mother Gonzague did change her opinion, and some of the sisters believed that the superior's enlightenment was one of Thérèse's first miracles.

Thérèse usually managed her difficult feelings toward the superior with prudence and exquisite finesse. She did not participate in the community gossip or complain about the superior. On at least one occasion, however, Thérèse outwardly challenged Mother Gonzague's abuse of authority.

The superior had decided on a course of action that would have delayed the profession of two of the sisters whom Thérèse had under her care. Thérèse thought that Mother Gonzague's decision was capricious and unjust. She felt that the superior needed to be corrected. It was one of the few times that Thérèse reacted sharply and in public, allowing her disagreements and annoyances with Mother Gonzague to surface.

In the presence of fifteen or so community members who were working together, one of the sisters who approved of the superior's decision stated that Mother Gonzague could impose her arbitrary decision as a way of testing the obedience of the young sisters. Thérèse responded abruptly and forcefully, *There are some trials that should not be given* (TLMT 114).

Later she addressed Mother Gonzague privately and directly. Speaking forthrightly and with love for the superior as well as for the community and the sisters who would be affected by the decision, Thérèse told her superior that the decision was not compassionate, nor was it just. The superior listened to Thérèse and, respecting Thérèse's judgment, changed her position.

I am now certain it is my duty to speak

During her early years in the convent and while still in the novitiate, Thérèse noticed that one of her sister novices, older than herself, had fallen into the same trap of emotional attachment to Mother Gonzague as she herself had. Knowing from her own experience the darkness of such an emotional entanglement, Thérèse also knew the pain that the light of truth would cause this sister if she were to be confronted with the dangerous path she was on. Thérèse, however, felt that the sister needed correction for her own good so that she could avoid the snare she was entering.

Thérèse prayed for several months to be in peace and without fear so that she would have the inner freedom and creativity to speak with compassion and with words that the sister could hear. The truth would set her companion free, but Thérèse knew that the heart is not always ready to bear the pain of the truth. She herself had not been able to hear the truth when her Uncle Isidore had confronted her as a child about the trap of self-pity she had fallen into following her mother's death. So as Thérèse prepared to speak with her companion sister, she *begged God to place sweet and convincing words in my mouth, or rather that He speak through me* (SS 236).

Thérèse was also taking a personal risk in addressing the issue. If the sister were to become defensive and tell Mother Gonzague that Thérèse was trying to damage their relationship, Thérèse could have fallen under the wrath of the superior and could possibly have been dismissed from the convent. But after her long discernment, she confided to Pauline, *I am now certain it is my duty to speak; I must not consider the consequences* (GC 758).

Having experienced the same slavery of attachment to Mother Gonzague, Thérèse could empathize with the sister and be disarmingly gentle, even as she was direct in her compassion. Thérèse told the sister forthrightly that her affection for the superior had nothing supernatural about it. It was not real love; it was perilous infatuation. For the sister novice, cultivating her dangerous feelings and allowing herself to be controlled by them were ways of poisoning her heart.

Thérèse explained to the sister: *Your fondness for Mother Prioress is too natural. She is doing your soul a great deal of harm, because you love her passionately, and those kinds of feelings displease God; in nuns they are poison. You did not become a Carmelite to satisfy your natural longings; you did so to mortify them and die to yourself* (STL 223). Then with a severe bluntness, Thérèse told her that the kind of relationship she was establishing with Mother Gonzague was really like *a dog . . . attached to its master* (SS 237). Thérèse knew the sister's emotional state was subhuman. It was bondage to her neediness and her inordinate passions.

To soften the sting of the truth, Thérèse shared the story of her own personal slavery to her earlier infatuation with Mother Gonzague. The sister was astonished at Thérèse's insight into her feelings and behavior and was grateful for Thérèse's honesty. The young sister was ashamed and then enlightened. She saw that she had been indulging and deceiving herself. Thérèse and her companion wept together in the glow of being freed from the bondage of false love and the poison of self-indulgence and attachment (cf. EIG 176–77).

When Thérèse wrote, *Love is nourished only by sacrifices, and the more a soul refuses natural satisfactions, the stronger and more disinterested becomes her tenderness* (SS 237), she could have been speaking to this young sister now free from self-deception and the self-violence of attachment, or she could have been reflecting on her own earlier relationship with Mother Gonzague, or she could have been simply reminding herself of an important truth that she needed to remember constantly.

Thérèse had learned that one of the basic sacrifices that nourishes love is detachment from the grip of self-indulgence to the feelings of neediness. Such feelings arose spontaneously, she knew, but there was a hidden falseness in them, and to cultivate them was to undermine inner freedom and begin to walk the way of self-violence. Her complete conversion had been the fundamental source of this wisdom.

If I'm not loved, that's just too bad!

When Thérèse was entrusted with mentoring the newer candidates in the convent lifestyle, she needed to be vigilant, honest, determined, and detached. She was discrete and prudent but truthful with them, and while being compassionate, she was firm when correcting them. Thérèse was quite direct and sometimes forceful. They regarded her as being very firm, even rigid. Her willingness to accept her responsibility to correct these sisters cost Thérèse dearly, since she was more naturally prone to try to please, and she did not have a naturally assertive or demanding nature.

When she knew what she had to say would be difficult for the young sisters to hear, she especially relied on her natural sensitivity in a spirit of faith and prayer. But finally, she was resigned: *If I'm not loved, that's just too bad! I tell the whole truth and if anyone does not want to know the truth, let her not come looking for me. We should never allow kindness to degenerate into weakness* (HLC 38).

Honest with the sisters she guided, Thérèse also invited them to be honest with her. She was willing to sacrifice her own feelings so that the sisters would not be inhibited in their interaction. She was willing to not take personally their criticism, right or wrong. *You understand,* she wrote to Mother Gonzague, *that everything is permitted to the novices; they must be able to say what they think, the good and the bad* (SS 243–44).

This openness with the young sisters made Thérèse vulnerable to their immaturity and bluntness. *God lifts the veil which hides my imperfections, and then my dear little Sisters, seeing me just as I am, no longer find me according to their taste. With a simplicity which delights me, they tell me all the struggles I give them, what displeases them in me* (SS 244).

On one occasion, her own sister Céline, now a member of the community under Thérèse's direction, was particularly abrupt with her. Thérèse took the occasion to deepen her own self-knowledge and detachment: *Yes, it is the Lord who has commanded* [Céline] *to say all these things to me. And my soul enjoyed the bitter food served up to it in such abundance* (SS 245).

An older member of the community also *served up* some *bitter food* to Thérèse when she remarked to her during recreation, "You should be tending to your own direction instead of directing others!" (HLTT 107).

In the judgment of most of the members of the community, however, Thérèse appeared to be quite successful in her work of mentoring the young sisters. She was aware of this adulation, but she also understood that this road of success was dangerous because it led to the temptation of self-righteousness and arrogance. In her prayer, she recognized that God allowed her to be admired for doing her work successfully because the work would have been impossible if she had been seen as she truly was, *filled with faults, incapable, without understanding or judgment* (SS 244). While acknowledging the success of her work, she also acknowledged that she was prone to faults and weaknesses, especially in her emotions and motivations.

Both her successes and failures were true, but neither was the whole truth. The whole truth was that it was God's work of love in her and through her. *If He pleases to make me appear better than I am,* Thérèse said, *that is none of my affair since He is free to act as He likes. . . . God has cast a veil over all my interior and exterior faults; . . .* [but] *there is always present to my mind the remembrance of what I am. In the eyes of creatures I succeed in everything . . .* [but] *in the depths of my soul,* God allows many humiliations (SS 244). God's mysterious love filled her life.

I then very quickly take care to excuse the Sister

As a young sister herself, Thérèse had experienced the severity of Mother Gonzague and the inconsiderateness of some of the sisters trying to help her adjust to the ways of the community. Thérèse had indeed made many mistakes that needed prompt correction for her own enlightenment as well as for the proper order of the community. Some sisters at times had even acted harshly toward her, and she could have done similarly with the young sisters under her care. She knew, however, that in addition to behavioral change, there was the more important necessary change of heart.

More significant, she also had now come to recognize the violence in severity and in being judgmental toward others, and she was not willing to participate in violence. When Thérèse corrected the behavior of the young sisters with firmness, it was without harshness and with compassion, intending to help the sisters develop a Gospel consciousness as well as to accept the behavioral changes that were in their interest and necessary for the peace of the community (cf. EIG 257ff.).

Scolding and harshness were methods Thérèse saw as cruelly violating the dignity of the person and not the way of Jesus' love and mercy. She sometimes seemed to act sternly toward the young sisters as she tried to move them along the path of love, but she was really adapting her words and actions to fit their needs, to meet them on their own terms. Her sternness was not an expression of her anger, nor was it punitive. In her firmness she followed Jesus, who seemed to be uncompromising but was actually accommodating his teaching to those who would not have understood it if addressed in any other way.

She never suggested to the young sisters that they reproach themselves for their misdeeds or be antagonistic toward themselves because of their mistakes. She never suggested that they cultivate thoughts or feelings that belittled themselves or showed a lack of respect for themselves. She did not teach change by guilt or fear. She constantly suggested that they acknowledge their mistakes but not become enemies to themselves. Rather, she advised that they be patient and kind with themselves even as they increased their self-discipline for the sake of self-transcendence. She had learned this from her own experience.

In guiding the younger sisters, she needed to be discerning and make good judgments regarding the rightness or wrongness of their behavior. She also recognized that making these kinds of judgments was not being judgmental. Being judgmental carried with it condemnation and even hostility. Being judgmental, Thérèse understood, often included self-righteousness and an adversarial attitude, and was a step on the path of violence. Making a good judgment was an act of love on behalf of the good of the community, and for Thérèse, it was necessary for her discernment regarding the good of the young sisters as well.

She saw her own tendency toward being judgmental as a fault, and she acknowledged that it had lingered within her. *Formerly, when I saw a Sister doing something which displeased me and appeared to be against the Rule, I said to myself: Ah, if I could only tell her what I think and show her she is wrong, how much good this would do for me!* (SS 245). Thérèse noticed in retrospect that at that time in her life, her evaluation of the sister's behavior had come from a sense of what would benefit her own self-centered ego and was not necessarily what would benefit the sister or the community.

As Thérèse matured and when she became the mentor for the younger sisters, her attitude changed: *Ever since I have practiced a little the trade of correcting, I assure you, dear Mother, that I have entirely changed my attitude. When it happens that I see a* [older, professed] *Sister perform an action which appears imperfect to me, I heave a sigh of relief and say: How fortunate! this is not a novice* [under my charge]; *I am not obliged to correct her.* Then Thérèse added from a more mature love, *I then very quickly take care to excuse the Sister and to give her the good intentions she undoubtedly has* (SS 245).

When Thérèse was personally disturbed by a professed sister's behavior— even if that behavior was a fault—she rarely directly confronted the sister and requested her to change her ways. Instead, Thérèse moved into a spirit of welcoming God's providence into the situation. By surrendering her expectations and lingering judgmental attitude, her feeling about the disturbing behavior changed. Regaining her inner freedom, she could then deal creatively and compassionately with the sister's behavior and continue to walk the path of love.

CHAPTER 12

When I Am Charitable, It Is Jesus Alone Who Is Acting in Me

BEARING WITH THE FAULTS OF OTHERS

Throughout her years in the convent, Thérèse tried to act charitably toward the sisters, but the main focus in her early years had been on her love relationship with Jesus and on her love of God. In the last years of her life, she came to understand more deeply the connection between love of God and love of neighbor. She saw more clearly that Jesus desired her to come to him in union with her sisters. Particularly as she had continued to meditate on Jesus' words at the Last Supper to love one another as he has loved us (John 13:34), the "new commandment" of love, she understood deeper secrets in *the science of love*.

Toward the end of her life, she recognized that *God has given me the grace to understand what charity is* (SS 219). This grace included a clearer vision into a reality that she had glimpsed earlier: that her love for her sisters was Jesus loving in her. She was loving God when she was loving her sisters because Christ Jesus within her was doing the loving. She now understood with clarity that her love for God and her love for her sisters were really not two separate loves (cf. EIG 260ff.).

Her new awareness of what charity is brought with it a great freedom in her relationships with the sisters. She no longer felt the necessity of refusing all human consolations, *for my soul is strengthened by Him whom I wanted to love uniquely. I can see with joy that in loving Him the heart expands and can give to those who are dear to it incomparably more tenderness than if it has concentrated upon one egotistical and unfruitful love* (SS 237).

During her first years in the convent, Thérèse had *seen many souls, seduced by this false light* [of false friendships]—*the empoisoned cup of a too ardent love of creatures*, as she had written earlier (SS 83). The compromising relationships among the sisters reinforced her natural tendency to shyness and mistrust of her own capacity for authentic friendship with those beyond her family. From her experience with her little friend in her school days, she feared that she could *have allowed myself to be taken and my wings to be clipped, and then how would I have been able to "fly and be at rest"?* [Psalm 55:7] (SS 83). She feared human friendships would compromise her love of God.

Now, however, in the last years of her life, Thérèse's human relationships with her sisters blossomed. She relaxed into appreciating and enjoying her sisters in open expressions of friendship, understanding *above all that charity must not remain hidden in the bottom of the heart* (SS 220). It was a profound discovery in *the science of love* and a giant step for Thérèse on the path of love. Her heart opened in expressions of affection and in gratitude.

You know better than I do my weakness and imperfection

Thérèse received even more light on love of neighbor as she reflected on the original commandment of charity from the Old Testament, "Love your neighbor as yourself" (Leviticus 19:18), and compared that commandment with Jesus' new commandment to "love one another as I have loved you" (cf. John 13:34).

The reference point of the new commandment caught her attention and challenged her. Jesus had said to love "as *I* have loved." She was not to love others as she loved herself, but as Jesus loved. The first challenge that she recognized was that her own love for her sisters certainly did not have the depth or inclusivity of Jesus' love.

The second challenge Thérèse noticed was that Jesus' love for his disciples was not diminished by their faults, their rudeness, or their sinfulness. Thérèse was aware, however, that she continued at times to discriminate in her love. Those personalities who were more to her liking sometimes received more of her attention and affection. Now she felt herself being drawn to respond to these two challenges.

The seeds of the response to the first challenge, the call to love others as Jesus himself loved them, had already found a home in Thérèse's heart when she had placed herself at the foot of the cross after her complete conversion and *experienced a great desire to work for the conversion of sinners* (SS 99).

At that time, she had seen that her place was to receive Jesus' love and share that love with inclusivity. But only toward the end of her life did she see with forceful clarity that this receptivity and sharing of Jesus' love was the very essence of the fulfillment of the new commandment. She could love her sisters as Jesus loved them only with Jesus' own love. *Ah! Lord, I know that you don't command the impossible,* she wrote. *You know better than I do my weakness and imperfection; You know very well that never would I be able to love my Sisters as You love them, unless You, O my Jesus, loved them in me* (SS 221). Her failures to love her sisters taught her that she needed to get ever closer to the only source of love.

Thérèse was consoled by the fact that Jesus had given this new directive to his disciples precisely at the Last Supper. That was a special time of Jesus' own self-giving love in the Eucharist and in the unfolding paschal mystery. Just as the command to "love your enemy" was not really a command but a description of the reality of authentic love, so Jesus' words to "love one another as I have loved you" was also the reality that would occur if she more fully welcomed Jesus' self-giving love into her life.

Only in union with Jesus' love in her heart through a spirit of faith and self-surrender would she have the capacity and the energy to love authentically. That was why Jesus had spoken of his love for his disciples at the very time he offered them the sacrament of his love, the sacrament of his very presence. In asking them to love one another as he had loved them, he provided them with the grace and power—the presence of himself—that enabled them to fulfill his wish. This truth, Thérèse said, *gives me the assurance that Your Will is to love in me all those You command me to love!* (SS 221).

As she reflected on her interaction with the sisters over the years, Thérèse was certain that when her heart had opened in real charity, especially to the difficult sisters, these were occasions when Jesus, in fact, was actually loving through her. *Yes, I feel it, when I am charitable, it is Jesus alone who is acting in me, and the more united I am to Him, the more also do I love my Sisters* (SS 221). Thérèse could respond to the new commandment only by becoming more and more united in a spirit of availability to Jesus, the source of love. In this way she would become more lovingly available to her sisters in healing, in compassion, and in works of charity.

Love does not seek its own interest

Thérèse had also noticed that her heart was blocked from being lovingly available to the sisters by some of her negative feelings about them. Whereas Jesus extended his love to all, she sometimes discriminated in her love according to her preferences. This was the second challenge.

In particular, she recognized that Jesus loved his disciples even though they were crude and sinful. *Why did he love them?* Thérèse asked herself as she meditated on the Gospels. She knew the answer: *Ah! it was not their natural qualities which could have attracted him* (SS 220). She was confirmed in believing that Jesus was asking her to relate to the difficult sisters toward whom she felt natural antipathy and even repugnance in the same loving manner as he himself would. Thérèse wrote at the end of her life, *I understand now that charity consists in bearing with the faults of others, in not being surprised at their weakness, in being edified by the smallest acts of virtue we see them practice* (SS 220).

Years before, her confessor had also confirmed one of her early intuitions about loving Jesus: "Yes, you are right," her confessor had written in reply to one of her letters. "It is better to love Jesus on His terms" (GC 559). This idea of loving on the other's terms now became a deep conviction as she loved her sisters. *Love does not seek its own interest*, she said simply (TLMT 108).

If she loved her sisters as Jesus loved them and not according to her own preferences or expectations, she would be following *Jesus' counsel: "If anyone take away your coat, let go your cloak also."* To give up one's cloak is, it *seems to me, renouncing one's ultimate rights*, Thérèse reasoned at the end of her life. *It is considering oneself as the servant and the slave of others.* Then she added knowingly as she was approaching death, *When one has left his cloak, it is much easier to walk, to run* (SS 226–27).

In the final months of her life, Thérèse would often sit outside under the chestnut trees, confined by her extreme weakness to a wheelchair—the very wheelchair that her dying father had used. There, as these insights into *the science of love* developed and while writing in her manuscript her final recollections focused on loving her sisters, she was sometimes distracted by these same sisters wanting to be charitable and saying kind words of encouragement to her. These interruptions, even though well-intentioned, became a burden to her. Thérèse, however, now relying on the blessings of *the grace to understand what charity is* (SS 219), willingly accommodated the sisters and graciously received their kindnesses. Sensing the humor in these distractions helped her to adapt her response to meet, on their own terms, the needs *of more than one good charitable sister* (SS 227).

She began to amuse herself by anticipating each annoyance, and at times she engaged in wordplay with these *charitable sisters*. Describing the scene, she wrote, *I want it; I count on it* [the interruptions to her work of composing the last pages of her memoirs].

> *I don't know if I have been able to write ten lines without being disturbed; this should not make me laugh nor amuse me; however, for the love of God and my Sisters (so charitable towards me) I take care to appear happy and especially to be so. For example, here is a [sister] hay worker who is just leaving me after having said very compassionately: "Poor little Sister, it must tire you out writing like that all day long." "Don't worry," I answer, "I appear to be writing very much, but really I am writing almost nothing." "Very good!" she says, "but just the same, I am very happy we are doing the haying since this always distracts you a little." In fact, it is such a great distraction for me (without taking into account the infirmarians' visits) that I am not telling any lies when I say that I am writing practically nothing.* (SS 228)

In the period before her death, and even as Thérèse bore patiently the distractions, she tried to live more fully the charity that she was describing in the final pages of her manuscript. Throughout her life, Thérèse had been sensitive to the needs of others, overly sensitive at times. Accommodating others on their terms and disregarding herself had been Thérèse's practice in her early years, and at that time, it had proven to be a trap. Until her complete conversion, her focus on adapting to others had taken the youthful Thérèse off the path of authentic love and into the snare of codependence.

Now, however, she could enter this realm of accommodating love with confidence. In her psychological and spiritual maturity, especially in the last two years of her life, her increasing spirit of detachment and sense of humor helped her. She could bear the disturbing behavior of others and her own distressing reactions with more peace.

I should be compassionate toward the spiritual infirmities of my Sisters

From the time Thérèse had entered the community, the thought of being a burden to others deeply troubled her sensitivities. She wanted to be inconspicuous, not only in her acts of charity, but also in her needs and in her person.

At the time of her profession two years after she had joined the convent, she had prayed, O *Jesus, never let me be a burden to the community, let nobody be occupied with me* (SS 275). This was an impossible prayer in a community trying to live the Gospel, but Thérèse's intentions were clear.

So even as she was deeply grateful for all the care that the community and especially Mother Gonzague lavished on her during the final months of her life, she tried to minimize the care that she needed. *I tried not to make anyone suffer from my pains*, she confided to her confessor (HLTT 230). As a way of loving the sisters on their own terms, she asked for nothing special, and she was not happy that her cough and her raspy breathing caused by her illness were annoying some of the sisters.

Now sitting in the wheelchair under the chestnut trees and writing her reflections on charity, she recognized that in her physical weakness, she was receiving much kindness from the sisters and especially from Mother Gonzague. She also remembered that she had not always been able to extend kindness indiscriminately over the years. She acknowledged that she had not been fully patient and kind to some of the disturbing sisters in their emotional weakness. Reflecting on this, she wrote, *I told myself that I should be as compassionate towards the spiritual infirmities of my Sisters as you are, dear Mother* [Gonzague], *when caring for me with so much love* [in my physical infirmities] (SS 245).

This comment was a confession on Thérèse's part and summarized some of her written reflections. It was also a warm and sincere statement of gratitude to Mother Gonzague. But the comment may have been a kind of loving invitation to the superior as well. Thérèse was writing her manuscript on charity for Mother Gonzague, and in it she made this observation directly to her.

The comment came after Thérèse had recounted in such detail the difficulties she had experienced in trying to fulfill Jesus' command to love all the sisters without exception and on their terms. Thérèse's allusion to needing to be *compassionate toward the spiritual infirmities* of the difficult sisters and her numerous stories of bearing the inconveniences of the sisters' thorny behavior, as well as her references to her own struggles to befriend her negative feelings and respond to difficult sisters with patience and without harshness—all of these stories and references pointed directly to the pattern of charity to the sisters that the capricious Mother Gonzague herself needed to cultivate.

Perhaps among the reasons Thérèse offered these examples of her discoveries of what love looks and feels like, especially in the presence of "the enemy," as well as her insights into how love can be blocked in the human heart, was to enlighten Mother Gonzague. Perhaps Thérèse was writing in part to invite her superior to move from her sometimes condemnatory and harsh manner to a more creative way of loving the troubled sisters under her care. If this were the case, it is another example of Thérèse's great capacity to respond compassionately and creatively to others' needs on their own terms—in this situation, to the needs of Mother Gonzague, whom she had finally come to love in the full light of *the science of love*.

And there is yet one other comment that Thérèse made on her deathbed that applied to loving indiscriminately. It was a witty remark about loving "enemies" that she made to accommodate the sisters caring for her and to lighten their burden. Her sister Pauline reported that during the last weeks of Thérèse's life, as she lay in the infirmary, one of the sisters "was trying to kill the flies that were pestering her and Sister Thérèse made this rather disarming observation: *They are the only enemies I have, and since God has told us to love our enemies I am glad they give me this opportunity to do so. That is why I always spare them*" (STL 51).

Offered to amuse those who were so upset by her suffering and to dispel the seriousness of the deathbed scene, Thérèse's comment testifies to the degree of psychological and spiritual maturity that she had finally reached on her path of love. Like St. Francis, who loved all of nature, and like St. Augustine, who seems to have been troubled with the existence only of mosquitoes, Thérèse tried to have no adversarial feelings toward anyone or anything except, perhaps, toward flies! And these feelings she was willing to forego and humorously invited her sisters to forego as well.

In her final months, she also spoke of spending her time in heaven doing good on earth. Thérèse extended her willingness to love indiscriminately well beyond the sisters of her community. It was her desire to respond throughout all of time to the needs of others on their terms, to the needs of everyone without exception. It was Thérèse's glorious desire to participate in the fullness of God's redemptive love for all creation.

Thérèse's Experience of Engaging the Spirituality of Her Time

Thérèse at twenty-two years old, in 1895,
seated second from the left in the second row

CHAPTER 13

Love Lowers Itself and Transforms Nothingness into Fire

CONFRONTING JANSENISM, PERFECTIONISM, AND PELAGIANISM

In addition to Thérèse's interactions with the sisters in their ordinary daily community activities, there was another experience of convent life that was formative in helping her recognize the heart qualities of love and understanding *the science of love*. Developing out of the seeds of her conversion and concurrent with her growth in love for the sisters, Thérèse's third formative experience unfolded as she attempted to remain true to the spirituality of the Gospel even as she saw that truth negated by the popular image of God and contaminated by the false ideal of Christian holiness presented in her day.

The common preaching of the era, as well as the ordinary teaching in the spiritual books, fostered mistaken notions of both the nature of God and the essence of Jesus' call to holiness. These false ideas came partly from the three interrelated spiritual errors of Jansenism, perfectionism, and Pelagianism, circulated in various forms throughout the Church. They burdened most of the ordinary faithful with a religion of fear.

Jansenism was officially condemned as a heresy as early as the seventeenth century. It distorted authentic Christian truth by promoting, among other errors, the false image of God as wrathful, punitive, and vindictive. The harsh, vengeful God of Jansenism demanded perfection, requiring sinners to attain moral worthiness.

Perfectionism, not officially a heresy but a prevailing attitude among many religious teachers, presented the false idea that the Gospel call to holiness was a command to strive to be perfect in the sense of acquiring all virtues and eliminating all sins and defects. This perfectionism, actually a caricature of authentic Christian holiness, was mistakenly taught as being the only way a person could be worthy to satisfy Jansenism's vindictive God of justice.

Pelagianism, a heresy condemned very early in Church history, was commonly understood to teach that by human effort alone, often in the form of willful and if necessary violent forms of religious asceticism, a person could successfully acquire at least the beginnings of perfectionism and appease the wrath and merit the love of Jansenism's God.

The chief motive for good moral behavior was the dreadful fear of the God of Jansenism, and the chief means of attaining perfection was the willful human effort advocated by Pelagianism. As for those sinners who fell short of acquiring moral perfectionism, Jansenism's God demanded reparation for sin by self-punitive, even self-violent mortifications.

Thus, these three erroneous ideas twisted the Gospel notion of holiness into the knotty moral business of striving for an unattainable perfection and bound the Christian with tangled cords of anxiety, guilt, shame, and fear. In this way, Christian holiness was often effectively reduced to a morality of terror, negating the fundamental mystery of the Incarnation. It annulled the authentic Gospel call to receive in joyful faith and share in humble charity God's freely given intimacy of divine union established in Christ.

We would prefer to die rather than to offend Him

Thérèse had no theological or scriptural education to theoretically oppose these false spiritual teachings, but she did have her own experience of bouts with scrupulosity, which she called *a terrible sickness, . . . a martyrdom* (SS 84; GC 580–81, note 7; 585; 598; 767–68, note 5). She also knew from the confidences of others the wreckage that lingering fear and excessive guilt could cause in the human heart (cf. GC 565–66, note 1; 567). Moreover, she had reflected on the truth of her own experience of human love, of God's love, and of Jesus' teaching. Jesus' words touched her deeply: "If you then, who are wicked, know how to give good gifts to your children, how much more will your heavenly Father give good things to those who ask him" (Matthew 7:11).

Contemplating the Gospel and her own experiences, Thérèse knew that the Father of Jesus was not truly represented by the popular wrathful Jansenistic image. She knew also that she had been called to holiness and had *measureless desires* (SS 197) to become a saint and to live a life of love. Yet especially in the early months of her convent life, even with her best efforts, she recognized that she was not acquiring the ideal of perfectionism. She could not rid herself of all her faults, acquire virtue, or accomplish great spiritual works.

She had questioned her *measureless desires* to love and wondered if they were *only but a dream, a folly* (SS 197). Yet she held on to the conviction that God's love was infinite and that God's justice was not vindictive. God's justice, she believed, is *clothed in love* (SS 180) and is expressed in compassion;

it differs from human justice, just as the peace that Jesus gives differs from the peace of this world (John 14:27). At the deepest level in her heart, Thérèse was confident that her desire for sanctity would be fulfilled, but how this might happen became clear to her only in the last years of her life (cf. HLTT 147ff.; EIG 221ff.).

As a child she had received the affection of her parents, who reached down in love to raise her up; and she was convinced that God, who is love, would do nothing less. *Yes, in order that Love be fully satisfied, it is necessary that It lower itself, and that It lower Itself to nothingness and transform this nothingness into fire* (SS 195). In the Holy Eucharist, Thérèse believed that God had especially lowered himself in order to transform *nothingness into fire*. Yet during the school retreats associated with receiving her First Communion, the youthful Thérèse heard nothing of God's love.

At that time, Thérèse was eleven years old, still suffering bouts of melancholy over the loss of her mother and becoming more and more sensitive to her own mixed motivation and spiritual weaknesses. Fr. Domin, the school chaplain of forty-one years, preached the First Communion retreat from a mentality tinged with the spiritual errors of the day. *What Father told us was frightening*, she wrote in her retreat notebook. *He spoke about mortal sin, and he described a soul in the state of sin and how much God hated it* (GC 226). He threatened the young children with God's wrath and warned them of their capacity of making a sacrilegious First Communion that would eternally condemn them to hell (cf. HLTT 54).

Thérèse had expected to hear Fr. Domin speak about God's coming down in love into her heart in a special way in the reception of the Eucharist. She had longed to hear the preacher invite her to contemplate God's infinite love and mercy. Instead, Fr. Domin was telling her to meditate on her ability to commit serious sin and perhaps her inevitability of being alienated from God in this life and separated from her Beloved eternally.

Talks of being rejected by God and damned to hell did not inspire Thérèse to virtue; they simply distressed her and aroused the fear that contributed to the scrupulosity that would last the next eighteen months. Hearing from the school chaplain that no one knew whether they were worthy of God's love or God's hatred, Thérèse was completely distraught and simply broke down and wept.

It was only many years later, as she became more spiritually confident, that she was consoled in knowing that God's love transcends the issue of human worthiness. She later wrote with conviction, *Jesus gives us the grace of feeling at the bottom of our heart that we would prefer to die rather than to offend Him* (GC 729). Certain of this grace of preferring death to offending God, Thérèse came to rely on her clear conscience, even though she would continue to hear in the preaching during the annual retreats in the convent that *no one knows if one is just or sinful* (GC 729; cf. 731, note 8). Throughout her life such sermons aroused fear in her; she reacted to these kinds of false ideas even in her later life as she had in childhood—by sometimes getting physically ill. She noted in recalling the convent-preached retreats that they were *more painful to me than the ones I make alone* (SS 173).

I shall have only my desires to offer Him

To one Jesuit retreat director who preached the community retreat several months before her profession, she confided, *I want to become a saint.* Fr. Blino, who also seems to have been ensnared in a mentality poisoned by the errors of the time, responded paternalistically, "What pride and what presumption! Confine yourself to correcting your faults, to offending God no longer, to making a little progress in virtue each day, and temper your rash desires" (GC 623, note 8).

However well-intentioned this response was, Thérèse did not hear it describing a God of love who stoops down *to nothingness and transforms this nothingness into fire.* She heard an echo of Jansenism. But now Thérèse was not intimidated by the priest's response. She knew that God was completely different from what Fr. Blino's advice suggested, and she also knew that she was on a completely different spiritual path from the one such a response implied.

Sanctity, for Thérèse, was not a matter of tempering her rash desires, her *measureless desires*, but of cultivating them. She believed that the Holy Spirit would inspire her only with desires that could be fulfilled and that her deepest desires were really God's desires in her, needing only her willing cooperation (GC 1015). As she neared her death, she wrote with boldness: *When I shall appear before my Beloved Spouse, I shall have only my* [cooperation with His own] *desires to offer Him* (GC 1054).

But for now, she replied to Fr. Blino with a certain simplicity. *Father, I don't think that these are rash desires; I can aspire to sanctity* (GC 623, note 8). Thérèse was not striving for perfectionism; she was longing for God. The sanctity to which Thérèse aspired was the holiness of the Gospel, inviting her to be available to God's love and to be willing to reciprocate and share that love. If sanctity were a matter of tempering her desires, of being without faults, and of making a little progress in virtue each day, Thérèse would have despaired long ago.

More receptivity to her union with God was her focused spiritual intention. In her growing maturity, she surrendered into the reality of who she was with her gifts and weaknesses, allowing God's mercy and love to correct any faults that would be corrected and to prompt any spiritual progress that would be made. She had already learned in her conversion experience that *Jesus in one instant* could transform her and that all he needed was her *good will* (SS 98). And she did not doubt Jesus' power or the focus of her goodwill.

My good will was never lacking

From her early years, Thérèse was disturbed by the notion that sanctity was equated with perfection. After entering the convent, she also became aware of the mixed motivation of the sisters who confided to her the weaknesses of their own spiritual lives. Even though Thérèse had heard the admonition "Strive to be perfect" and had heard the religious life sometimes presented in the spiritual teaching of the day as the "state of perfection," she did not find herself or her companions participating in that perfection.

She had, in fact, become distrustful of the very notion of "striving" in the spiritual life. She was not questioning the energy of determination, but she was suspicious of the attitude of "striving" accompanied by a mind-set of predetermination that endorsed an unreflective rigorism. She saw in the effort of striving only willfulness, and based on her own experience, she was suspicious of willfulness in trying to acquire virtue or getting rid of defects. Her earlier striving to overcome her excessive sensitivities and to practice virtue following her mother's death had involved a willfulness that prompted practicing virtue *in a strange way* (SS 97), a way of self-centeredness.

Thérèse had often meditated on her complete conversion experience and knew that it had not been achieved by striving. It had come to her as a complete gift of God. Her part had been only her spirit of willingness to surrender herself into God's hands. Her only contribution was that, as she wrote, *my good will which was never lacking* (SS 98). Jesus could not take hold of her clenched fist of willful striving, but Jesus did grasp her outstretched repentant hand of willing patience and surrender. Her willful striving had been useless, but ironically, it did have a spiritual benefit. Although contrary to the contemplative spirit, her striving had resulted in her deepest contemplative awareness—her total inadequacy and her complete need of God's love.

She had also become aware of the dubious consequences and the merely temporary results of the sisters' strivings to correct the wrongs in themselves, in one another, and in her. Willful striving to be perfect and to overcome evil sometimes resulted in the sisters being violent to themselves as well as being cruel toward one another in a spirit of rivalry, jealousy, or self-righteousness.

To attempt to combat evil by willfulness, Thérèse now suspected, was to try to destroy evil with evil, fire with fire, malice with malice, making the last state of self-righteousness or discouragement sometimes worse than the first (cf. Mark 3:23; Matthew 12:43-45). She would continue to respond as best she could to doing God's will and never give up her willingness to be available to Jesus with open hands. *I am not always faithful,* she acknowledged, and in her willingness, she added, *but I never get discouraged* (GC 801). She came to understand that ultimately, any acquisition of virtue or elimination of faults would finally be Jesus' work, and he could do it *in one instant* (SS 98; cf. GC 794–96; 800–01).

She knew also that she could not physically perform the self-disciplinary actions that were usually associated with perfection and striving to be perfect. Even though confident of her sincerity and of the *measureless desires* of her heart, she was not seeing much personal progress along the path of perfection. She wondered and she prayed.

A new commandment

Thérèse was aware that Jesus' words recorded in the Gospel to "be perfect, just as your heavenly Father is perfect" were sometimes used to prove that the call to Gospel holiness was indeed a call to flawless moral perfection and that willful striving to be perfect was the means to sanctity (Matthew 5:48). Thérèse had no scriptural resources or authorities to validate her insights, but as she read more and more of the Gospel and as she contemplated Jesus' life, she became certain that Jesus was not teaching perfectionism but was proclaiming a new kind of holiness.

Even within the immediate context of Jesus' words to "be perfect, just as your heavenly Father is perfect," she noticed that Jesus was primarily speaking about a "new commandment." In this fifth chapter of the Gospel of Matthew, Jesus had been repeating the theme of former religious teachings, and he was contrasting it with his own new teachings: "You have heard that it was said . . . But I say to you . . . "; "It was also said . . . But I say to you . . . "; "You have heard that it was said to your ancestors . . . But I say to you . . ." (Matthew 5:27-28, 31-32, 33-34)

Having set up this contrast between the old and the new commandments, Jesus reached the climax of his teaching with the final and most important commandment of all: "You have heard that it was said, 'You shall love your neighbor and hate your enemy.' But I say to you, love your enemies, and pray for those who persecute you. . . . So be perfect, just as your heavenly Father is perfect" (Matthew 5:43-44, 48).

Jesus' new commands fulfilled the law by refining and superseding the teachings of the past. Thérèse recognized that the directive to "love your enemies" was the most important of these new teachings precisely because it revealed the essence of God's perfection, which consisted in God's universal mercy. "For if you love those who love you, what recompense will you have? Do not the tax collectors do the same? And if you greet your brothers only, what is unusual about that? Do not the pagans do the same?" (Matthew 5:46-47). God is perfect, Thérèse realized, in extending all-inclusive love so that "he makes his sun rise on the bad and the good, and causes rain to fall on the just and the unjust" (5:45).

Thérèse understood that Godlike perfection consisted in loving even "the unjust" and "the bad," even those who were enemies, who rejected love. God's love was freely given to all, even God's enemies, and did not insist on any kind of willful striving or on any prior condition of perfection. Jesus' command that his disciples be perfect as "your heavenly Father is perfect" was not, therefore, a command for moral perfectionism willfully achieved. Rather, it had to do with the inclusivity of authentic love.

Thérèse noticed also that the parallel text to that of Matthew's "Be perfect, just as your heavenly Father is perfect" was the verse in Luke that enjoined compassion, not perfection. Luke stated Jesus' new teaching this way: "Be merciful, just as your Father is merciful" (6:36). In Luke's text, Thérèse believed Jesus was stating clearly that God's perfection consisted in love and compassion.

Jesus was inviting his disciples to be Godlike by being as merciful and compassionate as God was merciful and compassionate.

In contemplating the life of Jesus, Thérèse had also recognized that in the wider context of the complete Gospel, the command to "love your enemies" described how Jesus himself was acting in his own life. His life was lived with inclusive love and in patience and kindness, even toward those who rejected his love. Jesus' love extended even to his executioners. He told Peter, who was trying to defend him, to "put your sword into its scabbard" (John 18:11), and from the cross, Jesus prayed, "Father, forgive them, they know not what they do" (Luke 23:34).

These Scripture texts confirmed for Thérèse that Jesus was calling his disciples to participate in God's perfection not by moral perfectionism but by compassionate loving. They validated and nourished a seed that had been planted at her conversion and had been growing over the years in her interactions with the sisters in the convent—the inclusivity of love without violence.

CHAPTER 14

I Find Perfection Very Easy to Practice

UNDERSTANDING GOSPEL PERFECTION

As Thérèse understood Jesus' words to "be perfect as your heavenly Father is perfect" beyond the realm of willful striving for perfection and within the kingdom of God's compassion, two other New Testament passages became clearer to her. They, in turn, shed additional light on Jesus' words. Illuminating one another, these three passages also became increasingly important as Thérèse continued to probe *the science of love* and to discover the heart qualities of love. One of the two texts was the story of Zacchaeus the tax collector (Luke 19:1-10); the other was Jesus' parable of the Pharisee and the publican (18:9-14).

During a private retreat four years after she had entered the convent, Thérèse received the spiritual insight that the downward path of Zacchaeus, who had been invited by Jesus to descend from his treetop perch, would be her own spiritual path. *What science* [of love] *is Jesus about to teach us?* Thérèse wrote. *Let us listen to what He is saying to us: "Make haste to descend, I must lodge today at your house." Well, Jesus tells us to descend* (GC 761; cf. GC 757).

By allowing Jesus to find lodging in her heart, she would more and more accept herself with her weaknesses and gradually be purified of her attachments to creatures, to her feelings and expectations, and even to her spiritual ambitions. Thérèse was being invited to embrace a form of spiritual poverty that at the end of her life she acknowledged as a great grace: *I can depend on nothing, on no good works of my own in order to have confidence,* she said. *This poverty, however, was a real light and a grace for me. I was thinking that never in my life would I be able to pay my debts to God; this was real riches, real strength for me. . . . We experience such great peace when we're totally poor, when we depend upon no one except God* (HLC 137).

Complete dependence on God, complete trust in God—the total opposite of the attitude of striving for perfection—confirmed Thérèse's path and became the essence of her little way of spirituality.

Jesus Tells Me to Descend

At this time of Thérèse's insight into her call to accept the inner poverty of the downward path of Zacchaeus, her sister Céline was still at home with their beloved father. As he neared death, he was losing his mental capacities. A short time after Thérèse had left the family to enter the convent, their father had suffered a series of strokes that gradually weakened him physically, emotionally, and mentally. Thérèse was grieving deeply as her beloved "king" stumbled into the terrible, inaccessible world of the mentally ill. Yet she tried to support her sister in her emotionally distressing and physically wearying task of nursing their father.

Thérèse assured Céline that God's love was asking them both to embrace together the self-emptying poverty of letting go of their dearly beloved father. Thérèse wrote to Céline, sharing what she would continue to learn as she contemplated Jesus' words to Zacchaeus: *In our dear Father, Jesus has stricken us in the most sensitive exterior part of our heart; now let us allow Him to act, He can complete His work in our souls. . . . What Jesus desires is that we receive Him into our hearts. No doubt, they are already empty of creatures, but, alas, I feel mine is not entirely empty of myself, and it is for this reason that Jesus tells me* [like Zacchaeus] *to descend* [Luke 19:5] (GC 762).

Thérèse was not yet twenty years old when she had this spiritual awareness of the richness of the spirit of poverty and self-emptying. The importance of self-surrender, or self-abandonment, as she would later often refer to the spirit of willingly embracing God's will, was to become more apparent to Thérèse throughout the rest of her life. Thérèse's way of love would not be the path of doing great things, multiplying spiritual riches, and establishing spiritual security by attaining perfection. Rather, it would be the path of Zacchaeus—the path of descending, of responding to Jesus' call to "come down," to be with Jesus and let Jesus' love transform her as he wished.

I considered that I [too] *was born for glory,* Thérèse had thought as a teenager when she had read the story of Joan of Arc. She had known intuitively at that time, and now, in her maturity, she knew from experience that unlike Joan's call to glory, her glory would be in hiddenness. *God made me feel that true glory is that which will last eternally, and to reach it, it isn't necessary to perform striking works but to hide oneself and practice virtue in such a way that the left hand knows not what the right is doing* [Matthew 6:3]. She understood that her greatness would consist in her *becoming a great saint,* but a hidden saint (SS 72). In these reflections she was also deepening the love and imitation of her beloved Mother Mary, in whose Magnificat Thérèse had originally discovered the spirit of littleness and poverty.

Especially in the final months of her life, Thérèse imagined herself, like Zacchaeus, "descending," being welcomed by Jesus now into *his* home, his embrace. In death she would be coming to Jesus *with empty hands,* offering herself to God's mercy in complete spiritual poverty. She had prayed in her act of offering: *After earth's Exile, I hope to go and enjoy You in the Fatherland, but I do not want to lay up merits for heaven. I want to work for Your Love alone. . . . In the evening of this life, I shall appear before You with empty hands, for I do not ask You, Lord, to count my works. All our justice is stained in Your eyes. I wish, then, to be clothed in Your own Justice and to receive from Your Love the eternal possession of Yourself* (SS 277). She desired to die emptied of herself and to be taken by Love.

It is a matter of taking hold of Jesus by His heart

The other Scripture passage that helped Thérèse understand her path of love was the parable of the Pharisee and the publican (Luke 18:9-14). Jesus taught this parable precisely to those who believed that achieving perfection had to do with eliminating all moral weaknesses and with having acquired the righteousness of spiritual riches that made love exclusive. Thérèse recognized in this parable not only two men seeking to pray but two radically different paths of spirituality. The path personified by the publican embraced love and arrived at sanctity. The path personified by the Pharisee included violence and led to ruin.

In the parable, the Pharisee reported to God in a kind of pseudo-prayer, stating the religious successes that he thought consisted of his moral perfection. Thérèse noticed that this path attempted to establish a connection with God based on legalities and was founded on responses to obligations and law, devoid of any desire for union with God in authentic love. The Pharisee gave an account of himself to God as a clerk might give an account of his transactions to a demanding superior.

The Pharisee was not seeking God; he was seeking legal confirmation of his own perfection. He thanked God, not for God's inclusive love, but because God had made him "not like the rest of humanity" and, in particular, "not like this tax collector [publican]" (Luke 18:11).

In his comparison with the publican, the Pharisee further established his moral credentials by building his goodness on the comparative weaknesses of the publican. The Pharisee assumed that God's wrath and justice excluded the sinful publican from love, and so the Pharisee made the publican his enemy.

If the Pharisee had had his way, Thérèse could see, he would have followed his fundamental insecurity and fear and would have violently ejected from the Temple his adversary, the publican. The path of the Pharisee was a path of striving for perfection that eventually led to violence in his heart against the sinful publican.

The publican, however, came before God not in self-righteousness but in spiritual poverty. He had not achieved any level of perfection. Rather, he "stood off at a distance" (Luke 18:13), humbled himself before God, and by not comparing himself with the Pharisee, kept his distance also from his would-be adversary. He did not have to exclude anyone from his love; he did not support himself by condemning anyone else. He did not have an agenda of self-promotion, and he had no need to build his virtue on anyone else's weakness. The path of the publican was the path of asking for and receiving God's compassion and, by accepting the presence of the Pharisee, sharing that compassion. The publican, aware of his own sinfulness and confident of God's mercy, did not need to be an enemy to anyone.

The Pharisee did not ask for God's mercy; he did not think he needed it. The publican, however, prayed, "O God, be merciful to me a sinner" (Luke 18:13). Thérèse recognized the publican's plea as a profound, redeeming prayer because it expressed the honest acknowledgment of weakness and sinfulness and a total willingness and trust to receive God's infinite mercy. The prayer of the publican, a prayer that Jesus himself gave in the parable, resonated with Thérèse's own insight that *I find perfection very easy to practice. . . . It is a matter of taking hold of Jesus by His heart* (GC 965–66). In the publican's prayer, Thérèse found the essence of Jesus' call to authentic holiness.

The difference of heart between the Pharisee's attitude of striving for perfection and the publican's spirit of receiving God's compassion resonated with Thérèse's intuitions and insights into the fundamental nature of Gospel holiness. Thérèse's path of receiving God's love and mercy would imitate that of the publican and was the same path of downwardness and spiritual poverty that Zacchaeus had followed into intimacy with Jesus.

The publican's prayer for God's mercy was really a plea that God unite him, a sinner, into the very essence of God, since love and mercy are not separate from God's essence (1 John 4:8). When the publican was asking for God's mercy, Thérèse recognized, he was asking for God. God does not give mercy and love as a kind of merited handout. God *is* love and mercy. The publican was seeking a deeper union with God.

Desiring a more profound intimacy with God as well, Thérèse made the publican's prayer her own. Acknowledging her own sinfulness, she would welcome God's love, the Holy Spirit, into her soul. She would be totally available to God's love, Christ's love, the Holy Spirit surging within her. With God's own love, the Holy Spirit of love, she would love herself, love God, and love her sisters. It would all be one love because it would all be God's love in her. The two great commandments, to love one's neighbor as oneself and to love God, were really only one commandment, just as Jesus had said, because the love that fulfilled them was one: the Holy Spirit.

God's love, Thérèse knew, sustained her, for "in him we live and move and have our being" (Acts 17:28). As she continually welcomed God's Spirit of love into her heart, she did not then need to "generate" love within herself to give to God and others. She needed, rather, to unblock the movement of the Holy Spirit within her. The Spirit of divine love, available through her willing self-surrender, would become, as Jesus had said, a fountain of living water surging up and abiding in her as her love for God, her love for herself, and her love flowing to others (John 4:14).

To bear with one's imperfections, that is real sanctity!

The parable of the Pharisee and publican, together with the story of Zacchaeus, further confirmed for Thérèse that union with God was God's gift, not dependent on her moral achievements. The spirit of the parable was the opposite of the spirit that Fr. Blino had advised, and it negated the popular erroneous teaching of Jansenism, perfectionism, and Pelagianism. Her union with God was being accomplished, not by her efforts and achievements, but was a gift she was receiving from the God of love stooping down in mercy and raising her up in her weakness and sinfulness.

Thérèse made her own the spirit of willingly and humbly receiving God's mercy in repentance and trust that was manifested by the publican. She was willing to be aware of her weaknesses and to acknowledge her inability to acquire perfection. She was also willing to be patient with herself in her sinfulness, not to be discouraged, and to return as often as necessary to the path of doing God's will as best she could.

In addition, she who was so ready to endure any pain in doing God's will also abandoned her need even to be successful in her suffering. To her sister Céline, she wrote, *Let us suffer the bitter pain, without courage! . . . And still we would like to suffer generously, grandly! Céline, what an illusion! We'd never want to fall?* Then turning her attention to God's mercy, Thérèse continued: *What does it matter, my Jesus, if I fall at each moment; I see my weakness through this and this is a great gain for me. You can see through this* [weakness] *what I can do and now You will be more tempted to carry me in Your arms. If You do not do it, it is because this pleases You to see me on the ground. Then I am not going to be disturbed, but I shall always stretch out my arms suppliant and filled with love! I cannot believe that you would abandon me!* (GC 557).

On one occasion, her sister Céline, now in the convent with her and having developed quite a demanding nature, became impatient even with Thérèse. Later when Céline apologized, Thérèse's reply included an empathetic comment and a reference to the publican, who had "stood off at a distance" at the back of the Temple. She wrote to Céline, *Yes, it suffices to humble oneself, to bear with one's imperfections. That is real sanctity! Let us take each other by the hand, dear little sister, and let us run to the last place . . . no one will come to dispute with us over it* (GC 1122).

Thérèse recognized an even further dimension to the spirit of poverty, of not being perfect. She noticed that some sisters with demanding temperaments like Céline, frustrated by failure in their willful efforts to acquire the perfection of all the virtues, continued to fall into the trap of willfully striving to be perfect at least in the virtue of charity.

During Thérèse's early years in the convent, some of the sisters had tried to be charitable to her by a punitive, hostile attitude, employing harsh reprimands and lingering resentments. Thérèse noticed that when the sisters had attempted to correct her youthful mistakes, they expressed the same willful attitude that they used in their violent and failed attempts to correct their own weaknesses. Such willful efforts carried a subtle self-righteousness similar to the Pharisee's attitude, an attitude that contaminated authentic love. No matter where it was applied, even in the seemly good cause of correcting oneself or others as an expression of charity, the attitude of willfulness poisoned the heart and sowed the seeds of violence.

This wisdom of the futility of willfulness in the spiritual life became important for Thérèse in understanding *the science of love.* The spirit of willingness, therefore, became a significant psychological indicator, a heart quality, a major stepping-stone on the little way. It became an essential insight in Thérèse's wise teaching to the young sisters whom she was guiding.

I must bear with myself such as I am with all my imperfections

Contrary to speaking of willful efforts to get rid of defects and acquire virtue, Thérèse told the sisters under her care to become more patient and kind with themselves and others and, in the spirit of the publican, to open themselves to receive God's compassion in the humility of their own sinfulness. God's mercy would enliven the sisters to become authentically charitable by the Spirit of love surging in their hearts.

As Thérèse herself had become more available to God's love and less willful, she had experienced less need to be defensive and self-centered. This same downward path of authentic humility would also reduce the sisters' need to impose their willfulness on one another. Thérèse was confident that this downward path would purify their hearts, and their behavior would be transformed as well.

Thérèse assured the sisters that the way of the publican and Zacchaeus could lead them to be free from comparisons and from the bondage of needing to gossip or to harbor a spirit of blame or rivalry. They could allow one another to have idiosyncrasies without cultivating feelings of being personally offended or hostile. They would have less need to fuss about having everything in themselves, in others, and in the convent perfectly in place, completely squared away, properly arranged, and precisely organized—fuss that was actually a dimension of striving to be perfect.

At one time in her life, Thérèse herself had almost despaired as she took her first and sometimes mistaken steps on the path of love. *I really made a big fuss over everything! I was just the opposite of what I am now,* she wrote in her maturity almost twenty years later. *When I think of the past, my soul overflows with gratitude when I see the favors I have received from heaven. They have made such a change in me that I don't recognize myself* (SS 91).

St. John of the Cross, St. Teresa of Ávila, and St. Paul, her important mentors, had taught Thérèse by their words and example that as the saints advanced on the authentic path of holiness, they had been less prone to thoughts and acts that could be identified as sin, yet they spoke often of their continued sinfulness. Willingly embracing God's love, they experienced their own sinful tendencies even more, and this awareness and repentance constituted their humility and their release from many acts of sin.

Now on her downward path, Thérèse had noticed this same pattern unfolding in her own life, and she spoke of her willingness to *bear with myself such as I am with all my imperfections* (SS 207). *I am not disturbed at seeing myself weakness itself,* she acknowledged in bold confidence at the end of her life. *On the contrary, it is in my weakness that I glory,* she wrote, referring to St. Paul (2 Corinthians 12:5), *and I expect each day to discover new imperfections in myself* (SS 224).

On one occasion, she sent a note to her sister Marie, who was with her in the convent and who desired to know what Thérèse had been learning about *the science of love.* Thérèse shared with her sister insight into the essence of the prayer of the publican. *What pleases God is that He sees me loving my littleness and my poverty, the blind hope that I have in His mercy* (GC 999).

As she neared her death, Thérèse remarked, *I have my weaknesses, but I rejoice in them. . . . I will be tormented by a foolish thing I said or did. Then I enter into myself, and I say: Alas, I'm still at the same place as I was formerly! But I tell myself this with great gentleness and without any sadness! It's so good to feel that one is weak and little!* (HLC 73–74). She contemplated with gratitude these words of Jesus: "I did not come to call the righteous but sinners" (Matthew 9:13; Mark 2:17; cf. SS 84; HF 337; GC 825). Without complacency or presumption, she remarked that she was content to be a sinner because Jesus came for sinners.

Thérèse had also glimpsed a special aspect of wisdom in the pseudo-prayer of the Pharisee. The Pharisee's "prayer" reaffirmed that she needed to continue to be attentive to her own motivation and self-righteousness. *If [a] soul takes delight in her beautiful thoughts and says the prayer of the Pharisee,* Thérèse considered, *she is like a person dying of hunger at a well-filled table where all his [God's] guests are enjoying abundant food and at times cast a look of envy upon the person possessing so many good things. Ah! how true it is that God alone knows human hearts* (SS 234).

The reality was that Thérèse wanted to know herself as God knew her in the reality of the Spirit of truth. She did not want to deceive herself as the Pharisee did. The false prayer of the Pharisee, containing as it did a ledger of "good" deeds, reminded her of the importance of self-awareness. The authentic prayer of the publican, expressing the deep truth of helplessness on the spiritual path without God's mercy, deepened her certainty that her weaknesses could become stepping-stones on the path of love.

As a child preparing for First Communion, Thérèse, mentored by her sister Pauline who had just entered Carmel at that time, had kept a ledger of all of her sacrifices as well as her lapses. But as she matured, she intuitively rejected any similarity to the practice of the Pharisee and entirely abandoned the practice of record keeping that might keep her focused on her own progress. In the spiritual life, she rejected all sense of accounting, all legalities and bookkeeping. She rejected everything less than loving.

She had noticed early on that by keeping records, she could have been lured into self-centeredness and willful striving for holiness, and she resisted. *Directors have others advance in perfection by having them perform a great number of acts of virtue, and they are right; but my director, who is Jesus, teaches me not to count up my acts,* she stated boldly. *He teaches me to do all through love, to refuse Him nothing, to be content when He gives me a chance of proving to Him that I love Him. . . . It is Jesus who is doing all in me, and I am doing nothing* (GC 796).

She told one of the younger sisters who was still preoccupied with recording her good deeds and her defects, *There is a science God doesn't know, arithmetic* (TLMT 74–75). Thérèse's way became focused simply on doing everything as best she could for God, as each moment required. For Thérèse, a person in love does not keep accounts. She wrote these words in a poem:

Living by Love means "Give unendingly,
Claiming no earthy wage." I do not doubt
This . . . I have stopped all counting up. I see
That when one loves, one doesn't measure out! (CP 72)

I always feel the same bold confidence of becoming a great saint

Expressing the bold confidence of the publican, Thérèse said to one of the young sisters, *We are not saints who cry over our sins; we take delight in them because they serve to glorify the mercy of God.* The young sister was startled by the audacity of Thérèse's comment, understanding how contrary it was to the ordinary spiritual teaching of the time. Many years later, after Thérèse had been canonized, the sister, still astonished by Thérèse's spiritual boldness, remarked, "What canonized Saint has ever spoken in this way?" (GC 1122).

Her holiness, Thérèse saw more clearly as she matured, had nothing to do with her worthiness or her achievements or her striving. Her sanctity had everything to do with her availability to God's Spirit at every moment and her willingness to do God's will in acts of love. Personally resonating with the truth of the publican's prayer, Thérèse wrote, *I always feel . . . the same bold confidence of becoming a great saint because I don't count on my merits since I have none, but I trust in Him who is Virtue and Holiness. God alone, content with my weak efforts, will raise me to Himself and make me a saint, clothing me in His infinite merits* (SS 72).

At the end of her life, seeking a prayer that would embody her way of love, Thérèse made her plea an echo of the prayer of the publican. To Mother Gonzague she wrote, *Dear Mother, this is my prayer. I ask Jesus to draw me into the flames of His love; to unite me so closely with Him that He live and act in me* (SS 257).

In the final paragraphs of her writings, she makes an explicit reference to the prayer of the publican. *Since Jesus has re-ascended into heaven, I can follow Him only in the traces He has left; but how luminous these traces are! how perfumed! I have only to cast a glance in the Gospels and immediately I breathe in the perfumes of Jesus' life, and I know on which side to run. I don't hasten to the first place but to the last; rather than advance like the Pharisee, I repeat, filled with confidence, the publican's humble prayer.* To this reference to the publican, she added a final personal reference to Mary Magdalene. Most of all, Thérèse wrote in her notebook, *I imitate the conduct of Magdalene; her astonishing or rather her loving audacity which charms the Heart of Jesus also attracts my own* (SS 258–59). Thérèse would be as boldly confident as the publican and as lovingly audacious as Magdalene.

As she lay on her deathbed, she spoke from an intense awareness of God's love and mercy that had pervaded and empowered her life. From a depth of self-knowledge and with authentic humility, she said, *I see only the graces I've received from God. . . . I have lights only to see my little nothingness. This does me more good than all the lights on the faith* (HLC 144, 148).

With her own weaknesses illuminated by grace, she said simply, *I won't say like St. Peter: "I will never deny you"* (Matthew 26:35; HLC 83). It was a profound and honest acknowledgment that her willing receptivity to God's love in spiritual poverty, self-emptiness, and complete self-surrender was her spiritual path; indeed, her sanctity. God's love would be the holiness that Thérèse was willing to receive.

CHAPTER 15

Even God's Justice Seems to Me Clothed in Love

LEARNING FROM SCRIPTURE

Growing in confidence in her understanding of authentic sanctity and resisting the mistakes issuing from Jansenism, perfectionism, and Pelagianism, Thérèse had begun teaching the younger sisters under her care that what was required for holiness was not more self-concern about their spiritual progress, nor even interest in keeping records of their defects and virtues, and certainly not any willful effort or violent, self-punitive reparation for their faults and sins. She shared with them, rather, her own desire for ever closer union with God, that union with God already present and destined to extend even into eternal life.

The more You want to give, the more you make us desire

As a child, Thérèse had read the devotional book *The End of the Present World and the Mysteries of the Future Life* by Fr. Charles Arminjon. It was not a spiritual book of classic dimensions, but it was a confirmation of her own intuition that the rewards of heaven would not be something like a crown, a throne, or even just eternal happiness. Rather, the reward and joy of heaven would be *someone,* God himself. The eternal love relationship of full union with God would constitute the essence of eternal happiness. Fr. Arminjon, one of the few spiritual authors she appreciated, assured her that in the final hour of life, God would embrace the faithful, saying, "Now it is My turn! Can I respond to the gift which the saints have made to Me other than by giving Myself now without limit or measure? . . . Yes, it must be so: I am now the soul of their soul. I must penetrate them with My blessedness, as fire penetrates iron. . . . I must show Myself to their spirit cloudlessly, unveiled, without the medium of the senses, must unite Myself with them face to face." These words were among *the greatest graces in my life,* Thérèse said, and she understood that the beginning of this union with God was already available in this life in Christ (SS 102). What could all suffering amount to if, at life's end, her loving Father would say, "Now it is My turn!" (HF 129; cf. GC 450–51, note 5; cf. EIG 131ff.).

Her desires were nothing more than to allow that union with God to deepen in this life. She had no inclination to moderate her desires; truly they were not her own desires anyway. They were, she was now convinced, God's desires in her. *The more You want to give* [us], Thérèse prayed to God, *the more you make us desire* (SS 276; PST 53ff.). She experienced prayer as a *surge of the heart*—God's own desire surging in her desires (CCC 2558; SS 242). Thérèse, like her mentor Teresa of Ávila, was a woman of desire, moving toward fewer and fewer human attachments and deeper and deeper union with God.

Everything I did was done to please God: this was her ever-growing desire (HLC 118). Some of the younger sisters mentioned to Thérèse that their motivation for prayer and good works was more to make reparation for their sins or to gain a reward in heaven. Each morning as part of the community prayer, a translation of a verse from the Psalms was recited: "I have set my heart on keeping your commandments always because of the reward that might be merited" (Psalm 119:12; cf. Psalm 19:11b). Thérèse said this verse only reluctantly and confided to one sister, *Within myself I hastened* [in prayer] *to say: "Oh Jesus, you know very well that I don't serve you for the reward, but solely because I love you and to save souls"* (TLMT 93).

When Thérèse did succeed in practicing virtue, and particularly when she responded to the sisters with patience and small acts of kindness, she revealed: *It is not for the purpose of weaving my crown, gaining merits, it is in order to please Jesus. . . . When I do not have any* [such] *opportunities, I want at least* [in prayer] *to tell Him frequently that I love Him; this is not difficult, and it keeps the fire going. Even though this fire of love would seem to me to have gone out, I would like to throw something on it, and Jesus could then relight it. . . . Jesus is really powerful enough to keep the fire going by Himself. However, He is satisfied when He sees us put a little fuel on it. The attentiveness pleases Jesus, and then He throws on the fire a lot of wood. We do not see it, but we do feel the strength of love's warmth* (GC 801).

The Gospels sustain me

Because the Jansenistic image of a wrathful God permeated the spiritual atmosphere of the convent, pervading not only the preaching of the retreats but also many of the spiritual books in the library, most of the presentations at the community retreats and most readings of piety were of little help to Thérèse as she matured. After a time, she became completely uninterested in reading popular devotional books. Thérèse had become convinced that *Jesus has no need of books or teachers to instruct souls; He teaches without the noise of words* (SS 179; cf. TLMT 76). *Without showing Himself, without making His voice heard, Jesus teaches me in secret; it is not by means of books, for I do not understand what I am reading. Sometimes a word comes to console me such as this one . . . : "I want to make you read in the book of life, wherein is contained the science of LOVE"* (SS 187). She was certain that Jesus was teaching her *the science of love* by the everyday experiences of her own *book of life* in the light of the Gospel.

On one occasion, when Thérèse was standing by the doorway of the convent library, she whispered to one of the sisters: *Oh! I would have been sorry to have read all those books. . . . If I had read them, I would have broken my head, and I would have wasted precious time that I could have employed very simply in loving God* (HLC 261).

She was not, of course, against reading. The religious books enlightening her about eternal happiness had been important in her spiritual growth, and even before she entered the convent, she had put to memory the spiritual classic *The Imitation of Christ*. In her early years at school, she had been captivated by the sheer joy of reading. I *would have spent my life at it,* she said (SS 71).

Later in the convent, however, she experienced that *all books left me in aridity. . . . If I open a book composed by a spiritual author (even the most beautiful, the most touching book),* she wrote, *I feel my heart contract immediately and I read without understanding, so to speak. Or if I do understand, my mind comes to a standstill without the capacity of meditating* (SS 179).

Nor did she suggest that other sisters avoid reading. Some sisters were profiting greatly from the insights and meditations they found in the devotional books. But Thérèse's own way, as she grew in the simplicity of the spiritual life, did not include the multiplicity of devotional practices, the pious thoughts, and various litanies suggested even by the noted spiritual writers of her time. Thérèse was faithful to the convent schedule that provided time for the sisters to read spiritual books, and she focused her reading on the New Testament.

The epistles of St. Paul were fundamental to her spiritual understanding, but it was particularly the Gospels to which she returned again and again for her spiritual nourishment. *The Gospels . . . sustain me during my hours of prayer, for in them I find what is necessary for my poor little soul. I am constantly discovering in them new lights, hidden and mysterious meanings* (SS 179). The Gospel illuminated Thérèse's prayer and her love, guiding her on the authentic path of perfection and holiness through the thicket of the false spirituality of the time.

To preach the authentic wisdom of the Gospel had always been one of the reasons Thérèse had desired to be a priest (cf. EIG 307; HLTT 173). This desire was fulfilled in a kind of vicarious way when about sixteen months before she died, she was assigned by her superiors to pray especially for two seminarians about to become priests who had each requested prayers.

In addition to her prayers, Thérèse also began to correspond with each of them and became their spiritual mother and mentor as well as their spiritual sister. By this time in her life, she was not hesitant to teach her understanding of the path of love and Gospel holiness. She knew that the understanding of the Gospel that she shared with them would not only transform them but also enlighten them to proclaim the same authentic wisdom to others. In this way the truth of the Gospel, she was delighted to think, would be preached in mission areas.

To one she wrote with conviction and with a sense of humor directed at herself what she knew to be the essence of the Gospel: *At times, when I am reading certain spiritual treatises in which perfection is shown through a thousand obstacles, surrounded by a crowd of illusions, my poor little mind quickly tires; I close the learned book that is breaking my head and drying up my heart, and I take up Holy Scripture. Then all seems luminous to me. . . . Perfection seems simple to me, I see it is sufficient to recognize one's nothingness and to abandon oneself as a child into God's arms. [Leave] to great souls, to great minds the beautiful books I cannot understand, much less put into practice. . . . I am very happy there are many mansions in God's kingdom, for if there were only the one whose description and road seem incomprehensible to me, I would not be able to enter there* (GC 1093–94). Thérèse spoke from her heart and her own experience, confident of being led by the Holy Spirit.

Never did words more tender and more melodious come to give joy to my soul

Although living in the convent, Thérèse did not have easy access to the Old Testament. According to the practice of the time, the complete Bible was not ordinarily available to the faithful, even though pious reading of the Bible in many French families was beginning to develop (HLTT 22; 173–74). It was feared that without further explanation by the Church, reading the Old Testament could easily mislead the faithful.

During the celebration of the liturgy of the Mass and while reciting the Divine Office with the Carmelite community, Thérèse did daily reflect on the Psalms and readings from the Old Testament. But only after she had been in Carmel six years, when her blood sister Céline had joined her, did Thérèse read for the first time certain meaningful passages of the Old Testament.

Céline brought with her to the convent, not a complete Bible, but a personal notebook in which she had copied some passages of the early books of the Bible. Meditating on the texts that Céline shared, Thérèse was jubilant in noticing that they completely validated and expanded her own insights.

Thérèse was grateful to read in the Book of Proverbs that God treasured especially the little ones. Her translation read: "Whoever is a little one, let him come to me" (Proverbs 9:4). She had always considered herself to be numbered among the "little ones" in the reign of God. Also, the words of the Book of Wisdom further assured her, in the translation Céline shared, that "to him that is little, mercy will be shown" (6:7). Thérèse responded to this passage with silence and tears of joy.

In addition, she read passages from the Book of Isaiah and was delighted to know that "as one whom a mother caresses, so will I comfort you; you shall be carried at the breast, and upon the knees they shall caress you" (cf. 66:12-13). With Isaiah's image of God as a loving mother, Thérèse rejoiced. *Ah! never did words more tender and more melodious come to give joy to my soul* (SS 208; cf. SS 188). She loved to imagine herself in the arms of her loving God and was further enchanted by the truth of Isaiah's words: "God shall feed his flock like a shepherd; he shall gather together the lambs with his arm, and shall take them up in his bosom" (cf. 40:11).

Reading these passages inspired Thérèse and filled her with joy. *After having listened to words such as these there is nothing to do but to be silent and to weep with gratitude and love* (SS 188). Her own intuitive image of God stooping down and embracing her in a union of love was confirmed by God's own word.

Inspired by these passages of Scripture, she now knew for certain that it was true: God was like a father and a mother, and her own mother's love and her father's *truly maternal love* (SS 35) had been but faint images of the divine infinite love.

In her inadequacy and littleness, Thérèse wanted to rest in union with God, and she understood that to do so was really to participate in the life of the Trinity, living in Christ and filled by the Holy Spirit, the Spirit who sanctified her. Experiencing herself as a little one in need of mercy and desirous of being held by God, Thérèse settled into these truths as she had settled securely as a child into the arms of her parents.

I want only to sing of Your Mercies

With the illumination of these four texts from Proverbs, Wisdom, and Isaiah validating her *measureless desires*, Thérèse matured considerably in her understanding of *the science of love*. She began to formulate more confidently and clearly what she would later teach as her little way. She prayed, *O my God, You surpassed all my expectation. I want only to sing of Your Mercies* (SS 208).

Thérèse was now more convinced than ever that the Jansenistic images of God in some spiritual books, often taken from the Old Testament and portraying God as vengeful and supporting violence, were corrected by images of God as a loving parent. Was it possible that some human images of God were more accurate than others, even if both were in the Scriptures? Although images of God such as a warrior, judge, or eternal rock of shelter were in the Scriptures, and although each image might contain an element of truth, did one image portray God more fully than another? Thérèse knew that no one image of God could adequately reveal the reality of the mystery of God. The incomprehensibility of the nature of God was one reason why the Scriptures presented so many images of God. But she was also convinced that, yes, the image of God as a loving parent was more nearly accurate than any other image.

Not only had the image of God as a loving parent arisen from her own experience and from her reading of the New Testament, but it had now been confirmed by the Old Testament passages that she had recently discovered. Even more important, Jesus himself had addressed God tenderly as *"Abba,"* as loving Father, as "Daddy."

Also contemplating Jesus' life and teaching in her prayerful study of the Gospels, Thérèse saw that all the various images of God in the Old Testament had to be balanced by the reality of Jesus, and Jesus himself is not a humanly invented image of God but God-made-man. The passages from Isaiah, Proverbs, and Wisdom portrayed God as a loving parent, and Jesus himself had acted like a loving parent.

Jesus, it was true, was firm, even at times unrelenting. She saw that Jesus spoke with force and strength in his words against those who opposed him. She also noticed that Jesus acted with power in some situations, in particular with the money changers in the Temple. She believed, however, that Jesus thought and acted, not in a willful, violent, or wrathful spirit, but with the power and force needed to alert those in his audience to their plight. They would have been attentive to nothing less. Knowing Jesus as she did, she was certain that he was using power in a compassionate way to help those who needed healing in their soul. She was confident that the Father whom Jesus was manifesting also always acted in love, even if that love came disguised as pain and suffering.

Thérèse had no way of consulting the biblical scholars on these matters. Her contemplation of Jesus, however, and now having read the Old Testament texts describing the tenderness of God assured her that Jesus, the Son of God, was manifesting the way of his Father. The Father of Jesus and Jesus himself were in love with the world and could not be on the side of wrath and revenge (John 3:16). The spiritual writers who shared the false notions of Jansenism might be able to quote the Old Testament to try to prove God was wrathful and full of vengeance, but they were wrong in not understanding that Jesus' life placed everything in the Bible in a new perspective.

That is why Jesus came: to show us a life completely filled with God and lived fully in God's love. God is love and God is in love with us, Thérèse was certain. God wants us to live heart-to-heart with him, not as servants who are fearful and distant (1 John 4:8; John 15:15). If God had simply wanted obedient, fearful servants, it would have been enough for God to have sent only the writers of the Old Testament who imagined God to be vindictive to the disobedient. But God's inclusive love extends even to his enemies, and his blessings continue to fall on the good and the bad. Jesus is the light that illumines the entire Bible.

What a sweet joy it is to think that God is . . . perfectly aware of our fragile nature

The new devotion to the Sacred Heart was arising in the popular spirituality of Thérèse's day, but even that was contaminated by the Jansenistic tendencies to equate God's justice with wrath and revenge. By emphasizing not God's love but rather the need to make reparation to God's justice, the popular devotion to the Sacred Heart of Jesus was filled with penitential acts.

Responding to this emphasis of appeasement in the devotion to the Sacred Heart, Thérèse wrote to Céline: *You know that I myself do not see the Sacred Heart as everybody else. I think that the Heart of my Spouse is mine alone, just as mine is His alone, and I speak to him then in the solitude of this delightful heart to heart, while waiting to contemplate Him one day face to face* (GC 709). For Thérèse, *the Heart of my Spouse* was a heart flowing with love toward creatures, welcoming full union in an eternal face-to-face encounter. Jesus' Sacred Heart was not a heart turned inward with grievance, expecting and needing reparation.

Thérèse taught the sisters that God was not on the side of violence—not the so-called "good" violence connected with combating evil in oneself or others, and not even in the "sacred" violence associated with worship and reparation. However, this was new teaching for the sisters, and one young sister, thinking of the Jansenistic image of God, challenged Thérèse. The sister pointed to a psalm in the Divine Office that in the common translation said divine justice "extended over the whole earth." The sister understood God's "justice" to mean God's "vengeance." And by "extended over the whole earth," she believed the psalmist meant that God's wrathful violence would be meted out everywhere for every wrong.

Thérèse did not deny that such a passage was in the Psalms. She also knew that spiritual books would not have helped the sister correct her image of God. Nor on this occasion did she fully explain her own vision that even God's justice *seems to me clothed in love* (SS 180). However, she did know that further reading in the Scriptures, especially in the Gospels, would give a more accurate understanding of the Father of Jesus. For now, however, Thérèse simply paged to another psalm that said that *God's Mercy reaches to the heavens* (cf. Psalm 36:6; SS 181). This meant, Thérèse told the sister, that God's mercy and love enfolded and surpassed justice.

By turning to another psalm, Thérèse, in effect, guided the sister into an important principle of biblical interpretation that Thérèse herself used to great profit. Thérèse invited the sister to consider the principle that Scripture passages shed light on one another, and that a broader scriptural context would help the sister know that no one human image of the infinite mystery of God could possibly be completely true. Jesus would confirm that the image of God not as a vindictive judge but as a loving parent is the most nearly accurate one. The sister was eventually convinced that Thérèse's teaching of God's mercy was true, and she became Thérèse's most important disciple within the community.

Later Thérèse wrote about her understanding of the oneness of God's justice and mercy. *"How GOOD is the Lord, his MERCY endures forever!"* [Psalm 118:1]. *It seems to me that if all creatures had received the same graces I received, God would be feared by none but would be loved to the point of folly; and through love, not through fear, no one would ever consent to cause Him any pain* (SS 180).

Then with the insight flowing from her contemplation of God's mercy and justice, she added: *All of [God's] perfections appear to be resplendent with love; even His Justice (and perhaps this even more so than the others) seems to me clothed in love. What a sweet joy it is to think that God is Just, i.e., that He takes into account our weakness, that He is perfectly aware of our fragile nature. What should I fear then? Ah! must not the infinitely just God, who deigns to pardon the faults of the prodigal son with so much kindness, be just also toward me who "am with Him always"?* (cf. Luke 15:31; SS 180).

This photograph of Thérèse was taken in late 1894 or early 1895, about two and a half years before her death.

CHAPTER 16

He Instructed Me Secretly in the Things of His Love

OBLATION TO MERCIFUL LOVE

Thérèse's appreciation of the unity of God's justice and mercy continued to deepen over her lifetime. She wrote to one of the newly ordained priests she had been mentoring:

> *I know one must be very pure to appear before the God of all Holiness, but I know, too, that the Lord is infinitely just; and it is this justice which frightens so many souls that is the object of my joy and confidence. To be just is not only to exercise severity in order to punish the guilty; it is also to recognize right intentions and to reward virtue. I expect as much from God's justice as from His mercy. It is because He is just that "He is compassionate and filled with gentleness, slow to punish, and abundant in mercy, for He knows our frailty, He remembers we are only dust. As a father has tenderness for his children, so the Lord has compassion on us!!" [Psalm 103:8, 14, 13] . . . How would He allow Himself to be overcome in generosity? . . . This is, Brother, what I think of God's justice; my way is all confidence and love. I do not understand souls who fear a Friend so tender. . . . I rejoice at being little since children alone and those who resemble them will be admitted to the heavenly banquet.* (GC 1093–94)

Expressing herself with simplicity and conviction, Thérèse invited her spiritual brother, as she invited her sisters, to be among the first to join her on the path of *the science of love*, her little way maturing within her.

God willed to have His mercy shine out in me

About two years before her death, Thérèse was inspired to offer herself to God's merciful love in a special way. By this time she had become certain, without any remaining doubt, that *because I was little and weak, He lowered Himself to me, and He instructed me secretly in the things of His love*. In this weakness God *willed to have His mercy shine out in me* (SS 105). Ordinarily not concerned with adding devotions to the usual community prayers already required of her, Thérèse nevertheless felt drawn to write a prayer of self-offering acknowledging her weakness and letting divine mercy radiate to her and through her.

Thérèse recognized that just as each person expressed love in an original and creative way, so each person was called to manifest holiness in a unique manner. She believed that her specific calling was to honor in a special way the mercy of God. *I understand . . . that all souls cannot be the same, that it is necessary there be different types in order to honor each of God's perfections in a particular way. To me He has granted His infinite Mercy, and through it I contemplate and adore the other divine perfections!* (SS 180).

Now as she contemplated composing a prayer of self-offering, she also understood with crystal clarity another dimension of *the science of love.* That dimension concerned an aspect of Gospel wisdom sown years earlier as she had positioned herself at the foot of the crucifix, and which had been further clarified especially by her contemplation of the story of Zacchaeus and the parable of the Pharisee and publican. This spiritual knowledge given especially to little ones, to those like Magdalene and the prodigal son who had experienced their own littleness, was the truth that to love God was not a matter of struggling to evoke sentiments of love for God and then directing those sentiments to God. Rather, to love God was fulfilled in complete abandonment and gratitude in the spirit of the publican. To love God, she now knew clearly, was to let God reach down to embrace her in God's own transforming love. Thérèse was now certain that for her to love God required her to abandon herself to God's love already uniting her with God. She was inspired to compose a prayer expressing these sentiments and offering herself totally in self-surrender to God's love.

Is Your disdained Love going to remain closed up within Your Heart?

As she prepared to compose the prayer of self-offering, Thérèse learned that a sister living in another French Carmelite convent had already written such a prayer. This sister, although renowned for her holiness, was following the piety of the day by offering herself in reparation and expiation as a victim to God's vengeance and justice. Her prayer, regretting that God's justice was being neglected and needing to be appeased, asked God to punish her as a victim of divine rage as she herself took the place of unrepentant sinners.

This offering [by the pious sister] *seemed great and very generous to me,* Thérèse wrote, *but I was far from feeling myself attracted to making it* (SS 180). Actually Thérèse felt repulsed by the image of God as vengeful. She also felt helpless attempting to duplicate the severe austerities that the prayer implied. But most important, she was convinced that God did not need to be appeased and was not vindictively reserving punishment for sinners.

Jesus' thirst on the cross was God's begging for love, longing for the return of sinners so that a reestablished bond of love could be extended into eternity. The sinner's punishment was not the act of a vengeful God of justice, but the pain of the sinner's own willful alienation from divine love, refusing, as the Pharisee refused, to accept union with God and return love for love. Divine mercy, more than any other divine attribute, Thérèse believed, was unknown, ignored, and rejected. Divine mercy needed to be acknowledged, accepted, and proclaimed.

O my God! Thérèse implored, reflecting on the good intentions of the pious sister:

> *Will your justice alone find souls willing to immolate themselves as victims? Does not your Merciful Love need them too? On every side this love is unknown, rejected; those hearts upon whom You would lavish it turn to creatures seeking happiness. . . . They do this instead of throwing themselves into Your arms and of accepting Your infinite Love. O my God! Is Your disdained Love going to remain closed up within Your Heart? It seems to me that if You were to find souls offering themselves as victims of holocaust to Your Love, You would consume them rapidly; it seems to me, too, that You would be happy not to hold back the waves of infinite tenderness within You.* (SS 180–81)

It is my weakness that gives me the boldness of offering myself

Thinking again of the young sister's concern about God's justice, Thérèse continued, *If Your Justice loves to release itself, this Justice which extends only over the earth, how much more does Your Merciful Love desire to set souls on fire since Your Mercy reaches to the heavens. O my Jesus, let me be this happy victim; consume Your holocaust with the fire of Your Divine Love!* (SS 181).

Thérèse's heart surged with the passion of these sentiments as she now composed a complete self-offering to divine mercy. Thérèse's offering would not be about the vengefulness and violence of God. She would not ask a vindictive Jansenistic God to scapegoat and victimize her with violent retribution for the offenses of sinners. Rather, she would offer herself in complete self-surrender and gratitude to be willingly embraced by God's love and to willingly share the overflowing mercy of God. She would pray for God to reach down to embrace her in God's loving mercy (cf. HLTT 155ff.; EIG 232ff.).

I am only a child, Thérèse prayed, *powerless and weak, and yet it is my weakness that gives me the boldness of offering myself as VICTIM of Your Love, O Jesus!* (SS 195). Like the publican, her very weakness and her sincere plea for God's mercy were enough to draw her into divine love and mercy.

In her prayer of offering, Thérèse would use the identical words found in the popular victim prayers of her day. She would use, in fact, the very words the pious sister used in her prayer: the words "oblation," "consume," "martyr," "holocaust," and "victim." Thérèse, however, would deliberately subvert and transform the meaning of these words from images of violence into images of love and devotion.

She would offer herself to God as a "victim," not to be victimized by God's alleged rage, but to be completely available to God's love. She would be a "martyr," not to be destroyed in God's supposed wrath, but to surrender in gratitude to the embrace of God's loving union. She would be a "holocaust," not to be annihilated by the fire of sacrificial violence, but to be "consumed" by being enveloped in God's purifying and transforming love. She would be an "oblation" to be poured out into the ocean of God's mercy.

She would open her soul. She would *choose all* (SS 27) and become an oblation, a martyr, a holocaust, a victim of divine mercy. She would unite her will with God's will and *ask God to consume me incessantly, allowing the waves of infinite tenderness shut up within God to overflow into my soul* (SS 277). In this way she would become a "martyr" and die of divine love.

Thérèse was sensitive to the feelings of fear that these violent words aroused, so when she invited Céline to join her in reciting the Act of Oblation to Merciful Love that she had just composed, she confided to her soul mate, *We have nothing to fear from this Act. From this Oblation of self to God's love we can expect mercy alone* (MSST 92). She asked another sister rhetorically, *Do you know what God requires of us by way of preparation* [to make this act of offering]?

He requires us to admit our unworthiness. Since He has already given you this grace, give yourself up to Him without fear (TLMT 87).

O my God! Most Blessed Trinity, I desire to Love You and to make You Loved

Thérèse recited her Act of Oblation to Merciful Love on June 9, 1895, just two years and three months before she died. She knelt before the statue of the Blessed Mother, the same statue she had seen smile on her in childhood, with Céline, her *spiritual sister* (SS 103) at her side. This prayer embraced all that she had thus far learned of *the science of love* and contained the essence of her little way.

Thérèse and Céline joined their voices and hearts:

O my God! Most Blessed Trinity, I desire to Love You and to make You Loved, to work for the glory of the Holy Church by saving souls on earth and liberating those suffering in purgatory. I desire to accomplish Your will perfectly and to reach the degree of glory You have prepared for me in Your Kingdom. I desire, in a word, to be a saint, but I feel my helplessness and I beg you, Oh my God! to be Yourself my Sanctity!

Since You loved me so much as to give me Your only Son as my Savior and my Spouse, the infinite treasures of His merits are mine. I offer them to You with gladness, begging You to look upon me only in the Face of Jesus and in His heart burning with Love.

I offer You, too, all the merits of the saints (in heaven and on earth), their acts of Love, and those of the holy angels. Finally, I offer you, O Blessed Trinity! the Love and merits of the Blessed Virgin, my dear Mother. It is to her I abandon my offering, begging her to present it to You. Her Divine Son, my Beloved Spouse, told us in the days of His mortal life: "Whatsoever you ask the Father in my name he will give it to you!" [John 15:16]. I am certain, then, that You will grant my desires; I know, O my God! that the more You want to give, the more You make us desire. I feel in my heart immense desires and it is with confidence I ask You to come and take possession of my soul. Ah! I cannot receive Holy Communion as often as I desire, but, Lord, are you not all-powerful? Remain in me as in a tabernacle and never separate Yourself from Your little victim.

I want to console You for the ingratitude of the wicked, and I beg of You to take away my freedom to displease You. If through weakness I sometimes fall, may Your Divine Glance cleanse my soul immediately, consuming all my imperfections like the fire that transforms everything into itself.

I thank You, O my God! for all the graces You have granted me, especially the grace of making me pass through the crucible of suffering. It is with joy I shall contemplate You on the Last Day carrying the scepter of Your Cross. Since You deigned to give me a share in this very precious Cross, I hope in heaven to resemble You and to see shining in my glorified body the sacred stigmata of Your Passion.

After earth's Exile, I hope to go and enjoy You in the Fatherland, but I do not want to lay up merits for heaven. I want to work for Your Love alone with the one purpose of pleasing You, consoling Your Sacred Heart, and saving souls who will love You eternally.

In the evening of this life, I shall appear before You with empty hands, for I do not ask You, Lord, to count my works. All our justice is stained in Your eyes. I wish, then, to be clothed in Your own Justice and to receive from Your Love the eternal possession of Yourself. I want no other Throne, no other Crown but You, my Beloved!

Time is nothing in Your eyes, and a single day is like a thousand years. You can, then, in one instant prepare me to appear before You.

In order to live in one single act of perfect Love, I OFFER MYSELF AS A VICTIM OF HOLOCAUST TO YOUR MERCIFUL LOVE, asking You to consume me incessantly, allowing the waves of infinite tenderness shut up within You to overflow into my soul, and that thus I may become a martyr of Your Love, O my God!

May this martyrdom, after having prepared me to appear before You, finally cause me to die and may my soul take its flight without any delay into the eternal embrace of Your Merciful Love.

I want, O my Beloved, at each beat of my heart to renew this offering to You an infinite number of times, until the shadows having disappeared I may be able to tell You of my Love in an Eternal Face to Face! (SS 276–77; PST 53ff.)

I beg You to choose a legion of little Victims worthy of Your LOVE!

To the text of her self-offering, Thérèse signed her religious name preceded by her baptismal name, an acknowledgment that this act of offering was about *the fire* of the Holy Spirit that she had received in a special way at her Baptism. The offering expressed the fulfillment of the grace of her religious vocation as well. It also expressed the many graces and insights into *the science of love* that she had received over the years (cf. HLTT 157ff.).

If you don't want to ever fear again do as I do, Thérèse told one of the sisters she was guiding, *take the means to force God not to judge you at all, by presenting yourself to him with empty hands. . . . Be assured: for the victims of Love, there will be no judgment. God will hasten to repay with eternal delights his own love that he sees burning in their heart* (TLMT 80–81).

O Jesus! Thérèse wrote at the end of her life, *why can't I tell all little souls how unspeakable is Your condescension? I feel that if You found a soul weaker and littler than mine, which is impossible, You would be pleased to grant it still greater favors, provided it abandoned itself with total confidence to Your Infinite Mercy. . . . I beg You to cast Your Divine Glance upon a great number of little souls. I beg You to choose a legion of little Victims worthy of Your LOVE!* (SS 200).

God had prepared Thérèse to receive the blessing of composing the Act of Oblation to Merciful Love by inspiring her to place herself at the feet of Jesus crucified, willingly uniting herself to the suffering Jesus. By grace she had come to the spiritual maturity to pray from the center of her being this act of offering: a prayer of complete self-surrender and total availability; a cry from the depth of her sublime faith, her *measureless desires* to love, and her profound hope.

One obtains from God what one hopes for, she had taught (STL 233). *It is impossible for God not to respond to that, because He always measures His gifts by how much confidence we have* (TLMT 86).

The Act of Oblation to Merciful Love is a complete denunciation of any violence in spirituality and specifically a total rejection of the violence inherent in Jansenism, perfectionism, and Pelagianism. As a proclamation of the fundamental elements of Gospel holiness, it is a significant contribution to Christian devotional literature. The Act of Oblation to Merciful Love, in the form of a prayer, expresses Thérèse's little way of love.

Thérèse's Little Way

CHAPTER 17

I Want to Seek Out a Means of Going to Heaven by a Little Way

FINDING THE LITTLE WAY

Over the years, as she continued to meditate on the poverty of spirit of her beloved Mother Mary and on the loving audacity of Mary Magdalene, Thérèse was encouraged to be bold with Jesus in her own little way. With Mother Mary and Magdalene, she had also found her spiritual home at the foot of the cross, receiving and sharing Jesus' outpouring of love. More recently, she had been enlightened when she prayed over the scriptural text of Jesus' word to "be merciful, just as your Father is merciful" (Luke 6:36) as that text was illuminated by the parable of the prodigal son but especially by the brilliance of the story of Zacchaeus (19:1-10) and the parable of the Pharisee and publican (18:9-14). She needed no further assurance that mercy and compassion, not perfectionism, was the Gospel call to holiness and that, for her, to love God was to receive God's love into her heart.

These understandings glowed even more intensely as Thérèse continued to pray in the radiance offered by the Old Testament passages. These verses had confirmed her spiritual intuition that God was both a loving father and a loving mother who cared especially for those who were humble in their weaknesses—the "little ones" who were called to sanctity but who could not attain the perfection that perhaps the "great ones" could achieve. She had now begun to discern more clearly the essence of another way to holiness, a new path *very straight* and *very short*: her *little way* (SS 207; cf. HLTT 153ff.).

The elevator which must raise me to heaven is Your arms, O Jesus!

The mistaken idea of holiness often suggested was that sanctity was a matter of willful effort well beyond the ordinary person. Holiness was portrayed as laboriously ascending the stairway of perfection, climbing the ladder of humility, struggling through the stages of virtue, attaining exalted levels of prayer, and scaling the rugged heights of severe mortification. Sanctity was not for the "little ones."

The stairway of perfection, or *the rough stairway of fear* (GC 1152) as Thérèse once referred to it, recalled to her mind the actual impossible stairway that she had faced as a two-year-old when she had tried to climb to the second floor of her family home. At that time, her mother had described Thérèse's attempting the unattainable: *She will not climb the stairs all alone, but cries at each step: "Mamma, Mamma!"* (SS 18; cf. GC 1218).

Recognition of her personal inadequacy in her early convent days made her acutely aware that she simply could not, by her own efforts, overcome her weaknesses and climb that rough, impossible, fearful stairway of perfection. She needed the help of a loving parent, and she was willing to receive that help from her loving Father.

Once before, on the Christmas Day of Thérèse's conversion, she had received God's help on a stairway. At that time, she had learned the important truth that she could, by the sheer grace empowering her, physically and emotionally take her next step, even in great distress. Then God had given her the help she needed, and now in her Carmelite vocation, she asked for God's light and mercy.

Could there be a way to advance in holiness without this attempt at unattainable achievements, without this striving and often violent effort? God had inspired in her the great desire to be holy *and since God never gives desires that He cannot realize, I can, then,* Thérèse knew, *in spite of my littleness, aspire to holiness. It is impossible for me to grow up,* Thérèse wrote. *But I want to seek out a means of going to heaven by a little way, a way that is very straight, very short, and totally new* (SS 207).

Was it possible, she wondered, that such a straight, short, and new way could actually be found in the spiritual life? Perhaps it could because, after all, as she noted enthusiastically, *We are living now in an age of inventions* (SS 207). Thérèse had, in fact, come upon a new invention that made climbing physical steps unnecessary. She had experienced it when she was fourteen years old during a stopover in Paris on her pilgrimage to Rome to ask the pope's permission to enter the convent. The new invention was in the large department store where she and Céline shopped with their father (HLTT 72; cf. GC 306–7, note 2). It was the elevator, the lift. Thérèse was delighted to learn from experience that the elevator did make it possible to *no longer have to take the trouble of climbing stairs* laboriously, step-by-step (SS 207).

If only there were an elevator in the spiritual life that would replace the *rough stairway of perfection,* everything would be different, and then the weakness of the little child could be overcome in a *totally new* way (SS 207). And Thérèse knew immediately that the spiritual life did have such an elevator. She was filled with conviction and joy that *the elevator which must raise me to heaven is Your arms, O Jesus!* (SS 208).

She would, then, *abandon* herself *as a child into God's arms* (GC 1094). Her loving God, who was already stooping down to her, was ready to take her up. She would remain spiritually the little child, and God would do the heavy lifting. It was that simple. With the image of the elevator, Thérèse had captured a profound insight into the fundamental mystery of the Incarnation, the essential message of the Gospel.

Already in her prayer, Thérèse had glimpsed an important secret of God's love, a secret that often eluded the wise and learned who could and did climb a certain number of steps on that *rough stairway of perfection*. It was the secret revealed to the little children who were too small to do any climbing at all. Thérèse's secret was in knowing that *the nature of love is to humble oneself* (SS 14), and that it is the nature of divine love to stoop down and lift her up and transform her.

Now in her spiritual maturity, she was certain that it was to the little ones who were inadequate in the spiritual life—*the child who knows only how to make . . . feeble cries; [and] . . . the poor savage, who has nothing but the natural law* [and who doesn't even know about stairways or ladders]—*it is to their hearts that God deigns to lower Himself. . . . When coming down in this way*, she wrote, *God manifests His infinite grandeur* (SS 14). This conviction that the infinite God *deigns to lower Himself* in union became Thérèse's peace and joy, and the continuous deepening of this union with God gradually became Thérèse's life.

I had to remain little and become this more and more

Thérèse knew that union with God had already been established by God's love stooping down in bringing her into existence and then blessing her in Baptism, which united her with Jesus in his paschal mystery, in his mystical body, and with the Trinity. That union was constantly nourished by Jesus continually lowering himself in the Eucharist, sharing his risen life. Moreover, that union was daily being actualized by God's love reaching down in divine providence, sustaining her in every situation. Now she wished to accept more fully that union, appreciate it, and express it in each present moment by doing God's will. Being embraced by her loving Father who scooped her up was the answer to Thérèse's *measureless desires* of holiness and love.

As in her early childhood when she had found security resting in the arms of her parents, now Thérèse found great consolation resting in God's arms. She no longer needed to struggle up a difficult, frightful, impossible stairway. She would be lifted up by divine love. And further, to be lifted up meant that the entire need to grow up and to grow out of inadequacies in order to reach holiness was transformed.

If Thérèse were to be carried in the elevator of God's arms, then, as she said, *for this I had no need to grow up, but rather I had to remain little and become this more and more.* It was not, then, that being weak and little, she needed to become strong; it was, rather, that she needed to remain little so as not to be a burden when God reached down to lift her up. *I can,* she now said with complete conviction, *despite my littleness, aspire to holiness* (SS 207–8; cf. GC 836; 784; 786, note 3).

Her totally new way would mean deepening her spirit of self-surrender to God's will, becoming more and more willing to run toward her prodigal Father, taking the downward path of Zacchaeus, remaining little in her weaknesses and spiritual poverty, and living the prayer of the publican in total confidence and love.

In order to be raised up by God, Thérèse needed to die to herself, to die to her egocentricity. She now understood Jesus' invitation in the Gospel and in the paschal mystery of everyday life. She needed to die daily to any selfishness that might be hidden in her heart, even the self-centered ambition of becoming perfect through possessing holiness, and instead, let Holiness more and more possess her. *Perfection consists in doing His will* (GC 795), of cooperating with God's desires unfolding in the very ordinary, everyday experiences of life.

In this way her prayer would be fulfilled: *May Your will be done in me perfectly, and may I arrive at the place You have prepared for me. I desire to accomplish Your will perfectly and to reach the degree of glory You have prepared for me in Your Kingdom* (SS 275–76). God would lift her to the degree of perfection that God had prepared for her. It would not be her doing; it would be all God's work in her.

Although Thérèse spoke of searching for a *totally new* way, the way of spirituality that the Holy Spirit was inspiring in her was actually the Gospel way of holiness, the fundamental Christian way. Thérèse's genius was that she recognized and rediscovered authentic Gospel holiness, which had begun to be lost to ordinary Christians of her time.

Rather, how much you have to lose

During the last two years of her life, as Thérèse became more and more confident of her grasp of authentic Gospel spirituality, she found herself mostly alone in her convictions. All of the sisters she lived with, even Pauline who had been her second mother and her early spiritual guide, still lived the spiritual life mostly nourished by the common teaching and did not fully appreciate Thérèse's mature and profound spiritual insights.

Nevertheless, fully convinced, Thérèse taught her little way to the younger sisters by her example and through her spiritual guidance. She also influenced the community through the personal counsel she extended to the sisters who had begun seeking her help. Through the poems she wrote at the request of some of the sisters and through the dramatic plays that she composed for various community feasts days, she also taught her little way to the community.

In particular, Thérèse taught her little way to her soul mate, Céline, who since she entered the community had come under Thérèse's care. Having been Céline's intimate friend throughout her life, Thérèse had a deep insight into Céline's nature. Céline had a somewhat aggressive, determined way. When she came to Carmel, she applied that same willful spirit to acquiring holiness. That willfulness was the false way that Thérèse had noticed earlier in herself and had completely rejected. Now she tried to help her sister understand her newly discovered little way.

Céline, who had been surprised on that Christmas Day to see the teenage Thérèse peacefully abiding her feelings of hurt at her father's remark, was truly amazed now, some eight years later, to see the maturity of her sister in her role at the center of convent life. She saw Thérèse's remarkable ability to humbly accept her strengths and weaknesses without fuss, to act in love even toward the difficult sisters, to guide in patience the young sisters, and to be a compassionate presence in the rigors of the community life, bridging differences and hostilities.

Céline was especially challenged because she herself was not as psychologically and spiritually mature as Thérèse. In her relationships with the community,

Céline was experiencing her weakness in a way she never had before. Céline was impetuous and often had outbursts of impatience. She could not help but compare herself with Thérèse, who was almost four years younger but who seemed to be at peace with all the pinpricks of the convent life. Céline did not yet feel at peace; she felt self-conscious and inadequate. She was annoyed by the troublesome sisters and resisted the rigor and perfectionism of the community. Unlike Thérèse, she reacted with irritation and then became dissatisfied with herself for not being a better religious (cf. GC 552).

On one occasion, under the pretext of seeking advice, Céline came to Thérèse actually to complain. She did not criticize any of the sisters; rather, in her distress and frustration, she complained about herself. She was upset by her own harsh reactions to some of the difficult sisters. She found fault with herself for not being able to act with charity, as she would have liked. "Oh, when I think how much I have to acquire!" Céline remarked to Thérèse.

Thérèse responded out of a wisdom that had been growing especially since she had applied to herself the publican's prayer, *Be merciful to me a sinner,* as well as Zacchaeus' truth, *Jesus tells us to descend* (GC 761). It was the wisdom that she had learned from her Mother Mary, but also from Mary Magdalene, who *found what she was seeking by always stooping down and looking into the empty tomb.* Thérèse wrote of herself, *So I, abasing myself to the very depths of my nothingness, raised myself so high that I was able to attain my end* (SS 194).

It was the same wisdom, in those last months of her father's life as he slowly entered his mental darkness, that Thérèse had understood in her devotion to the Holy Face. The image of the Holy Face had become for Thérèse an image of her own father's suffering as well as an icon of the teaching of both St. Paul and St. John of the Cross on self-surrender and total self-emptying.

From her reflections, Thérèse replied to Céline by offering the fundamental wisdom, the basic paradox of the spiritual life. Céline needed to go up by going down, to increase by decreasing, to live by dying to self, to acquire by self-surrendering, to achieve by total self-abandonment, to desire everything by desiring nothing. If Céline would come to him who is everything, she must come by way of nothing. To Céline's lament that she had so much to acquire, Thérèse responded, *Rather, how much you have to lose* (MSST 28).

How much you have to lose: it was an expression of Thérèse's little way of spirituality in a brief maxim. Thérèse now shared that truth with Céline, but in a short time, she herself would be asked to embrace it more fully than she imagined possible. As Thérèse entered into the dreadful physical and spiritual suffering of the final eighteen months of her life, God would ask of her a total self-surrendering and the loss of everything less than himself. But for now, she was to focus on teaching that truth more and more explicitly to the sisters under her care, as well as to all the members of the community.

CHAPTER 18

If You Are Willing to Bear Serenely the Trial of Being Displeasing to Yourself

TEACHING THE LITTLE WAY

In conformity with the spirituality of the times, Céline had imagined that spiritual growth was a path of striving and acquisition. So Thérèse's response suggesting that Céline had *much to lose* (MSST 28) took Céline by surprise. Thérèse then used another occasion to further clarify her little way to her sister.

On this second occasion many months later, Céline, still frustrated in her efforts to conquer her faults and especially her lapses in charity, was reproaching herself as a failure. She was still not the holy person that she willed to be, and she was still not being acknowledged and respected as a saintly person by the other sisters. She wrote a despondent and self-reproving note to Thérèse (cf. GC 1036–37, note 1).

Céline wrote her note at Christmastime, and Thérèse wished to encourage her to welcome the Christ child into her heart despite her faults. In responding to Céline's self-condemnation and frustration, Thérèse did not suggest that Céline ignore her failings, nor did she suggest that her sister exert more effort to correct them. Thérèse said simply, *If you are willing to bear serenely the trial of being displeasing to yourself, then you will be . . . [for Jesus] a pleasant place of shelter* (Collected Letters of St. Thérèse of Lisieux, translated by F. J. Sheed, 303; cf. GC 1038 for a slightly different translation).

When we accept our disappointment at our failures, God immediately returns to us

Thérèse was expressing a truth that she had pondered since her conversion, that *when we accept our disappointment at our failures, God immediately returns to us* (HLC 181). It was the essence of the little way that Thérèse herself now understood so clearly. Céline needed to lose what blocked the Holy Spirit of love from surging within her. Thérèse saw that Céline's own feelings of self-rejection and her willful striving for self-improvement were hindering her movement along the little way and limiting the Holy Spirit's action in her.

These feelings and willfulness were causing a war within Céline and making her an enemy to herself. Thérèse had experienced this in her own life in the presence of the sister toward whom she had a *natural antipathy* and with whom she sometimes experienced a *violent* struggle (SS 222–23).

Céline needed to be willing to be patient with herself and to let go of her hostile feelings toward herself, especially her failure to appreciate herself and her discouragement. Céline needed to "come down," abandon her perch in the Zacchaeus tree, and accept Jesus into her dwelling as she was and without self-condemnation. Céline needed to adopt Jesus' own self-emptying spirit and, in the spirit of the publican's self-surrender, simply seek God's mercy.

In particular, Céline needed to lose her willfulness that drove her to strive for self-improvement. That harsh willfulness was itself a kind of disguised violence obstructing the power of the Holy Spirit. By expressing her willpower in an attitude of willingness to accept her spiritual poverty in humility, Céline would make her heart *a pleasant place of shelter* and welcome for Jesus. Relinquishing her willful desire to be someone other than who she was and embracing a spirit of self-surrender and gratitude would put her on the little way, the path of transformation. Céline's weaknesses were actually providing an opening for grace, and her willingness to bear her faults peacefully would allow her to do the good works, as best she could, that God wished her to do. God would transform her in God's time and in God's way.

But Thérèse, knowing Céline's impetuous nature, did not expect Céline to succeed in bearing her faults in peace. She simply invited Céline to be *willing* to bear them—or to be willing to be willing. She invited Céline not to become impatient with herself for being frustrated with her own spiritual inadequacies and with the limitations of the sisters. Céline would have to learn, as Thérèse herself had learned, when to put boundaries on her own feelings by temporarily fleeing situations that she could not bear.

The wisdom and transforming power contained in Thérèse's words *how much you have to lose,* as well as in the invitation to be *willing to bear serenely the trial of being displeasing to yourself,* had been germinating in Thérèse for many years. Her first fleeting glimpse of this truth happened when she had borne her feelings as she climbed the steps after the Christmas midnight Mass, courageously enduring the pain of her father's words of criticism without self-rejection or retaliation.

This truth had enlightened her even more deeply after she had positioned herself at the foot of the cross following her complete conversion. During the years in the convent, this truth had become a stepping-stone on her spiritual path, as she had willingly borne serenely, as best she could, her own negative feelings toward the many idiosyncrasies of the sisters. She had also gradually shared this truth with the sisters she guided, and now she would continue to teach it especially by her own personal example, as she serenely bore the reality of who she was in the arms of Jesus in her little way.

I abandon myself into the arms of Jesus

Since Thérèse encouraged the young sisters under her care to be honest and frank with her, they sometimes questioned her about her own spiritual path. They were curious to know how she handled her own failures. One of the young sisters asked her what she did when she felt herself to be inadequate and a sinner. Did Thérèse ever get discouraged?

In her response, Thérèse did not reveal the details and history of her struggles with her excessive feelings. But she knew that it was true that as a child, after her mother's death, she had fallen into a state of melancholy that had plagued her for ten years and that did include feelings of discouragement. During a period at the time of her First Communion, she had deliberately confronted her despondency and resolved that she would not become discouraged (cf. TLMT 119; STL 174; EIG 101ff.). This willful resolve did not, of course, end the matter, and she was often distressed and dangerously close to discouragement while in the grip of her scrupulosity over the next years.

She was also near the realm of discouragement in her inability to remain faithful to her own heart after her childhood cure by the smile of the Blessed Virgin. At that time, by revealing her secret to her sister Marie, she had broken the promise to herself that *I never will tell anyone* (SS 66). She had done violence to her true self and fell into deep disappointment with herself. At that time, she prayed, *O my good Blessed Virgin, grant that your little Thérèse may stop tormenting herself* (PST 37; cf. EIG 93ff.). In her teenage years, the grace of her complete conversion finally healed Thérèse of the youthful melancholy that had plagued her soul, poisoned the joy of her childhood nature, and held her at the edge of discouragement.

Years later Thérèse wrote words of self-revelation echoing the resolution she had made at the time of her First Communion: *I am not always faithful, but I never get discouraged; I abandon myself into the arms of Jesus* (GC 801). She had put her tendency to discouragement within the context of self-surrender to God stooping down to her. *To be little,* she wrote, describing what she meant to be walking the little way like a child embraced by God, *is not to become discouraged over one's faults, for children fall often, but they are too little to hurt themselves very much* (HLC 139).

Even as she neared the end of her life, however, as she endured the distress and utter darkness of her trial of faith, she wrote to Mother Gonzague confessing that if this trial had occurred *a little earlier, I believe it would have plunged me into a state of discouragement* (SS 214). The possibility of discouragement was always near.

Throughout her life, when Thérèse failed in love because of weakness, she did not harbor or cultivate feelings of discouragement; rather, she returned again and again to the Heart of Holiness. In the spirit of the publican, she said, *I entrust to Jesus my failings, I tell Him all about them; and I think, so bold is my trust, that in this way I acquire more power over His heart and draw to myself in still greater abundance the love of Jesus who came to call sinners, not the righteous* (HF 337). She brought her weaknesses to her prayers as she brought all of her trials and joys to prayer, telling God *all about them.*

To her prayer she also brought her repentance, confident in her little way that *when we cast our faults with entire filial confidence into the devouring fire of love, how would these not be consumed beyond return?* (GC 1133–34; cf. SS 181).

She experienced deep grief and repentance when, failing in love, she violated her true self, but she did not cultivate self-condemnation or discouragement as Céline was prone to do. *When I commit a fault* [especially against charity] *that makes me sad,* she said, *I know very well that this sadness is a consequence of my infidelity, but do you believe I remain there? Oh! no, I'm not so foolish! I hasten to say to God: My God, I know I have merited this feeling of sadness, but let me offer it up to you just the same as a trial that You sent me through love. I am sorry for my sin, but I'm happy to have this suffering to offer to you* (HLC 71). Sad that she had failed again, Thérèse used her feelings to become more available to God's mercy.

On one occasion, a young sister, herself near discouragement by all her distractions during her private prayer, asked Thérèse whether she also had distractions at prayer. Thérèse responded with honesty and simplicity and with a bit of humor at her own weakness. *I have a lot of these,* she said, *but as soon as I perceive them I pray for the persons that occupy my imagination and this way they benefit from my distractions* (TLMT 25). Thérèse, who often fell asleep during her prayers and who had been scolded by her ordinary confessor for those lapses (GC 659; 717), now was telling the young sister that she also had lots of distractions, even when she stayed awake. She turned her distractions into prayer, however, and in that way, she benefited not only herself by resuming her prayer but also those whose memories had distracted her by praying for them. It was a creative, intuitive solution without self-condemnation. She had found a way that avoided discouragement and enabled her to *bear serenely the trial of being displeasing to* herself in her weaknesses.

Really, I am far from being a saint

Reflecting on her prayer over the years, Thérèse wrote toward the end of her life a description of prayer that flowed from her understanding of her little way. *For me,* she noticed, *prayer is a surge of the heart; it is a simple look turned toward heaven, it is a cry of recognition and of love, embracing both trial and joy.* She had experienced each of these ways of prayer: the surge of her heart, the movement of the Holy Spirit within her beating with God's heart, the simple look of contemplative awareness at God's presence in her life, and the willing embrace of both *trial and joy* as she reflected on her experiences (CCC 2558; SS 242; cf. EIG 44ff., 201ff.).

Her experience of each of these moments of prayer was not limited to her formal prayer times, but came to her even more so when she simply remained in a spirit of prayerfulness during the ordinary activities of the day. *Never have I heard Him speak,* she wrote, *but I feel that He is within me at each moment; He is guiding and inspiring me with what I must say and do. I find just when I need them certain lights that I had not seen until then, and it isn't most frequently during my hours of prayer that these are most abundant but rather in the midst of my daily occupations* (SS 179). She also believed *it is Jesus Himself hidden in the depths of my poor little heart . . . acting within me, making me think of all He desires me to do at the present moment* (SS 165). In her little way, her prayer and life had become one.

Nevertheless, throughout her life, Thérèse continued to struggle with her tendency to fall asleep during her formal time of personal prayer. With all of her goodwill, she was even overcome with drowsiness during the special prayer time after receiving Communion. She did not, however, attribute her fatigue in a self-blaming way to a lack of fervor, even though that would have been the logic of the spirituality of the times. She was confident of her heart's desire, and with spiritual courage, she took a certain bold delight in her weakness.

Two years before her death, Thérèse wrote these words:

> *Really, I am far from being a saint . . . ; instead of rejoicing, for example, at my aridity, I should attribute it to my little fervor and lack of fidelity; I should be desolate for having slept (for seven years) during my hours of prayer and my thanksgivings after Holy Communion; well, I am not desolate, I remember that little children are as pleasing to their parents when they are asleep as well as when they are wide awake; I remember, too, that when they perform operations, doctors put their patients to sleep. Finally, I remember that: "The Lord knows our weakness, that he is mindful that we are but dust and ashes"* (SS 165; cf. Psalm 103:14).

Rather than being discouraged and condemning herself for the absence of a felt sense of devotion, Thérèse trusted in her own sincere desires and was confident of her willingness to be available to God. *O Jesus!* she prayed with confidence, *grant me the grace in all I do to please You alone* (PST 48). She accepted in self-surrender and gratitude the reality of who she was in the arms of Jesus. It was her little way.

Do not fear to tell Him you love Him even without feeling it

Of course, on one level Thérèse wished that she had more devotional feelings in her personal prayer, but when she lacked such feelings, she was undaunted. She offered her weakness to Jesus and noted that *no doubt this* [little way] *does not displease Jesus since he seems to encourage me on this road* [of spiritual poverty] (SS 173). Thérèse trusted that God, knowing her frailty and her desires, would continue to love her nonetheless. Thérèse was confident that God was a loving parent and a healing doctor and not a harsh critic or a demanding judge. She was *willing to bear serenely the trial of being displeasing to* herself.

During her entire nine years of convent life, aridity in prayer was her dominant experience. She recited the Divine Office, the Rosary, and other prayers in community, comforted in her drowsiness and lack of pious feelings by the hope that the fervor of her sisters would make up for her own deficiencies. To make sense of her dryness and drowsiness, she attributed them not to herself but to Jesus' own fatigue. Jesus, she imagined, *was sleeping as usual in my little boat* (SS 165).

Jesus was disheartened and wearied, she imagined, with having always to respond to requests. *Since Jesus wants to sleep why will I hinder Him? I am only too happy that He doesn't bother with me,* she wrote shortly after entering Carmel, *for He is showing me that I am not a stranger when treating me this way, for, I assure you, He is going to no trouble about carrying on a conversation with me!* (GC 500). *I see very well how rarely souls allow Him to sleep peacefully within them. Jesus is so fatigued with always having to take the initiative and to attend to others that He hastens to take advantage of the repose I offer to Him* (SS 165).

She would respect Jesus' repose and not make any demands. She would be patient with her aridity. She would simply let Jesus sleep, confident that he would *more quickly grow tired of making me wait than I shall grow tired of waiting for Him. He will undoubtedly awaken before my great eternal retreat,* she wrote, reflecting on her desire to be eternally face-to-face with her Beloved. Then she added with her characteristic boldness, *But instead of being troubled about it* [her lack of feelings of fervor] *this only gives me extreme pleasure* [to offer myself to God in the poverty and pain of my weaknesses] (SS 165; GC 612, 803–4).

Since the time she had positioned herself at the feet of Jesus crucified, she had *understood more than ever how much Jesus desires to be loved* (SS 180). She simply wanted to give Jesus the joy of having his love received even if her feelings remained arid. She advised one sister suffering from a lack of consolation during prayer: *Do not fear to tell Him you love Him even without feeling it. That is the way to force Jesus to help you, to carry you like a little child too feeble to walk* (GC 1117).

On her little way, Thérèse expected God to carry her when she was *too feeble to walk* alone. And to be carried in the arms of God meant to be free of discouragement or self-condemnation. But when God gave her the grace to manage, she did not simply walk the little way in childlike confidence and love;

she seemed to skip boldly along the way with the freedom of delight and creative, grateful joy. She could be playful in her confidence of God's love. Even the troublesome sisters, at first disturbed by what they thought was Thérèse's immaturity, came to appreciate her youthful enthusiasm, spontaneous joyful smile, simple gaiety, and quiet humor. In her maturity Thérèse had become completely detached from her need to appear to be good according to the perfectionistic standards of her day.

CHAPTER 19

Don't Think That the Path of Love Is Full of Consolations

UNDERSTANDING THE LITTLE WAY

Thérèse's understanding of the little way was clearly not, of course, founded on childish thinking, indifference, or irresponsibility. Rather, it was established on Jesus' teaching that the free love of God was to be accepted in faith and gratitude and responded to with good works of justice and charity. It was also founded on Jesus' teaching to embrace the way of the cross daily by enduring the sacrifices and suffering inevitable in a life of love.

One of the young sisters wanted to share Thérèse's teaching of the little way with her parents. Thérèse cautioned her: *Be very careful; our "little way" could be mistaken for quietism or illuminism if it is badly explained* (STL 236). Thérèse was concerned that her way would be misunderstood as a kind of quietism, an error allied to passivism, which was almost the opposite of perfectionism and which taught that since God's love was free and inclusive, we should do nothing to receive it. Thérèse, of course, was not advocating that the spiritual life make no demands or that human freedom and free will had no role to play in holiness. Rather, God required her *good will* that was the free willingness to accept God's love and to patiently and faithfully do the good works that love demanded. Self-surrender into God's arms was itself Thérèse's primary but not only work of *good will,* and self-surrender was not the same as giving up or doing nothing (cf. SS 98; GC 1015).

The most beautiful thoughts are nothing without good works

In her teaching, Thérèse repeated the wisdom of her spiritual mother, Teresa of Ávila, who emphasized that goodwill and selfless good works of justice and charity were the fruits of prayer and of self-surrender into God's will. *I do not hold in contempt beautiful thoughts which nourish the soul and unite it with God,* Thérèse wrote, clarifying her little way, *but for a long time I have understood that we must not depend on them and even make perfection consist in receiving many spiritual lights. The most beautiful thoughts are nothing without good works* (SS 234).

To one of the sisters under her guidance, she explained further that even though a little child cannot climb the *rough stairway of perfection*, she can at least *raise* [her] *little foot. You won't succeed in reaching the first step, but God requires you only to demonstrate your good will* [by good works]. *Soon conquered by your futile efforts, he will descend himself, gather you up in his arms, and carry you off to his kingdom forever* (STL 240).

Thérèse was telling the sisters from her own conversion experience that even if they had gotten onto the mistaken path of Pelagianism and perfectionism and were willfully striving to achieve perfection, God would use their inevitable failure on that path to bring them back onto the Gospel path. When they failed in their good resolutions, she counseled the sisters, they should not get discouraged; they would surely fall, but they should stand up again and go on. *Then Jesus will be moved by your good will, and will himself be your strength* (STL 240). They would learn by their fall, not only about the depth of their own weakness, but also about the depth of God's love, and they would know that God himself was their sanctity.

Thérèse continued to explain her teaching to the young sisters: *Don't think that to follow the path of love means to follow the path of repose, full of sweetness and consolations.* She was trying to prevent a misinterpretation of the little way as some kind of self-indulgence or an escape from responsibility, a neglect of good works or a resistance of unavoidable sacrifices—*it is completely the opposite. To offer oneself as a victim to Love means to give oneself up without any reservations to whatever God pleases, which means,* Thérèse added to further clarify that the little way was founded on taking up the cross and dying daily, *to expect to share with Jesus his humiliations, his chalice of bitterness* (TLMT 89).

Thérèse taught her sisters that the role of human freedom and willpower was not properly directed in willful efforts to acquire God's love, since God's love was already a reality. Gospel holiness consisted in willingly recognizing, receiving, rejoicing in, and sharing God's love already embracing us. God's love, Thérèse knew, cannot be attained or possessed. Rather, God's love possesses souls who are empty and available to God in the present moment of life. Life is to be lived in trust and faith in God's love, fulfilling responsibilities by the good works of justice and charity.

Thérèse recognized that good works are not the reason for God's love or God's grace. The reason for God's mercy is God's essence. God is love, and

God's love, if willingly received and appreciated, blossoms into good moral behavior and works of love. She had experienced that in her own life, especially in her relationships with her sisters in community.

Thérèse also knew that it was not the spiritual accomplishments and the exemplary works of the saints that made them saints. Rather, those accomplishments flowed from their holiness and sanctity, which in turn arose from their union with God. The saints lived a prayerful life of availability to God and did good works so they could accept more deeply in themselves and share more generously with others that greatest good—God himself. To do good works was to share Love, to share God. Doing good works for a lesser reason would be another example of moving mountains but amounting to nothing, as St Paul had warned (1 Corinthians 13:1-3). And Thérèse was aware of that truth also; before her conversion she had noticed how she had performed virtue *in a strange way*.

Thérèse's desire to foster the human attitudes that were the heart qualities of love was the same desire to cultivate her availability to receive more fully God's love and share that love with others. Her primary concern was to avoid and to let go of what blocked her from being available to union with God and to do this without violence of any kind. She rejected the motivation of fear. She had learned, especially from her interactions with the younger sisters under her care, that cultivating feelings of fear, guilt, or shame became obstacles to being available to God's love and actually hampered gratefully sharing love with others.

Thérèse taught the little way not as a way of fear, not the way of the Pharisee for whom good moral works substituted for the desire for union with God, and not the path of quietism or doing nothing. The little way was a way of availability to deeper union with God.

Jesus is pleased to teach her, as He did St. Paul, the science of rejoicing in her infirmities

When Thérèse at one time explained her little way by saying that *perfection seems simple to me*, she was clearly not speaking of moral behavior, especially that interior behavior of pure motivation that had constantly eluded her. When she continued by saying that to be perfect or holy, *it is sufficient to recognize one's nothingness and to abandon oneself as a child into God's arms* (GC 1094), she was also not suggesting simply doing nothing, since she had already taught that the *most beautiful thoughts are nothing without good works* (SS 234) and that a heart *burning with love cannot remain inactive* (SS 257–58). And when she acknowledged that *now I am simply resigned to see myself always imperfect and in this I find my joy* (SS 158), she was obviously multiplying statements that identified a way of self-awareness and self-abandonment that was completely different from Jansenism, perfectionism, and Pelagianism.

By proclaiming a merciful God who was the opposite of the wrathful god of Jansenism and by saying that *perfection seems simple to me*, Thérèse was declaring a way of holiness that rejected the self-righteousness implicit in the striving for perfectionism and advocated a spirit of self-surrender that opposed the willful efforts at the core of Pelagianism. She was, in fact, directly opposing the spirituality of her time by changing the understanding of the meaning of the word "perfection," just as she had, in her Act of Oblation to Merciful Love, deliberately subverted and changed the understanding of the meaning of the words "oblation," "martyr," "holocaust," and "victim."

Thérèse wrote to her cousin, explaining her understanding of the way of "perfection."

You are mistaken, my darling, if you believe that your little Thérèse walks always with fervor on the road of virtue. She is weak and very weak, and every day she has a new experience of this weakness, but . . . Jesus is pleased to teach her, as He did St. Paul, the science of rejoicing in her infirmities [cf. 2 Corinthians 12:5]. *This is a great grace, and I beg Jesus to teach it to you, for peace and quiet of heart are to be found there only. When we see ourselves as so miserable, then we no longer wish to consider ourselves, and we look only on the unique Beloved!* (GC 641)

Given the mistaken spiritual teachings of her day, however, Thérèse was not exaggerating when she cautioned her sisters, *Be very careful; our "little way" could be mistaken . . . if it is badly explained* (STL 236). Even Pauline seems to have at first misunderstood the depth and importance of Thérèse's teaching and only came to appreciate it years after Thérèse's death. Then Pauline was able to describe the little way more accurately: "Sanctity does not consist of this or that practice; it consists in a disposition of heart which makes us humble and little in the arms of God, conscious of our weakness, and confident to the point of audacity in the goodness of our Father" (HLC 129, note 1; cf. EIG 309).

Pauline had finally understood that the little way was not the multiplication of pious practices or the perfection of good morality. She had gained the insight that the little way consisted in being aware of our weakness in faith, in accepting our littleness in poverty of spirit, and in willingly desiring deeper union with God. The little way, Pauline came to understand, was to be confidently and gratefully in the arms of the God of love.

Thérèse herself, at the end of her life, had repeated the essence of this teaching: *Look at little children: they never stop breaking things, tearing things, falling down, and they do this even while loving their parents very, very much. When I fall in this way, it makes me realize my nothingness more, and I say to myself: What would I do, and what would I become, if I were to rely upon my own strength?* (HLC 140).

In addition to her caution that her little way could be mistaken for quietism and passivism, Thérèse also feared that it might appear to be something special and distinct from the message of Jesus. This was the error of illuminism that she had warned the sister about.

Illuminism was the notion that to attain sanctity, it was necessary to possess some secret truths beyond Jesus' teaching. Thérèse was confident that her understanding of *the science of love,* expressed in her little way, was the fundamental truth of Jesus' message, having nothing to do with a special or distinct revelation outside of the Gospel.

If at first Thérèse had suggested that the little way was *very straight, very short, and* [even] *totally new* (SS 207), she quickly recognized that it was not new in the sense that it was not an alternative to the Gospel way. It embraced the suffering of dying daily that Jesus had identified as intrinsic to the Gospel way of love.

Indeed, the suffering inherent in the little way, although having flowed through all of her life, was, as she approached her death, about to fill Thérèse to almost overflowing. The little way was a way of embracing the sufferings of love and not a path *full of sweetness and consolations* (TLMT 89).

It was in the example of her dying that Thérèse taught with particular clarity her little way of confidence and love.

Thérèse lying ill in the cloister, August 30, 1897

CHAPTER 20

Everything Has Disappeared on Me, and I Am Left with Love Alone

DYING IN THE LITTLE WAY OF CONFIDENCE AND LOVE

Suffering opened wide its arms to me and I threw myself into them with love, Thérèse had written of her first experiences on entering the convent when she was fifteen years old (SS 149). Through the hidden trials of her inner struggles, by the many little inconspicuous sufferings associated with her daily life of love, and by her prayers and offerings flowing from her desire for the salvation of all peoples, Thérèse was being slowly cleansed of selfishness. Thérèse's way had been a downward path into God's love and into the depths of less and less self-centeredness and self-righteousness. *My suffering,* Thérèse once remarked, *was all the more painful since I alone was aware of it. . . . Exteriorly nothing revealed my suffering* (SS 149). Now, in her final months, God carried Thérèse along her little way through purifying and redemptive sufferings that were both exterior and interior, in body and in spirit.

Preparing us to know Him as He knows Himself and to become God ourselves

During the last eighteen months of her life, Thérèse entered a period in which God completed the cleansing of her heart, the purifying of her faith, and the opening of her will to the full mystery of *the science of love.* It was the period that resonated with feelings that she had expressed a short time after she had entered the convent: *Alas, it does pain Him to give us sorrows to drink, but He knows this is the only means of preparing us to "know Him as He knows Himself and to become God ourselves"* (GC 450; cf. 1 Corinthians 13:12). She was confident that God was, throughout her life, preparing her to be totally embraced by God into God, but she could not have foreseen how God would fulfill this work of love during her last months.

Thérèse would now understand herself to be like iron in the furnace of God's love. She would experience the fire of God's love *in such a way that the fire* [would] *penetrate and drink up* [the iron] *with its burning substance and seem to become one with it. . . . This is my prayer. I ask Jesus to draw me into the flames of His love,* Thérèse wrote in her final days. Then, with all *the souls who will approach me . . . , the more these souls* [with her] *will run swiftly in the odor of the ointments of their Beloved, for a soul that is burning with love cannot remain inactive* (SS 257–58). She wanted to participate fully in the divinity of Christ who had participated completely in our humanity. She desired to draw all souls with her into God.

Although Thérèse had always had an intuition that she would die young and had noticed a few warning signs of physical weakness over the recent years, the certain indication of her complete physical deterioration was sudden (cf. GC 870, note 8; 873, note 6; 887; 896–97, note 2; 917–18, note 11; 967–68, note 8).

She approached Holy Week 1896 physically well. At about midnight at the close of Holy Thursday, after completing her period of adoration before the Blessed Sacrament at the altar of repose, she retired to her bed. It was the night of Good Friday. She recalled that

> *I had scarcely laid my head upon the pillow when I felt something like a bubbling stream mounting to my lips. I didn't know what it was, but I thought that perhaps I was going to die and my soul was flooded with joy. However, as our lamp was extinguished, I told myself I would have to wait until the morning to be certain of my good fortune, for it seemed to me that it was blood I had coughed up. The morning was not long in coming; upon awakening, I thought immediately of the joyful thing that I had to learn, and so I went over to the window. I was able to see that I was not mistaken. Ah! my soul was filled with a great consolation; I was interiorly persuaded that Jesus, on the anniversary of His own death, wanted to have me hear His first call. It was like a sweet and distant murmur that announced the Bridegroom's arrival.* (SS 210–11).

During those first hours of Good Friday night, Jesus had stooped down from the cross and was taking her up with him into his own suffering. She was twenty-three years old. She knew she was dying. She was at peace (SS 211; cf. EIG 273ff.).

In the morning, the community assembled to assist at the early hours of prayer and to ask pardon of one another in a spirit of reconciliation and self-offering on this day of Good Friday. Thérèse reported her experience of coughing blood to Mother Gonzague, the superior. But in the telling, she emphasized her present tranquil feelings of *my hope and my happiness. . . . I added that I was not suffering in the least (which was true) and I begged you, Mother, to give me nothing special* (SS 211). Mother Gonzague simply took her at her word and so was not alarmed.

Thérèse resumed her normal Holy Week routine of prayer, work, and fasting as the *hope of going to heaven soon transported me with joy.* That night she coughed up more blood. *Just as on the preceding night, good Jesus gave me the same sign that my entrance into eternal life was not far off* (SS 211).

Then on Easter Sunday, amid the rejoicing of the feast of such glory and hope, suddenly without warning, a spiritual terror burst upon Thérèse, sweeping away the *living faith* that she was so much appreciating (SS 211). Her physical condition had begun to deteriorate and now offered no resistance to an emotional collapse. Inner darkness totally overwhelmed her certainty of belief. She was seized by a radical, existential sense of meaninglessness. The structure of her faith convictions shattered into absolute chaos, and she was inundated by feelings of falling into a void. She was momentarily and completely overcome by fright and then blanketed by a descending *thick fog* of torment (SS 212).

Is He content with me?

Thérèse was entering a profound spiritual trial; *the darkest storm; the night of nothingness*, she called it (SS 190, 213). Her primal childhood feelings of being utterly abandoned and without a heavenly home to welcome her now surfaced to war against her spirit. She felt wholly devoid of the security of faith. She was clutched in the grip of dread. She had begun a long and solitary walk through a dark underground cavern, *a dark tunnel* with no light and no end. *This trial was to last not a few days or a few weeks, it was not to be extinguished until the hour set by God Himself and this hour has not yet come* (SS 211–12). And this hour would not come until her final breath. It would be a slow, laborious, lonely ordeal—eighteen months of emotional and spiritual desolation. There were to be momentary graces that brought Thérèse glimmers of consolation and joy, but then these graces would vanish, and in their disappearance they would drag her into yet deeper distress and aridity.

A month into the *darkness that obscures my soul*, with *the storm raging very strongly in my soul* (SS 213, 190), Thérèse had a dream. In the dream, as she described it to her sister Marie five months later, Thérèse *recognized Venerable [Mother] Anne of Jesus, Foundress of Carmel in France. Her face was beautiful but with an immaterial beauty. . . . Seeing myself so tenderly loved, I dared to pronounce these words: "O Mother! I beg you, tell me whether God will leave me for a long time on earth. Will He come soon to get me?" Smiling tenderly, the saint whispered: "yes, soon, soon, I promise you."* The reassurance that God, who now seemed so absent, was really stooping down to her in the mystery of her suffering and would take her soon filled her with peace. *I cannot express the joy of my soul,* she wrote (SS 191).

Then, in the dream, she asked of Venerable Anne the question that had constantly lingered in her heart. *I added: "Mother, tell me further if God is not asking something more of me than my poor little actions and desires. Is He content with me?"* (SS 191). This was the same recurring question that she had held within herself over the years as she searched *the science of love.* And now in her final agony, she was again compelled to wonder if her path had been true.

Venerable Anne's face *took on an expression incomparably more tender than the first time she spoke to me,* Thérèse remembered. *Her look and her caresses were the sweetest of answers.* Thérèse had received her assurance from Anne's countenance and gestures of love, but the blessing of the dream was even more explicit. *However, she said to me: "God asks no other thing from you. He is content, very content!"* Thérèse's heart was filled with joy. Even in the midst of her trial of faith, God's love had given her the kindness of consolation. She experienced deep peace and joy and prayed, *O Jesus, the storm was no longer raging, heaven was calm and serene. I believed, I felt there was a heaven and that this heaven is peopled with souls who actually love me, who consider me their child* (SS 191).

Five months later, as Thérèse was recounting her dream, she added this: *Several months have passed since this sweet dream, and yet the memory it has left in my soul has lost nothing of its freshness and heavenly charms. I still see Venerable Mother's glance and smile which was FILLED WTH LOVE. I believe I can still feel the caresses she gave me at this time* (SS 191).

The consoling grace of the dream *was only the prelude to the greatest graces You wished to bestow upon me,* Thérèse prayed (SS 192). For the *greatest graces* were to be those associated with her discovery of her vocation to be *Love in the heart of the Church* (SS 194). They were also to be realized and expressed in her parable in which she likened herself to the weak little bird who obtains *the favor of flying toward the Sun of Love with the Divine Eagle's own wings* and who is plunged *for all eternity into the burning Abyss of this Love* (SS 200). She was convinced now in faith that she was destined to be united fully to God's love—the Holy Spirit of love.

The dream, by releasing her from any final shred of doubt on her path of love, had prepared her to receive these *greatest graces.* She was being led into the depths of faith by the very trial of faith. The storm was raging in her feelings, but in the tunnel of darkness she was entering into a whole new dimension of *the boldness of . . . full trust,* confident that even with *all* [her] *infidelities . . .* [she would] *acquire in even greater fullness the love of Him who came to call not the just but sinners* (SS 199).

I don't believe in eternal life . . . and I am left with love alone

Thérèse considered the dream a blessing that helped her bear her cruel physical, emotional, and spiritual distress. She prayed in gratitude as she was recounting her dream to her sister Marie: *O Jesus, my Beloved, who could express the tenderness and sweetness with which You are guiding my soul! It pleases You to cause the rays of Your grace to shine through even the midst of the darkest storm!* (SS 190). Later, to Mother Gongazue, she wrote, *Never have I felt before this, dear Mother, how sweet and merciful the Lord really is, for He did not send me this trial until the moment I was capable of bearing it* (SS 214).

And yet over the subsequent months, Thérèse entered more deeply into the dark tunnel. As *the storm was raging* with increased intensity and her soul was becoming enveloped even more in the ominous fog, she wrote to Mother Gonzague words revealing the growing struggle tormenting her spirit: *Everything has disappeared! When I want to rest my heart fatigued by the darkness which surrounds it by the memory of the luminous country* [the Fatherland, heaven] *after which I aspire, my torment redoubles; it seems to me that the darkness . . . says mockingly to me: "You are dreaming about the light, about a fatherland; . . . you are dreaming about the eternal possession of the Creator of all these marvels.* She wanted to say no more, lest she blaspheme (SS 213).

During these last months of her life, Thérèse was drawn more and more deeply into this *sweet and merciful* but above all mysterious love of God. *It is true,* she wrote later, *that at times a very small ray of the sun comes to illumine my darkness, and then the trial ceases for an instant, but afterwards the memory of this ray, instead of causing me joy, makes my darkness even more dense* (SS 214). The graces surrounding the dream now became themselves a source of distress. As her torment continued, only rarely *a very small ray of the sun* appeared, and that ray was to be quickly eclipsed by the *dense darkness.*

Her little way, once so clear and consoling, suddenly appeared to be a fantasy. After the brief illumination of the graces surrounding her visionary dream, her union with God again seemed an illusion. The terror of total isolation and separation from her Beloved and the dread of the futility of her deepest desires again ravaged her soul.

The hope that God was going to stoop down to lift her to himself seemed a foolish fable. She was not going to be embraced by God and die of love as she had hoped when she had composed the Act of Oblation to Merciful Love the year before. She now had lapses into the scrupulosity of her childhood, feeling that she might be damned (HLTT 227). The sense of the certainty of heaven, her most precious security, the homeland toward which her whole life had been directed, suddenly vanished. In her final heavenly home, she had expected to be *face to face* with her Beloved in an everlasting embrace of love (GC 814). That hope was now overwhelmed in darkness and utter confusion.

To one sister at her deathbed, she acknowledged, *If you only knew what darkness I am plunged into. I don't believe in eternal life; I think that after this life there is nothing. Everything has disappeared on me, and I am left with love alone* (STL 195).

In the Fatherland, in that heavenly caress of her Beloved, she had not expected to simply rest. She had hoped to fulfill her desire of sharing God's inclusive love for all humanity: *If God answers my desires,* she had said months before, *my heaven will be spent* [spreading love] *on earth until the end of the world. Yes, I will spend my heaven doing good upon earth* (HLC 102; cf. GC 1074, note 11; CCC 956).

But now she wondered whether there was a heaven. Would she ever be held securely in the arms of her Beloved, and would she ever share God's love with those on earth? Would her *immeasurable desires* of love be simply and eternally extinguished? Would she ever be united with her beloved Mother Mary, her heavenly mother? Would she be separated from her earthly parents and her beloved human family forever? (cf. GC 816, 866). Had all her precious desires been madness, manipulated by herself for her own security? Had she wasted her entire life? Had she been living in some kind of dreadful, self-constructed fairy tale?

If I had not had any faith, I would have committed suicide

Throughout the eighteen-month-long tribulation, Thérèse's body gradually wasted away. Once so beautiful, she became emaciated in frightful physical suffering. Racked by the agonizing pain of advancing tuberculosis, she slowly suffocated to death.

Until the very last moment, her faith was buffeted by the battering storm, her hope was entombed in a tunnel of darkness, and her love was ridiculed by the fear of blasphemy. The dark and vicious fog of nothingness continued to prowl and menace her heart. Her intense physical suffering, her deepening emotional distress, and her spiritual trial of faith bound together to form an impenetrable wall of pain, a wall that surrounded and isolated her: *a wall*, she said, *which reaches right up to the heavens and covers the starry firmament* (SS 214).

She was besieged by hissing sounds in her ears; in her mind screamed the words of atheists, sneering words clamoring within her imagination and echoing through her feelings, ridiculing her, scoffing that there was really no meaning to her life after all. Her hope had been a charade, her little way a selfish invention, her confidence and trust in God an illusion. She was afraid that if she shared the depth of her spiritual suffering with her sisters, she might scandalize them. *I don't want to write any longer about it; I fear I might blaspheme; I fear even that I have already said too much* (SS 213).

Thoughts of suicide assaulted her. To one sister Thérèse whispered in confidence, *I couldn't even tell you to what degree the night is dark in my soul, for fear that I would make you share my temptations* (TLMT 33). At her bedside, she confided to Pauline: *Watch carefully, Mother, when you will have patients a prey to violent pains; don't leave near them any medicines that are poisonous. I assure you, it needs only a second when one suffers intensely to lose one's reason. Then one would easily poison oneself* (HLC 258).

Although she did not regain feelings of faith, Thérèse again revealed to Pauline, *Yes! What a grace it is to have* [the gift of] *faith! If I had not had any faith, I would have committed suicide without an instant's hesitation* (HLC 196). She grasped faith with the willingness of love.

Thérèse was in a particular way enduring the emotional trial of unbelief with those who did not believe, with those who refused to believe, and with those who rejected divine love through their own choices. In her excruciating trial of faith, the atheists, she said, became her *brothers* (SS 212). In feeling that she was stumbling in darkness on the way of nothingness, she no longer was separated from the impious and in no way was superior to the atheists. Rather, now experiencing emotionally what it was to be one of them, she could pray as one of them, and she could pray for them and with them.

It was during this time that Thérèse encountered the only unbeliever she would ever know in an interactive, personal way. Léo Taxil, a well-known atheist, entered her life. He had just revealed that he and his companion, Diana Vaughan, had been converted to Catholicism from Freemasonry and Satanism. This dramatic news circulated throughout the grateful Catholic community of France, and one of Diana's pious writings came to the attention of Uncle Isidore, now a journalist, who passed it on to the Carmelite community. Thérèse and the sisters discussed the piece with appreciation. At least one of Diana's writings had even been read and valued by the pope.

Pauline, and all of the community with her, wished to support the struggling new converts, and since Diana's conversion had come through her special devotion to Joan of Arc, Pauline sent her the photograph portraying Thérèse in the role of Joan in the play that Thérèse herself had recently written and performed for the community. Diana replied with a note of appreciation. Some of the community hoped that Diana might eventually join Carmel.

Diana had been in hiding for the last several years, fearing retaliation from the satanic sect she had renounced. So now to publicly introduce Diana, Taxil called a highly publicized press conference in Paris. Hundreds of reporters from the religious and national press attended.

Taxil had some astonishing news. He spoke clearly and directly: he had not been converted from Freemasonry! His story was a hoax! He had also completely invented the person, the story, and the writings of Diana Vaughan! The press conference climaxed Taxil's twelve-year diabolical travesty to ridicule the beliefs of the Church. Those attending were stunned and turned belligerent. But most significant, the photograph of Thérèse that Pauline had sent Diana was projected on the wall behind Taxil as he mockingly disclosed his charade and scoffed at the naive faith of the Carmelite dressed as Joan. The photograph appeared with a detailed commentary in the national press.

The Church in France was shocked and angry. The Carmelite community, and particularly Pauline, was shaken and totally embarrassed. Thérèse was deeply humiliated. In her distress she tore up the thank-you note from Diana, threw the pieces on the garden manure pile, removed Diana's name from her writings, and never spoke of the incident. Another blanket of darkness totally enshrouded her heart, and Thérèse again retreated into herself, bearing the suffering in silence and alone. She accepted the trial and prayed to forgive and love her enemies.

Prior to this time, she had admitted that she was unable to believe there were really impious people who had no faith. *I believed they were actually speaking against their own inner convictions when they denied the existence of heaven.* But now she knew that *there were really souls who have no faith, and who, through the abuse of grace, lost this precious treasure, the source of the only real and pure joys* (SS 211; cf. EIG 280–85).

Now, instead of anticipating heaven's eternal banquet, she felt that she must find a place at the table of those without faith. She was willing, if God so willed it, to dine with the atheist and the agnostic, *to eat the bread of sorrow as long as You desire it . . . and not to rise up from this table filled with bitterness at which poor sinners are eating until the day set by You* (SS 213).

In compassionate empathy with her unbelieving brothers and sisters, she begged pardon and mercy, praying that they would ultimately participate in God's presence. *I would like to save souls,* she wrote, *and forget myself for them; I would like to save them even after my death* (GC 1072).

What darkness! but I am at peace

In her own name and in the name of all those who suffered the emptiness of unbelief, Thérèse again prayed the prayer of the publican: *Have pity on us, O Lord, for we are poor sinners!* (cf. Luke 18:13). She continued to be confident that the publican's prayer was enough: *Oh! Lord, send us away justified.* Then she added a special prayer that embraced all those who lacked faith throughout all of human history: *May all those who were not enlightened by the bright flame of faith one day see it shine. . . . I am happy not to enjoy this beautiful heaven on this earth, so that He will open it for all eternity to poor unbelievers. . . . How sweet and merciful the Lord really is, for He . . . [is] taking away everything that could be a natural satisfaction in my desire for heaven. . . . The only grace I ask of You is that I never offend You!* (SS 212, 214).

Thérèse prayed in distress for safety from sin, *that I never offend You!* She prayed for perseverance and patience in her misery, clinging to faith with love against the forces of darkness and despair. She had always wanted to be a saint, and within a year of her entrance into Carmel, she had written to a sister echoing the sentiments that she had expressed as a teenager reading about Joan of Arc: *Ask Jesus that I become a great saint* (GC 520; cf. SS 72). Throughout her life, she had also been increasingly aware of her littleness, her sinfulness, her tendencies to be self-centered, self-righteous, and judgmental, and to show a lack of full charity to her sisters. These tendencies were "appropriate" kinds of weaknesses, the kinds of limitations that plagued the saints, even great saints. These were the kinds of faults that do not raise eyebrows. Thérèse had once remarked that *no human life is exempt from faults* (GC 1093), and these were the faults that she was imagining.

But what about the kinds of sinful tendencies that she was now suffering? Such tendencies would be unthinkable in the life of a saint, even a "little" saint. These were ignoble kinds of weaknesses—the egregious fault of blasphemy, for example, or the unforgivable folly of suicide, the dim-witted complicity in demeaning the holy faith of the Church, the frightful weakness of personal atheism, the rash presumption of having found a new way of spirituality, the stupidity of deceiving the community by false teaching, or the faithless despair that God had failed her. Did any of the saints ever succumb to such "inappropriate" temptations, particularly in their dying?

In the dark fog, with the storm raging, with heaven no longer a certainty, with the scoffing voices and the hissing sounds, Thérèse knew that such grievous, unthinkable faults were not beyond her. She struggled in humble prayer as a sinner, as one who felt the absence of God, for *the only grace . . . that I never offend You!*

She had once noted that the martyrs were often pictured as dying in glory, but that the king of martyrs had died in despair. Now her own sisters wanted her to die like a saint *should* die: to die on a day of liturgical importance, for example, or on a feast day of the Blessed Virgin. As she physically wasted away, as her breathing became more shallow and labored, as her coughing and vomiting increased, her prayer became one of simple patient endurance. She was no longer able to receive Holy Communion. This scandalized the pious sensitivities of some of the sisters, as did the fact that she was dying of a mysterious disease regarded as some in recent times have regarded AIDS—as associated with the marginalized, the outcast, and the unclean. Even uttering the name of the disease was considered taboo, and the convent physician attending Thérèse had simply called it "pulmonary congestion," although he had prescribed the remedies usually given for tuberculosis (cf. EIG 323ff.; HLTT 237ff.).

Was this any way for a saint, even a "little" saint, to be dying? Some of the sisters of her community did not think so. As for Thérèse, she had only the sincerity of her own conscience, the intensity of her love, and the focus of her hope to hold together in her heart the ironies and the sufferings, the peace and the pathos, of her dying.

In her physical suffering and spiritual torture, Thérèse surrendered into the reality of her nothingness, into the welcoming arms of God where she had always been from the beginning. Even though her little way seemed an illusion, she refused to abandon it; she blindly continued to live it. She was loving God by willingly embracing God's love for her, however painful that purifying love was. Now it was clearly no longer a matter of her trying to love God; it was all a matter of allowing God to love her.

Looking out the infirmary window at a particularly dark area in a grotto not far from the chestnut trees where she had sat in her father's wheelchair doing her final writing, Thérèse remarked, *Look! Do you see the black hole where we can see nothing; it's in a similar hole that I am as far as my body and soul are concerned. Ah! what darkness!* Then, resigned, she added, *but I am at peace* (HLC 173).

In the heart of the Church, my mother, I shall be Love

This period of overwhelming suffering was Thérèse's grace of personal purification. She was being cleansed of all that remained of her self-centeredness and self-righteousness, of any final trace of egotistic spiritual ambition and any lingering speck of willfulness—tendencies that had afflicted her throughout her life. Thérèse's early desire to love God so lavishly—that desire, too, was being purified by God into a willing spirit of total self-surrender to God's love and God's will. Her Beloved *was* truly stooping down, embracing her, uniting her completely to himself, but in a way that was beyond her imagining.

Jesus was raising her from the position she had taken at the foot of the cross, bringing her into his complete and intimate embrace. Jesus was making her one with himself in his own experience of physical annihilation, spiritual darkness, and total self-emptying. In feelings of complete isolation, Jesus had cried out, "My God, my God, why have you forsaken me?" (Matthew 27:46). Thérèse, too, felt abandoned, completely alone. She, too, felt suspended above nothingness. Jesus was drawing her fully to himself in his paschal mystery, allowing her to participate with him in his redemptive suffering for the world. She was "filling up what is lacking in the afflictions of Christ on behalf of his body, which is the church" (Colossians 1:24).

Having previously taken into her heart all those who had requested or needed her prayers, she had discovered that *when a soul allows herself to be captivated* [by Jesus, as she was now being taken] . . . , *she cannot run alone, all the souls whom she loves follow in her train. . . . Just as a torrent, throwing itself with impetuosity into the ocean, drags after it everything it encounters in its passage, in the same way, O Jesus, the soul who plunges into the shoreless ocean of Your Love, draws with her all the treasures* [the hearts of others] *she possesses.* In her final days, she prayed, *Lord, You know it, I have no other treasures than the souls it has pleased You to unite to mine* (SS 254).

Never would I have believed it was possible to suffer so much! Never! Never! Thérèse's words came as a whisper, laboriously and in gasps, as she spoke several hours before her death. She believed that her missionary desires were being fulfilled: *I cannot explain this except by the ardent desires I have had to save souls* (HLC 203).

In her final agony, as she desired to be consumed in the tender waves of God's love, she also desired that same consummation of love for all those in her heart—and for all humanity. With this intention, convinced that God in taking her into divine love would draw with her all creation, she prayed in one of her final prayers, *Jesus, draw me into the flames of* [Your] *love; unite me so closely with* [You] *that* [You] *live and act in me* (SS 257).

God was fulfilling her intense missionary desire to save souls and preparing her to *spend her heaven doing good upon earth* in a way that she could have never anticipated (cf. GC 578). Her Beloved was answering her prayer to *work* [by accepting her inevitable sufferings] *for the glory of Holy Church by saving souls on earth and liberating those suffering in purgatory* (SS 276; PST 53ff.).

In her continual desires to convert sinners, to participate in the mission of the priest, the apostle, and even the martyr and the universal missionary, she was being invited to embrace what she called the *greatest graces*—the calling of love. She wrote at the end of her life, *MY VOCATION IS LOVE! Yes, I have found my place in the Church and it is you, O my God, who have given me this place; in the heart of the Church, my mother, I shall be Love. Thus I shall be everything* [participating in the paschal mystery of Christ to save the world] *and thus my dream will be realized* (SS 194).

She understood *that love comprised* [the essence of] *all vocations, that love was everything, that it embraced all times and places—in a word, that it was eternal!* (SS 194). She wanted to share God's love with all of creation eternally, beyond space and time, beyond her family, beyond the sisters she lived with, and even beyond the time of her own life. Her desire was to be a compassionate companion of healing and hope to the entire human race until the end of time.

Embraced by God, sharing in Jesus' redemptive death, Thérèse was entering fully into the essence of her vocation to love. She frequently implored the assistance of her beloved Mother Mary and often gazed upon the image of the Holy Face. She was being lifted up with her beloved Jesus, bringing all of creation into the heart of divine love (John 12:32).

I count only on love

Until the moment of her death, Thérèse suffered the void of faith yet continued to make acts of faith. She never argued about the existence of heaven with those sneering voices within her imagination screaming that all of life was meaningless and nothingness and jeering that she had poured out her youthful passion in vain. In this spiritual combat, she was certain that a direct confrontation would actually have involved more bravado than bravery, coming from a last remnant of false self-confidence. Again she resorted to her *last plank of salvation, flight* (SS 224).

As her breathing became more and more hesitant and labored, with her life slowly draining away and her emotional stability on the edge of collapse, she acknowledged: *When my enemy* [thoughts of unbelief] *provokes me, . . . I turn my back on my adversary. . . . I run towards my Jesus. I tell Him I am ready to shed my blood to the last drop to profess my faith in the existence of heaven. . . . I never cease making acts of faith. . . . He knows very well that while I do not have the joy of faith, I am trying to carry out its works at least. I believe I have made more acts of faith in this past year,* Thérèse said, *than all through my whole life* (SS 213; HLC 257–58).

Thérèse had completed her way of love and had come to know *the science of love* with a profundity that she could not have envisioned. *Our Lord died on the Cross in agony, and yet this is the most beautiful death of love. . . . To die of love is not to die in transports. I tell you frankly*, she said to Pauline, *it seems to me that this is what I am experiencing* (HLC 73). *I do not count on the illness* [to cause me to die]; *it is too slow a leader,* she said. *I count only on love. Ask Good Jesus that all the prayers being offered for me may serve to increase the Fire which must consume me* (GC 1121; cf. TLMT 36).

During her last months, she frequently recited the Act of Oblation to Merciful Love that she had composed two years before. She now repeated as often as she could: *I offer myself as a victim of holocaust to your merciful love, asking You to consume me incessantly, allowing the waves of infinite tenderness shut up within You to overflow into my soul, and that thus I may become a martyr of Your Love, O my God!* And she wanted to believe: *May this martyrdom, after having prepared me to appear before You, finally cause me to die and may my soul take its flight without any delay into the eternal embrace of Your Merciful Love. I want, O my Beloved, . . . to tell You of my Love in an Eternal Face to Face!* (SS 276–77; PST 53ff.). Her prayer of being a martyr of both heart and body, *not through blood, . . .* [but] *through love* was being answered in a way that had been impossible for her to have foreseen (GC 440; cf. GC 577; SS 275).

I am not sorry for delivering myself up to Love, she whispered in her last agony. *Oh no, I'm not sorry; on the contrary!* Her final sigh was an echo of her entire life: *Oh, I love Him! My God, I love You!* (HLC 205–6).

"Death will come to fetch you," one sister had remarked earlier. Thérèse replied, *No, not death, but God! I am at the door of eternity.* And several months before, she had written to one of the priests she guided, *I am not dying; I am entering into Life* (GC 1128).

Her Beloved welcomed Thérèse into the fullness of that Life on September 30, 1897, at about twenty minutes after seven o'clock in the evening. It had been raining all evening, and now, just after seven o'clock, the rain ceased, the clouds parted, and the stars began to shine.

Her sisters noted that in her final moment, Thérèse raised her eyes and her face became radiant with an expression of total peace and sheer joy. *To love, to be loved,* was Thérèse's sole desire, *and to return to earth to make Love loved* (MSST 227; HLC 217). Now her *immeasurable desires* had been fulfilled. She had come into her homeland, had been embraced in the maternal love of her Mother Mary, and had indeed been united *with Love alone* (STL 195). She who had placed the entire world in her heart was now *caressed upon this Heart . . .* [she] *loved so much* (cf. CP 178; EIG 322ff.).

Thérèse had ended her memoirs several weeks before. Exhausted by pain, she had written her final words: *Yes, I feel it; even though I had on my conscience all the sins that can be committed, I would go, my heart broken with sorrow, and throw myself into Jesus' arms, for I know how much he loves the prodigal child who returns to Him. It is not because God, in his anticipating Mercy, has preserved my soul from mortal sin that I go to Him with confidence and love . . .* (SS 259; cf. GC 1093).

As the *bright flame of faith* had diminished within her heart, the *flames of His love enlightened and rejoiced* her spirit (SS 212, 257, 220).

Thérèse had finally come to know *the science of love:* she was now united completely with the Heart of Love.

Thérèse's Heart
Qualities of Love

CHAPTER 21

The Science of Love: The Road into God's Loving Arms

EXPLORING THÉRÈSE'S HEART QUALITIES OF LOVE

In our study of Thérèse's three formative experiences that taught her *the science of love* and led her to proclaim the spirituality of her little way, we noticed her struggle and her growth. Her struggle focused on the same problem that St. Paul observed when he said that he did not do what he wanted to do but rather did what he did not want to do. Paul also warned that we could perform acts of love but not have real love in our hearts (cf. Romans 7:15; 1 Corinthians 13:1-3). This was also the truth that Jesus had spoken about when he said, "This people honors me with their lips, but their hearts are far from me" (Matthew 15:8). Thérèse was ever conscious that her heart could be poisoned and that her love could be false.

In her spiritual journey, Thérèse discovered more clearly what she had recognized early in life: that a sense of inner peace was a primary grace assuring her that she was walking the true path of love. The loss of peace had warned her that she had taken a misstep, that her heart was self-centered and no longer God-centered. She had learned this in a new way in each of her three formative experiences.

Without inner peace, she knew that her motivation was not pure and that her heart was in some way being divided. The lack of peace had been her warning sign at the time of her complete conversion, and that same warning sign had arisen in her conflicted relationships with the sisters as well as in her personal distress when she encountered false ideas of Gospel spirituality.

Is pure love in my heart?

But questions still remained. What were the thoughts and feelings, the psychological dispositions, the heart qualities that allowed peace to find a home in her heart, assuring her that she was on the path of love? What were the personal attitudes indicating that the self-promoting ego was not manipulating her motivation and contaminating the purity of her intention to love? What did love look like and feel like at any given moment? These were the kinds of questions that Thérèse had continued to ponder over the years.

Thérèse was not concerned with narcissistic introspection or simple psychological curiosity, but rather, ever desirous of pleasing God, she wanted to let go of her self-centeredness, which blocked God's love and prevented her from extending love to others. Praying her experiences over a lifetime, Thérèse had come intuitively to some knowledge of the heart qualities of love, but even in the final months of her life, she wondered: *Is pure love in my heart? Is God not asking something more of me than my poor little actions and desires? Is He content with me?* (SS 197, 191).

In our reflections on Thérèse's growth in *the science of love,* we have noted certain of these heart qualities, although she herself rarely mentioned them explicitly and never analyzed them by psychological categories. Rather, she reflected on them in their presence, endured their absence, and whenever it was possible for her, she simply acted in their embrace and with their power. She proclaimed them by living them as best she could and by including them, usually implicitly, in her teaching.

Now in our study, we will highlight and further explore the six specific heart qualities that we have seen accompanying, cultivating, and expressing Thérèse's sense of peace and love. These heart qualities are (1) the sense of personal inner freedom; (2) the capacity for a creative response; (3) the spirit of empathy and compassion; (4) an attitude of willingness rather than willfulness in initiating and responding to her experiences; (5) the spirit of self-surrender, or as she came to call it at the end of her life, self-abandonment; and (6) a pervasive and enduring sense of gratitude.

These six psychological indicators were not chronological stages along Thérèse's path of love but were interdependent and interactive in her experiences. We do not list them in any particular order. We do point out, however, that inner freedom seemed to be her primary indicator. We also note that her ability to respond creatively and her spirit of compassion were closely related to one another and to inner freedom. Also closely related to one another were her willingness, self-surrender, and gratitude. The spirit of willingness, moreover, was perhaps the most subtle for Thérèse to discern and seemed to be the most challenging for her to embrace.

What follows is a summary of some previous observations from our study of Thérèse's three formative experiences. We will also provide some further insights and examples of how Thérèse understood, lived, and taught each of the heart qualities of her way of love.

1. Inner Freedom

The first heart quality that we identify, and the primary psychological indicator assuring Thérèse that she was walking the path of authentic love, was her ability to maintain her inner freedom and not be overwhelmed by her excessive feelings—to respect her feelings but not to allow her feelings to control her.

She glimpsed this heart quality at the time of her complete conversion. Her conversion alerted her that she was not acting lovingly toward others or herself; rather, under the power of her feelings, she was betraying her true self, losing her inner freedom, and acting in a driven, self-centered way. She referred to her experience of trying to practice virtue while being controlled by her feelings simply as *a strange way to practice virtue* (cf. SS 97).

Later in her interactions with the sisters in the convent, the issue of inner freedom arose again. Then she recognized more clearly that if she submitted to the force of her feelings, whether negative feelings or feelings of infatuation, she would actually no longer "have the feelings"; rather, "the feelings would have her." Enslaved by her feelings, she would lose her true self.

Moreover, in her desire to be at peace, she could not reject the energy of her feelings, nor could she simply reject the community members. She could not be a doormat, tread on by thoughtless companions and lamely submitting to the outside forces that evoked controlling feelings within her. Thérèse gradually became more capable of assessing her inner strength, determining what she could and could not tolerate, and establishing personal boundaries. She saw that patience with herself and patience with her sisters were fundamental to maintaining her inner freedom against the powerful feelings of her self-centered ego. Following St. Paul's teaching, Thérèse learned that patience and kindness, essential to love, flowed into and flowed out of inner freedom.

When she lost inner freedom under the impact of her strong feelings in the presence of the sisters who were irritating or contentious toward her, she became fearful, angry, and defensive. She simply fled the scene to avoid being driven to overreact. In fact, Thérèse admitted that with one sister, she was on the verge of overreacting *frequently* (SS 223).

For Thérèse, maintaining inner freedom and peace required constant awareness of her feelings, vigilance about her behavior, and patience with herself and others. Personally holding this spirit of awareness, vigilance, and patience and rejecting any form of being punitive toward herself—this formed the basis of the necessary self-discipline of her little way.

Indeed, it was partly because of her patience and wisdom that Thérèse had been appointed mentor of the newly arrived sisters in the convent. In her teaching to these sisters, Thérèse advised them again and again to hold on to their inner freedom by a spirit of detachment and by a willingness to be patient with themselves and with the other sisters.

Love your powerlessness

On one occasion a young sister was upset by some of the older sisters; she was unable to cope with their irritating behavior. To Thérèse she admitted her intolerance, and then in a self-critical tone, the young sister acknowledged that she needed to become more patient. Hearing the sister confess her impatience but especially noticing the sister's self-condemning spirit, Thérèse recognized that the penitent had not only lost her inner freedom by being excessively disturbed with the older sisters, but now was also being controlled by feelings of irritation with herself. The sister was condemning herself for her own inadequacy and blaming herself for not being better. Thérèse knew that the sister needed to become aware that she was allowing feelings of guilt and self-condemnation to control her. The sister had felt that she was on the path of becoming violent to the sisters who irritated her, but now the sister was becoming violent to herself by her self-condemnation. The sister had felt that her irritating companions were her enemy, and now she was becoming her own enemy as well.

Knowing that the young sister's transformation would begin in the process of loving herself even in her weakness of being impatient with the other sisters, Thérèse did not scold her. Thérèse did not contribute to the sister's impatience with herself, but rather offered advice similar to the recommendation she had offered Céline: *If you are willing to bear serenely the trial of being displeasing to yourself, then you will be . . .* [for Jesus] *a pleasant place of shelter* (cf. GC 1038). Thérèse responded to this sister: *If God wants you to be weak and powerless like a little child, do you think you will be less worthy?*

Consent, then, to stumble at every step, even to fall, to carry your cross feebly. Love your powerlessness; your soul will draw more profit than if, supported by grace, you achieve with a certain flair heroic acts which fill your soul with personal satisfaction and selfish pride (TLMT 79).

Thérèse was asking the sister these questions: "Can you pray with repentance to be better, but pray without self-condemnation? Are you willing and ready to be better without lacking in appreciation for yourself? Can you be patient with yourself until God gives you the grace to be patient with the sisters? Can you accept and love yourself and not become your own adversary? Can you bear serenely the distress and personal trial of knowing that you have the weakness of impatience? Can you accept your powerlessness without losing your inner freedom and without becoming negative toward yourself or others?" Success in virtue is not the point. Love—love of the sisters in their weakness and love of yourself in your inadequacy—*that*, Thérèse was trying to say, is the point.

Thérèse knew that an attitude of patience with herself would help the sister regain her inner freedom and, in a spirit of self-accepting love, accept God's love. The young sister's patient love for herself, even as she was willing to be better—if God willed it—was the first step in transformation. She would then be patient with others as best she could, not as an ego achievement, but in humble awareness of a common weakness. The young sister went away enlightened and remembered Thérèse's wisdom years later (TLMT 79). Thérèse had learned this wisdom from her own experience with the sisters toward whom she felt natural antipathy.

Thérèse offered the same advice to one of the priests to whom she had become a spiritual mentor. On one occasion, the priest confessed to her that he was a "miserable person." He told her with self-loathing sarcasm about the "beautiful years . . . I wasted, sacrificing to the world and its follies the 'talents' God was lending me" (GC 1125).

Thérèse tactfully ignored the implicit violence hidden in the self-condemnation and replied simply: *Do not think you frighten me by speaking "about your beautiful, wasted years." I myself thank Jesus, who has looked at you with a look of love as, in the past, He looked at the young man in the Gospel. . . . Ah! Brother, like me you can sing the mercies of the Lord, they sparkle in you in all their splendor* (GC 1133; cf. SS 13).

To the priest, Thérèse was pointing out that since Jesus had been patient with the rich young man who had effectively rejected him (Mark 10:21), God was certainly going to be equally patient with him, who was already acknowledging and regretting his weaknesses. Do not lose your inner freedom, she was telling him, which is more precious than even the specific "'talents' God was lending" you. By losing patience and kindness for yourself through your self-condemnation, she was implying, you are violating yourself. You are becoming your own enemy. You are negating God's love for you. Thérèse was advising him to follow her own strategy in prayer and in self-acceptance: to *sing the mercies of the Lord* (cf. SS 13). From her own experiences and not only from St. Paul's description of love, Thérèse had learned over and over that patience and kindness with oneself and with others were important ways of maintaining inner freedom essential to authentic love. And it was in patience that she maintained her inner freedom in her final suffering.

2. Creativity

The second heart quality of love for Thérèse, and closely related to inner freedom, was her capacity to be creative. Although she expressed creative skills in prose, poetry, and painting, Thérèse was most creative personally and spiritually in the way she lived her experiences, in her relations with others and in her relations with herself.

Thérèse had noticed that the path of authentic love was not predetermined but emerged as she took one step at a time in a spirit of spontaneity and adaptability, walking in freedom, patience, and kindness. Most often she did not know in advance what she would do as she tried to be loving, but she always knew in her mature creative love what she would not do: she would not do violence to herself or do violence to anyone else.

In her spiritual maturity, accepting her personal gifts and bearing her weaknesses creatively, Thérèse responded to each sister of the community with originality and in a unique way. Imitating the way others expressed love, Thérèse knew, was out of the question. She had her own gifts and faults, and she was called to love herself and others within the boundaries of those graces and limitations. Thérèse trusted her own creative capacity to accommodate each situation with as much inner freedom and adaptability as she could. When she manifested her love, especially by her healing presence and wise advice, she acted with genuine creative simplicity and spontaneity, without artificiality and without affectation.

As Thérèse developed personally and spiritually in her role of guiding the younger sisters, she came to know the truth that *there are really more differences among souls than there are among faces* (SS 239). To properly direct each of these sisters along a unique spiritual path of love, she interacted with each, not according to a predetermined plan, but creatively, accommodating each on the person's own terms. She became adaptable in her responses and directives and did not hold on to her own preferred expressions of love. *One feels it is absolutely necessary,* Thérèse concluded, *to forget one's likings, one's personal conceptions, and to guide souls along the road which Jesus has traced out for them without trying to make them walk one's own way* (SS 238).

In this creative spirit, she deepened her ability to listen and to be circumspect. She gradually had become detached from her own feelings, discreetly managing feelings of attraction and antipathy toward the sisters and their preferences. *With the grace of Jesus never have I tried to attract their hearts to me; I understood that my mission was to lead them to God* (SS 239).

Some of them I have to catch by the scruff of the neck

Although these feelings were gradually diminishing, Thérèse was challenged by her continuing need to please others and to feel close, to feel as if she belonged, and to feel bonded to others. She found it difficult to correct the faults and imperfections in the young sisters, since at one level of her nature, Thérèse really wanted to be their friend. But having been given the responsibility of guiding them, she could not follow her personal likings. *What cost me more than anything else was to observe the faults and slight imperfections* [of the young sisters] *and to wage a war to the death on these. I would prefer a thousand times to receive reproofs than to give them to others* (SS 239; EIG 256ff.). Even when she corrected a young sister by accommodating her nature creatively and meekly, nonetheless, Thérèse learned that the sister would still think, *The Sister* [Thérèse] *charged with directing me is angry,* [but] *all the blame is put on me who am filled with the best intentions* (SS 239).

Thérèse struggled interiorly not to take the sisters' criticisms personally but to respond creatively. She was able to become, as she expressed it, like a good shepherd *running after them, . . . speaking severely to them when showing them that their beautiful fleece is soiled,* as well as being *the little hunting dog . . . chasing the . . .* [rabbits] *all day long*; and also being *the watchman observing the enemy from the highest turret of a strong castle* (SS 239; GC 872; EIG 256ff.).

In fulfilling her responsibility, Thérèse sometimes expressed her concern for the sisters in ways that they experienced as tough love. She corrected fearlessly whatever the cost to herself, but at the same time, she adapted her challenges and directives to the unique temperament and specific needs of each sister. *Some of them,* she noted, *I have to catch by the scruff of the neck, others by their wingtips* (STL 31).

Toward one sister she was very gentle and flexible; to another, more firm and demanding. With one she shared her own inner struggles and offered encouragement; with another she concealed her own weaknesses and required conformity without undue words of support. To one she was stern; to another, humorous. She required one sister, who wept often, to drop her tears only in a small mussel shell that Thérèse supplied. The situation became so preposterous that the young sister was drawn out of her melancholy (TLMT 26).

Thérèse was equally creative in adjusting to the demands of each of the difficult older sisters in the community. She was as charitable as she could be to each sister on that sister's own terms, but Thérèse needed to do this within her own personal boundaries in order to maintain her inner freedom.

Even in her maturity, however, Thérèse continued to feel challenged in her capacity to respond creatively. She knew that she could be drawn into overreacting to contentious behavior. She could, if she lost herself, give a harsh word in retaliation to an angry word, returning injury for injury. When a sister had been disrespectful to her, Thérèse recognized that she was tempted *to answer* [the sister] *back in a disagreeable manner* (SS 223).

Thérèse always remained vulnerable to the underlying feelings of being rejected and not bonded with others. These were the lingering traces of her difficult feelings from childhood that aroused the self-defensive urges in her. She sensed the ominous power of these feelings and the controlling force of these urges in her temptation to retaliate in kind. Thus, the ability to manage her feelings and to respond creatively in difficult situations became an important psychological indicator to Thérèse that told her that she was on the path of love.

3. Compassion

An additional heart quality that alerted Thérèse that she was on the path of love, and which was psychologically interrelated with inner freedom and creativity, was her ability to act in a spirit of compassion.

As a small child, Thérèse witnessed compassionate behavior manifested in her family. The family had the custom of distributing food to the poor, sometimes inviting a poor person to share a meal at the family table. When the child Thérèse and her father took their Sunday walk together through the town, she was designated to extend to any poor person alms on behalf of the family. By this she learned to have pity and to be sensitive and generous—sentiments of compassion that filled her capacity as a child to act in charity.

But she had much more to learn about real compassion, and she did learn more from her experiences with the sisters in the convent. In particular, she learned that compassion had to do with "feeling with" as well as "being with." She learned that without the empathy of "feeling with," what pretended to be compassion could be an ego adventure or could be manipulating or patronizing. She also learned that true compassion brings healing and causes life to flourish.

During the months following her entry into the convent, Thérèse suffered much from the thoughtless behavior of some of the troubled sisters in the community. Thérèse refused to yield to self-pity or to gather support by complaining, blaming, or gossiping. Rather, in prayerfully remembering her own painful feelings and in imagining the inner experiences of the difficult sisters, she deepened her empathy.

On her natural sensitivity, on her tendency to please, and on her ability for self-awareness, Thérèse established her genuine empathetic desire to be able to suffer with the difficult sisters. Thérèse, too, was suffering emotionally in many of the same ways that she imagined that the difficult sisters must be suffering. She, too, felt lonely, rejected, and inadequate. With the wisdom of her own hurt feelings and a willingness to embrace the vision of seeing a hurting sister rather than just an angry, resentful sister, Thérèse was able to deepen her compassion and become a healing presence.

She understood that some of the sisters were troublesome because they were troubled; some were disturbing because they themselves were suffering inner disturbance. Some of the sisters were disrespectful because they had suffered from disrespect, and some were hard to please because they were in physical and emotional pain. These insights helped Thérèse to detach herself emotionally from the sisters' difficult behavior in an appropriate way, and most often she did not take personally their negative attitudes. She avoided being condescending or responding to needy sisters simply out of obligation and came to realize that the sisters who were the most difficult to love probably most needed her empathetic love.

If I had an infirmity such as hers, I would not do any better than she does

Thérèse also had noticed that when someone was physically ill, then others in the community seemed to be especially tolerant and responsive. But when a person was bothersome and troubled emotionally, then that person was ignored and isolated. In her own little way, Thérèse tried to remedy that community deficiency. On one occasion she remarked to her sister Pauline, who was complaining about one sister's conduct that Pauline thought was particularly reprehensible: *I assure you that I have the greatest compassion for Sister. If you knew her as well as I do you would see that she is not responsible for all of the things that seem so awful to us. I remind myself that if I had an infirmity such as hers, and so defective a spirit, I would not do any better than she does, and then I would despair; she suffers terribly from her own shortcomings. If you only knew how she is to be pardoned!* (STL 50–51). About one sister who had a difficult temperament, Thérèse remarked, *How she is to be pitied* (HLTT 111).

Thérèse knew what it was to suffer from one's own emotional limitations. She had been in that situation herself, especially during the ten years after her mother's death, *the most painful* period of her life (SS 34). At that time, Thérèse had entered a state of melancholy and mild depression. Now, to an emotionally disturbed and very discouraged young sister under her guidance, Thérèse, as an expression of her compassion for the sister, was able to admit that after the loss of her mother, when she awoke in the morning, *If I foresaw only troubles, I got up depressed* (TLMT 104).

To the physically ill, Thérèse had a special sense of care and compassion. She confided to Pauline that she would have liked the job of infirmarian so that she could have comforted the sick. To the sister infirmarian, Thérèse remarked, *You're lucky. You will hear our Lord say: "I was sick and you comforted me"* (STL 49).

For several months Thérèse herself did have the opportunity to care for the sick and dying sisters when an epidemic of influenza spreading throughout France swept into the convent. Thérèse, just celebrating her nineteenth birthday and still the youngest among the professed sisters, along with only two other sisters, remained healthy. They tended the sick and dying as best they could, dispensing the few remedies available. The epidemic was so severe, however, that three of the older sisters died within a week (cf. EIG 207).

In this distressing, deadly situation, Thérèse found herself thrust into a leadership role. Taking the initiative, she made many small but crucial decisions in the care of the sisters and in the daily business of the convent. *Now I ask myself,* Thérèse wrote several years later, *how I could have done all I did without experiencing fear.* And by way of explaining, she added that during that stressful time, *I had the unspeakable consolation of receiving Holy Communion every day* (SS 171–72).

By grace she was able to maintain her emotional balance. It was a time when the community experienced the energy of Thérèse's youth, faith, and courage. The sisters began to appreciate her practical, simple, peaceful, and prayerful way, as well as her healing presence, her self-giving, her wisdom, and her spirit of compassion and joy. And it was the time when the clerical superior of the convent who had opposed Thérèse from the time that she had requested entrance into the community finally recognized her maturity and acknowledged that "she is a great hope for the community" (HLTT 136).

When Jesus calls a soul to direct others, He has the soul experience the trials of life

Toward the end of her life, she was able to explicitly extend her compassion well beyond her family and the convent through her correspondence with the two seminarians, soon to become priests, assigned to her prayers and spiritual guidance. In the first letter she wrote to one of them, she expressed her empathy and sorrow for his spiritual distress, and with touching sensitivity, she assumed some responsibility for his failings. She suggested that since he was her *little brother* (SS 251), her own imperfections in prayer may have contributed to his lack of spiritual progress.

Her own failings had also prepared her to tell him that his weaknesses were providential. *When Jesus calls a soul to direct and to save multitudes of other souls,* she wrote him, *it is necessary that He have him experience the temptations and trials of life* (GC 1010). Reaching into the wealth of her own experience, Thérèse drew the insight that through his temptations and trials, God would use her spiritual brother to save souls. It was an insight of deep wisdom and an expression of compassion that she hoped would heal the distress of his spirit.

At the end of her life, as she lay ravaged by tuberculosis, Thérèse was cared for by the superior and the sisters who did what they could to meet her needs with their limited resources. Thérèse accepted their love graciously, but in her compassion, she also willingly tolerated inconveniences so as not to disturb the community. She prayed to her Mother Mary that she would not cough at night so that Céline, now her caregiver sleeping nearby her in the infirmary, would not be awakened. Later she said, *Here is what gives me the desire to leave* [to die quickly]: *I tire out my little sisters, and then I give them pain when being so sick* (HLC 174). She prayed *to cause my sisters no more pain; and in order to do this, that I go very quickly* (HLC 189).

She may have learned this disposition from her own mother who, nearing her painful death from breast cancer, took a room at night as far from family members as possible so that her cries would not disturb them. To the end, Thérèse, with her great gifts of sensitivity and empathy, was ready to forget herself and to accommodate others in a spirit of compassion.

4. Willingness

Interrelated with the three heart qualities of inner freedom, creativity, and compassion was Thérèse's experience of willingness, self-surrender, and gratitude. Since a spirit of willingness seems to have been elusive for Thérèse, we will examine this heart quality in slightly greater detail, providing additional examples of how Thérèse gradually allowed her willpower to be expressed in a spirit of willingness rather than willfulness.

I believed it was quite impossible for me to understand perfection better

As a child, Thérèse's willpower took the form of sheer stubbornness. Some of her tantrums were so violent that her mother became concerned. Describing Thérèse at about three and a half years old, her mother wrote that she "has in her an almost invincible stubbornness" and that she "gets into frightful tantrums" (cf. GC 1223, 1219; SS 23).

In her maturity, when Thérèse herself reflected on her childhood, she expressed her thanks that she had been raised so lovingly but also so firmly. To Pauline, she wrote, *I wonder at times how you were able to raise me with so much love and tenderness without spoiling me* (SS 44). Knowing that she was so prone to willfulness and intent on getting her own way, Thérèse was aware that if her family had treated her with the leniency that they had treated her sister Céline, who was less stubborn, they would have spoiled her.

Fearing the power and sensing the self-centeredness of her willfulness, Thérèse, at her First Communion when she was only eleven years old, had made the resolution that *I will try to humiliate my pride* (STL 174). Feeling inadequate in calming her willfulness, she simply resolved to combat her stubborn, willful streak and to become humble. Even many years later, she would continue to pray, *I beg of You to take away my freedom to displease You* (SS 276; PST 53ff.). She did not know that her resolution to humble the pride of her willfulness and her prayer that God take away the freedom of her willpower were desires that could not be fulfilled.

Freedom as an expression of the power of free will is an inherent part of human dignity, a sharing in the freedom of God. If Thérèse were to continue to remain the authentic human person that she was, she could not simply renounce her free will, and God could not remove it. Thérèse was also mistaken in thinking that humility could be achieved by a willful decision. The willful effort to become humble was itself a willful act of the self-centered ego, an act of hidden pride disguised as virtue. In answering her prayer, God did not take away her freedom but rather supported and transformed her will.

Thérèse's desire to curb her willfulness, however, echoed what she may have heard her father read to her as a child from the popular biographies of the saints as well as what she may later have read in the spiritual books in the convent library. Some of the saints were portrayed as having overcome their pride by sheer willfulness. And some of the saints were noted for having prayed to God to take away their will altogether. So it might be expected that Thérèse, in an immature piety, would have had a similar desire and a similar prayer. It was the attitude of willfulness, however, and not freedom or free will as such, that the saints were praying that God take away, and it was willingness, not willfulness, that would lead Thérèse to humility (cf. EIG 102ff.).

At the beginning of my spiritual life when I was thirteen or fourteen, Thérèse wrote in retrospect nine years later, *I used to ask myself what I would have to strive for later on because I believed it was quite impossible for me to understand perfection better* (SS 158). At that time, with a naivety that she herself later recognized, Thérèse had written that even the *learned . . . would have been astonished to see a child of fourteen understand perfection's secrets* (SS 105).

But over the years, with the lights that came to her through her trials and especially through the disappointments of her unfulfilled expectations accompanying her willful *strivings,* she began to recognize that she could *understand perfection better.* That better understanding focused on her awareness of the most profound of *perfection's secrets*—that in authentic perfection and holiness, there is no violence or willfulness.

This trial was all the more painful as I did not understand it

Over the years, Thérèse became more sensitive not only to *what* she desired but also to *the way* she desired. Her willpower was strong, and she wished to focus it on being available to God's love. But although the object of her desire was to do God's will, how could she be certain that she was not still driven by a disguised self-centeredness—a kind of ego adventure toward holiness, a self-seeking stubbornness now turned toward sanctity—but willful stubbornness nonetheless?

As a child, she had used her willpower for her own advantage in fits of self-seeking. Later she had used the power of her will to gain the needed permissions to enter the convent. In audaciously addressing the pope and in many other instances in her early life, she used her willpower to get her way because she was certain her way was God's way. Could some of those occasions have been disguised stubbornness coming from a hidden self-seeking? Thérèse did not think so at the time.

However, Thérèse tells us that especially as she prayed over her thwarted expectations and desires, she came to detect some secret self-centered willfulness. One such incident was when Thérèse finally gained permission to join the convent, but the date of entry that she herself had chosen was delayed. Her sister Pauline knew that Thérèse had been sickly as a child. As a member of the convent, she wished to protect Thérèse from some of the physical rigors of the convent life and pressed the superior to postpone her entry until after the penitential Lenten season—a three-month delay, from January 1888 to the first days of April.

Thérèse did not experience the delay as a favor. On the contrary, she felt *this trial was very great. It was all the more painful,* she remembered, *as I did not understand it.* She later wrote that she asked herself, *How did those three months pass?* (SS 143). She must have wondered at the time if she was just being stubborn in her desire to enter the convent on her own time schedule. If she were, would she sense some kind of inner disposition telling her that she was not on the path of authentic love?

Thérèse's awareness of her feelings and thoughts in this experience indicated that the answer to her question was yes. She was stubborn in wanting her own way, and she did finally have an inner sense that made her aware of her self-centered willfulness. She said as much when she revealed what she was thinking when she learned of the extended delay: *At first the thought came into my mind not to lead a life as well regulated as had been my custom* (SS 143).

Her first thought, now that the delay was official and out of her hands, was to make a fuss. In a kind of disguised interior tantrum, she would spend her time in a way not *well regulated,* even though that would sabotage her spiritual preparation to enter the convent. She would "get back" at the situation and exert her self-centered willpower in a kind of stubborn retaliation, refusing to surrender to what was being asked of her. Thérèse was not willingly abandoning herself into God's will in the here and now of the delay. She was acting against God's providence. She was cultivating a willful spirit and acting in violence to a situation that resisted her control.

But then, reflecting on the ambiguity of her motives, she continued her story: *Soon I understood the value of the time I was being offered. I made a resolution to give myself up more than ever to a serious and mortified life* (SS 143). Thérèse quickly reclaimed her inner freedom. Instead of "getting back" at the situation, she would become serious about living a life that would prepare her for the convent. In this way, she would willingly embrace the disappointment as God's will. In this spirit of willingness to accept God's will, she was able to experience the month of March, the last month of her delay, as *one of the most beautiful months of my life* (GC 390).

My intense desire to make Profession was mixed with great self-love

A similar situation arose when Thérèse was about to make her profession of vows. The clerical superior of the community, who from the beginning had opposed Thérèse's entering the convent at such a young age, now protested that at seventeen she was too young to take religious vows. As a concession to his objection, the community postponed the ceremony another eight months.

Once more, Thérèse was brought face-to-face with a situation in which her expectation and desire were thwarted. Questions similar to those that arose at the delay of her entry into the convent seem to have surfaced once again. *I found it difficult, at first,* she later wrote, *to accept this great sacrifice* [of having her profession delayed] (SS 158; cf. GC 902–4). Was she being stubborn again? Was she just desiring her own way? If she were, would she sense some heart quality that told her so? Once again, Thérèse found the answer to her questions to be yes.

The months of delay provided the opportunity for Thérèse to ponder her continuing struggle with mixed motives that were touching her will. It was to God that Thérèse brought her distress, and *one day, during my prayer,* she noted, *I understood that my intense desire to make Profession was mixed with great self-love* (SS 158; cf. EIG 190ff.).

Thérèse's prayer allowed her to recognize her self-centered ego in operation overpowering her true self, and in prayer she regained her inner freedom. *Since I had given myself to Jesus to please and console Him, I had no right to oblige Him to do my will instead of His own.* She prayed, *O my God! I don't ask you to make Profession. I will* [willingly] *wait as long as you desire, but what I don't want is to be the cause of my separation from You through my fault* [of willfulness] (SS 158). She was coming to know how willfulness poisoned her heart and how a spirit of willingness allowed her to walk the path of love.

I am simply resigned to see myself always imperfect

In these two instances of not getting her own way exactly when she wanted it, Thérèse discovered that she was still using her willpower with a refined kind of stubbornness and a willful self-centeredness. Clearly, her childhood awareness of her tendency toward willfulness and her childhood resolve to be different had not completely prevented future missteps. Perhaps by the time of her profession, Thérèse also knew that she would never be completely free from these spontaneous thoughts and first feelings of the self-centered ego willfully wanting its own way. Her prayer, however, had alerted her not to cultivate her tendency toward willfulness, which could poison her heart.

In her childhood stubbornness, Thérèse had not easily seen the self-centeredness and sense of retaliation that lay just below the surface of willfulness. Now her sensitivity and her prayer were illuminating most clearly the deep spiritual implication of the difference she had begun to feel in her heart between willfulness allied with self-centeredness and willingness associated with self-surrender to God's will.

She was gradually learning new aspects of *the science of love* that at fourteen she had barely glimpsed. *I learned very quickly since then* [during her teenage years], she noted in her maturity, *that the more one advances, the more one sees the goal is still far off. And now,* she added, *I am simply resigned to see myself always imperfect and in this I find my joy* (SS 158). Thérèse now recognized that acts of willing self-surrender into God's will were at the heart of peace and authentic love. She also learned that the tendency toward willfulness would not simply disappear. Her willingness to remain imperfect and surrender into God's will would become the essence of her little way.

Thérèse understood that willfulness did not just employ her willpower; it also included an attitude of inflexible attachment to her own choices and wants. It included desires to overpower adversarial situations and feelings of retaliation. Her willfulness was not manifesting authentic passion, resolve, determination, and power; rather, it was expressing inordinate passion, a sense of being driven, and an attitude of predetermination and a compulsion to overpower—all indicators of the seeds of violence. This attitude of willfulness—this sense of being driven, of predetermining a situation and attempting to overpower it—clearly opposed the spirit of inner freedom; it precluded creativity and eliminated compassion. Moreover, the vindictiveness and retaliation that sometimes erupted in an internal tantrum from thwarted willfulness were even more explicit indications of the violence lurking in willfulness.

All of this told Thérèse that willfulness could not be part of the path of love. She experienced this truth within herself in her prayers and reflections, but she also learned it from the personal revelations of the young sisters under her guidance. Willfulness, she learned, played a role in the condemnatory, judgmental spirit and spiteful actions of some of the sisters. She learned that willfulness could poison the heart of a community by sowing the seeds of violence in the form of gossip and cliques.

At the same time, Thérèse was noticing that as her desires became more and more purified through a sense of detachment and self-abandonment, she did not need to diminish her willpower. She came to recognize that on the path of love, God did not ask her to reduce her authentic passion nor to restrict her strong determination and power; rather, she was to maintain her willpower but in a spirit of willingness to do God's will. Thérèse saw that a spirit of willingness could carry her deepest desires and her strongest passions but also allow God to have the final word in all of her choices and preferences.

Willingness could focus her choices without attachment to their fulfillment, allowing God to fulfill them in God's time, God willing. Willingness could convey her preferences without the need to cling to those preferences. Willingness could carry the power of her intense desires and passion without substituting them for God's will.

Thérèse learned that a spirit of willingness would be the self-surrender of her will into God's will with the purification but without the elimination of her passions, preferences, or desires and without the negation of her freedom. As Thérèse prayed in her Act of Oblation to Merciful Love: *I am certain, then, that You will grant my desires; I know, O my God! that the more You want to give, the more You make us desire. I feel in my heart immense desires and it is with confidence I ask You to come and take possession of my soul* (SS 276; PST 53ff.).

Thérèse's childhood stubbornness had gradually calmed, but her capacity to focus her willpower and determination actually increased as she moved from driving her willpower in willfulness to deploying her willpower in willingness.

I made a resolution to give myself up more than ever to a serious and mortified life

All of these reflections about willingness and willfulness became one of Thérèse's most important lessons in *the science of love*. She recognized that the sense of willingness was a most significant psychological disposition indicating the path of love in day-to-day life situations. She also came to see that the tendency toward willfulness was a sure sign of the self-centered ego striving for identity, security, and self-worth, poisoning the best intentions of her heart and tending toward violence.

But there was an even deeper insight into willfulness that Thérèse was to discover as she continued to reflect on her reaction to the three-month delayed entry into the convent that Pauline had initiated. If she had followed her first thoughts and had been controlled by the original spontaneous feelings regarding the postponement, she would not have continued *to lead a life as well regulated as had been my custom* (SS 143). She would then have hurt no one but herself by compromising her deepest desires. That reaction, she saw almost immediately, would have been nothing but self-indulgent, willful retaliation against the situation and would have also been violence against her true self.

Her deeper insight, however, was revealed as she continued to tell the story of this experience. She remarked that when she *understood the value of the time I was being offered, I made a resolution to give myself up more than ever to a serious and mortified life* (SS 143). Thérèse had, after regaining her inner freedom, quickly recognized that she was moving on the wrong path and resolved to change her way. But did she see that there was an even more hidden danger within her new resolve to embrace more than ever a serious and mortified life?

Her new resolution to reestablish and even intensify her customary disciplined lifestyle could itself be a willful resolve. Was she making this resolution in an attitude of willfulness to achieve a certain self-discipline and reclaim virtue, or was she making her resolution in a spirit of willingness to conform to God's will? Was this new resolve coming from an even more deeply disguised attitude of self-centered willfulness, or was it a step on the path of authentic love of herself and a free, creative, compassionate response to God's will?

If the new resolution itself were another willful act, the self-centered ego would have achieved a subtle victory. It would now be perpetrating the "good" or "sacred" violence of self-inflicted pain in the disguise of achieving the good end of a *serious and mortified life*. Thérèse's new insight penetrated into the dimension of "good" violence.

Some mistaken religious preaching that Thérèse had heard endorsed "good" violence. Such preaching would have given God's approval to the "good" or "sacred" violence of self-inflicted, willful mortifications so that Thérèse's original "bad" impulse to abandon her *well regulated* life would be punished and corrected. But Thérèse, even at this young age of fifteen, intuitively sensed, at least dimly, that God never demands violence in any form. Perhaps Thérèse even had a faint awareness that the violence of self-inflicted, willful suffering to achieve holiness was like trying to drive out Satan by means of Satan (cf. Mark 3:23). The final situation was bound to be worse than the first, now with the spectacle of seven devils of self-righteousness parading where before there had been but one demon of self-centeredness (cf. Matthew 12:43-45). Although at the time of her First Communion Thérèse had not recognized the trap of trying to achieve humility by a willful resolve, perhaps now, as she waited to enter the convent, she had a sense of the trap poised by trying to overcome willfulness in a willful way.

When I say mortified, this is not to give the impression that I performed acts of penance

Thérèse was certainly aware of the trap of willfully attempting to overcome her willfulness when she wrote years later explaining the details of her resolution *to give myself up more than ever to a serious and mortified life* (SS 143). Immediately in her explanation, she made clear that at that time, she had never actually performed any severe, self-violent mortifications. She wrote of this with a sense of humor toward herself: *When I say mortified, this is not to give the impression that I performed acts of penance. Alas, I never made any. Far from resembling beautiful souls who practiced every kind of mortification from their childhood, I had no attraction for this. Undoubtedly this stemmed from my cowardliness, for I could have,* she remarked with some lightness, *found a thousand ways of making myself suffer* (SS 143).

She could have found *a thousand ways* to make herself suffer, but she did not desire suffering for itself. She did not love suffering in itself. She loved God and desired to be available to God. Thus, by using the words "mortification" and "mortified," Thérèse subverted and changed their meaning. Her meaning of the word "mortified" was not to suggest self-violence but to point to her readiness and self-surrender in being available to receive God's love. Mortifications for Thérèse were not acts of self-inflicted suffering to punish herself or to gain God's forgiveness. They were expressions of her willingness to fall deeper into the arms of a loving God at whatever the personal cost.

Thérèse's use of the expression "mortified life," then, is another example, as with her use of the words "perfection," "oblation," "martyr," "holocaust," and "victim," of the way in which she transforms the meaning of significant words used in the spiritual tradition by cleansing them of any suggestions of "good" or "sacred" violence. In a similar way, by her life itself, she was to transform the meaning of the word "saint."

Thérèse continued her explanation of what she meant by her *cowardliness* in avoiding ways to make herself suffer by saying with lightness that *instead of this I allowed myself to be wrapped in cotton wool and fattened up like a little bird that needs no penance* (SS 143). Then she detailed some of the mortifications and penances that she actually did perform. *My mortifications consisted in breaking my will, always so ready to impose itself on others, in holding back a reply, in rendering little services without any recognition, in not leaning my back against a support when seated, etc., etc. It was through the practice of these nothings that I prepared myself to become the fiancée of Jesus* [by entering the Carmelite community] (SS 143–44). Throughout her life, however, Thérèse's most ongoing mortification and self-discipline would be her willingness to bear in peace and repentance, and without violence, her own weaknesses and distressing feelings, and especially to bear her tendency toward self-centeredness and willfulness.

Profiting by all the smallest things and doing them through love

The mortifications that Thérèse imposed on herself at this time were acts of appropriate self-discipline and were not acts of punitive self-violence. They were acts of discipline for the sake of discipleship. She intended them to refocus her life, to regain her best self, to enhance her awareness of God's loving presence, and to sharpen her readiness to respond to God's will.

Breaking my will, always so ready to impose itself on others, was Thérèse's way of describing her deliberate use of willpower, in a spirit of willingness, to dissolve her self-centered readiness to get her own way. *Holding back a reply* was her way of describing how she tamed her willfulness, prayerfully managing her feelings and not overreacting in an attitude of defensiveness and retaliation, an attitude she noticed that still arose in her after years in the convent. The further mortification of *rendering little services without any recognition* was Thérèse's way of speaking of how she managed her continuing weakness of needing to please others and of needing to be affirmed. It was an important step along her way of being charitable inconspicuously. And *not leaning my back against a support when seated* was Thérèse's way of describing how she physically reminded herself of her willingness to be available to God's loving embrace, the only support she needed at every present moment (SS 143).

These were her penances. Each was without fuss or fanfare; each was hidden and little in its own way. Each helped her address her self-centered ego.

Each expressed the self-discipline of being vigilant, mindful, and faithful. Each fostered her self-awareness, especially to her tendency toward willfulness, and each was a reminder to her of her willingness to be available to God's will. But none were worthy of the name "mortification" as that was understood in the spirituality of her time. Thérèse was not focused on self-inflicted pain as a kind of reparation or as a way of improving herself. Her concern was the awareness of God's presence, the self-discipline to welcome God's will, and the faithfulness to respond in charity to others.

A year or so after her entry into Carmel, she noted again her practice of mortifications in relationship to charity toward her sisters and to her continued need to address her self-centeredness. Having given the examples of not complaining and of *not excusing myself,* she wrote: *I applied myself to practicing little virtues, not having the capability of practicing the great. For instance, I loved to fold up the mantles forgotten by the Sisters, and to render them all sorts of little services. . . . The only little mortification I was doing while still in the world, which consisted in not leaning my back again any support while seated, was forbidden me because of my inclination to stoop. . . . The penances they* [the Superiors] *did allow me consisted in mortifying my self-love, which did me much more good than corporal penances* (SS 159).

She would later tell one of the sisters under her guidance that such small acts of self-discipline related with charity toward others *don't attract people's attention and they have the advantage of keeping us spiritually alert and maintaining our sense of the supernatural* (STL 245).

By describing her cowardliness toward mortifications as *allow*[ing] *myself to be wrapped in cotton wool and fattened up like a little bird that needs no penance* (SS 143), Thérèse was humorously confessing that her youthful practices of self-discipline were rather trivial, and yet in her tendency to *really* [make] *a big fuss over everything* (SS 91), she could call them acts of mortification. She was also acknowledging that now in her maturity, she had come to a sense of peace over the interior pain that her little acts of self-discipline had required when she was young and continued to require throughout her life.

The imagery of the *cotton wool* and the *little bird* she later supplemented with another image of her willingness to bear inner sufferings associated with the small and inconspicuous acts of self-discipline that God's providence provided and that charity to others invited. It was the image of strewing flowers. She prayed, addressing Jesus: *I have no other means of proving my love for you other than that of strewing flowers, that is, not allowing one little sacrifice to escape, not one look, one work, profiting by all the smallest things and doing them through love* [inconspicuously and without making a fuss] (SS 196).

The image of gathering and strewing flowers became an important expression of her willingness to embrace the suffering of her little way. When describing what it meant for her to remain a little child before God, she said, *I've always remained little, having no other occupation but to gather flowers, the flowers of love and sacrifice, and of offering them to God in order to please Him. There is only one thing to do here on earth: to cast at Jesus the flowers of little sacrifices, to take Him by caresses; this is the way I've taken Him* (HLC 139, 257). The sacrifices of doing God's will that she willingly offered became rose petals strewn out spontaneously in love (cf. SS 29, 196; cf. GC 1232–33; GC 1134; CP 156, 209).

At the end of her life, in the spirit of her little way, she composed a love poem to the Child Jesus comparing her life of inconspicuous acts of love and sacrifice to a rose being willingly *un-petalled, joyously giving* itself up to life's very end, for Jesus' pleasure:

Delightful Child! The rose can deck Your Feast-days when
　It's at its height.
The rose, un-petalled though—thrown to the wind's will, then
　Blown out of sight!
That rose gives up itself—all artless—that it may
　No longer live.
Child Jesus! I, to You give myself up that way—
　Joyously [willingly] give!
Upon such petals then one walks without regret:
　And their debris
Are ornaments by no deliberation set—
　This now I see.
For You, I've strewn my life—my future, with what's gone:
　To mortal eye,
A rose that always will be withered from now on,
　I ought to die. (CP 209)

The glory of the rose *un-petalled* was the brilliant glow of its central bud of confidence and love. The petals were the self-sacrifice required by inner freedom and creativity, creativity and compassion, compassion and willingness, willingness and self-surrender, self-surrender and gratitude, all encircling and contributing to the radiance of the confidence and love of Thérèse's life offered as a living sacrifice.

Years later, as she reflected on the delay of her entry into the convent, she wrote simply: *I cannot express how much this waiting left me with sweet memories. Three months passed by very quickly, and then the moment so ardently desired finally arrived. I believe that . . . this trial was very great and made me grow very much in abandonment and in the other virtues* (SS 143–44). Indeed, Thérèse would continue to grow in the other virtues, and she would especially notice her need to continue to walk in willingness, but as her life in the convent unfolded, her attention would be especially focused on self-surrender as an expression of her self-emptying love.

5. Self-Surrender

An additional heart quality, interrelated with the other indicators and finally becoming, with gratitude, the fundament spirit of Thérèse's little way, was the spirit of self-surrender, or self-abandonment, to God. Her willing surrender into God's will would blossom into a lifestyle of complete self-abandonment.

To embrace this spirit, she was greatly helped by St. John of the Cross, her great spiritual father, whose writings she studied during those distressful months of her delayed profession. One of his sayings struck her forcefully: *You will not arrive at what you desire by your own path, or even by high contemplation, but through a great humility and surrender of the heart* (FGM 227, note 2). Praying through her feelings over the delay, she wrote these words: *The glory of Jesus, that is all; as for my own glory, I abandon it to Him, and, if He seems to forget me, He is free since I am no longer my own but His. . . . And He will more quickly grow tired of making me wait than I shall grow tired of waiting for Him!* (GC 612).

Three years after her profession, having been assigned to help in the guidance of the younger sisters, she began to write explicitly and with more conviction about the need for a spirit of self-abandonment and self-surrender: *Directors have others advance in perfection by having them perform a great number of acts of virtue, and they are right; but my director, who is Jesus, teaches me not to count up my acts. He teaches me to do all through love, to refuse Him nothing, to be content when He gives me a chance of proving to Him that I love Him. But this is done in peace, in abandonment, it is Jesus who is doing all in me, and I am doing nothing* (GC 796).

At the time of her father's impending death, as Thérèse suffered the inner turmoil of knowing that her "king" was slipping from her into the dark world of the mentally ill, she wrote to Céline, referring to herself in the third person: *What she must do is abandon herself, surrender herself, without keeping anything, not even the joy of knowing how much the bank* [of love] *is returning to her. . . . But this is done in peace, in abandonment* (GC 795–96). At this time also, Thérèse renewed her devotion to St. Cecilia, whom she now identified as *the saint of abandonment* (GC 553, 850).

The year before she died, Thérèse wrote this to her sister Marie: *I understand so well that it is only love which makes us acceptable to God that this love is the only good I ambition. Jesus deigned to show me the road that leads to this Divine Furnace* [of God's love], *and this road is the surrender* [self-abandonment] *of the little child who sleeps without fear in its Father's arms* (SS 188; cf. GC 994).

A fruit, that's sweet and rare—Abandonment is its name

As she was approaching death, Thérèse wished to live in the present moment every detail of her dying agony and thereby participate in union with Christ's redemptive suffering. She also desired to pass from this life to the place that God had prepared for her in heaven so that she could more completely fulfill her missionary desire to help all of humanity. She wished both to continue to endure and also to die into God. How was she to resolve her dilemma—to live or to die? She simply asked God to disregard her preferences totally. In a spirit of self-surrender and self-abandonment, she would let God's will unfold in her life in whatever way God preferred. In this spirit, six months before her death, she wrote to one of the priests she was mentoring, *I am asking Him* [God] *to be content with me, that is, to pay no attention to my desires of loving Him in suffering or of going to enjoy Him in heaven* (GC 1072).

As a child, Thérèse had willfully and aggressively reached for a basket of doll things and cried, *I choose all!* That gesture and those words, Thérèse had said, were a symbol for her whole life. She wanted to be a saint and to embrace all that her Beloved asked of her. *I don't want to be a saint by halves*, she wrote (SS 27). Now, as she lay on her deathbed suffering deep physical pain and emotional distress, when asked if she would rather live or die, she replied, *As God wills.* "And if you could choose?" she was asked. *I would not choose. I choose nothing. I abandon myself to God. I'll be falling into God's arms* (HLC 190, 188, 191). She expressed the fear that she had experienced as a child of her own willpower: *I fear only one thing: to keep my own will; so take it, for "I choose all" that You will!* (SS 27). That willpower had now been transformed into an active willingness and focused on her one desire to abandon herself in simplicity to her loving Father.

At this same time, a sister brought a sheaf of corn to Thérèse's bedside in the infirmary. Thérèse detached the most perfectly formed ear of corn and then said to Pauline, *This ear of corn is the image of my soul: God has entrusted me with graces for myself and for many others. . . . I feel so much that everything comes from Him* (HLC 131–32). Having abandoned herself into God's will, Thérèse was confident of God's love, the source of all her gifts. Echoing St. John of the Cross, Thérèse told one of the younger sisters, *Hold on tight to your confidence. It is impossible for God not to respond to that, because He always measures His gifts by how much confidence we have* (TLMT 86).

Thérèse quoted a sentence from Job that she had discovered in a book she had read when she was about eleven years old (TLMT 86). *This saying of Job: "Although he should kill me, I will trust in him"* [13:15], *has fascinated me from my childhood,* she said. It summarized her confident, hope-filled spirit of self-surrender. Then she added, *But it took me a long time before I was established in this degree of abandonment. Now I am there; God has placed me there. He took me into His arms and placed me there* (HLC 77).

A few months before her death, Thérèse wrote a poem she entitled "Abandonment Is the Sweet Fruit of Love":

And from its branches fair—
The tree is Love—there came
A fruit, that's sweet and rare—
Abandon is its name.

You've come here, from the Height,
Celestial Flame whose heat
Has warmed me! By its light
Abandon is complete. (CP 212–13)

Self-surrender into God's will had become her all-consuming desire, the passionate orientation of her willingness.

6. Gratitude

The sixth heart quality that helped Thérèse recognize that she was walking the path of authentic love was her ability to embrace a continuing spirit of gratitude. For Thérèse, gratitude was an all-pervading spirit, giving life to all the other heart qualities. Without gratitude, all the other heart qualities would have been somewhat reluctant, restrained, or imperfect. Gratitude, like a crowning jewel, recognized the giftedness and blessing of the qualities of inner freedom, creativity, compassion, willingness, and self-surrender, and expressed them in the only loving way possible—gratefully.

As a child, Thérèse had resolved never to complain (SS 30). Gratitude was implicit in that childhood resolve, and gratitude finally filled Thérèse's heart with peace, cleansing it of any trace of melancholy that had burdened her early years. Throughout her life, Thérèse allowed gratitude to flourish into an encompassing spirit that nourished her peace, fostered her joy, expressed her love, and, together with self-surrender and willingness, became the essential spirit of her little way.

Everything is a grace

Gratitude was her only appropriate response to God, who was ever stooping down to her, leading her and at times carrying her on her little way. It was at the heart of her love of God because, clothed in self-abandonment, it animated her willingness to receive God's love in all the moments of life. She was grateful for her very existence, for her union with Christ, for her faith, for the person she was, and for her life as it unfolded in God's providence. She was grateful for her spiritual and human gifts, for the peace and joy that permeated her life, but she was also grateful for her limitations and weaknesses and for the sadness and suffering that moved her closer to God. As the all-pervading spirit at the heart of love itself, gratitude was all-inclusive. And like love, gratitude for Thérèse *was everything, . . . it embraced all times and places. . . . In a word, . . . it was eternal!* (SS 194). *Everything is a grace,* Thérèse had insisted, and for everything thanks could be extended (HLC 98, 57).

By gratefully receiving God's love in all of her experiences, Thérèse also found the true meaning of loving herself. Her love of herself was not self-centered, egotistical delight. Her love of herself was the Holy Spirit prompting her to be grateful for who she was in the arms of God, who was loving her at every moment. As she had discovered that love of God and love of her sisters were one and the same love, so she also discovered that her grateful willingness to receive God's love and her love of herself were also one and the same love.

God as the source of love was the ultimate focus of Thérèse's gratitude. Gratefulness naturally arose from the sense of self-surrender, because she was not acquiescing to the hands of fate or destiny or chance; she was not resigning herself to an impersonal force. In self-surrender she was not submitting to discouragement; rather, she was allowing herself to be embraced in the arms of God. In the arms of the God of love, gratitude could be the only loving response. *Gratitude is the thing that brings us the most grace. . . . I have learnt this from experience,* she confided to Céline; *try it, and you will see. I am content with whatever God gives me, and I show him this in a thousand little ways* (STL 138).

Thérèse's gratitude not only was directed to God, to whom she directed the essence of her willingness and self-surrender, but gratitude also flowed horizontally, especially toward her family. She recognized that her family in a special way had mediated God's graces in her day-to-day childhood experiences. To understand God's love, she pondered again and again her formative childhood years. On her deathbed, she said to Pauline, Marie, and Céline, who were attending her, *Oh, my sisters, how much gratitude I owe to you. If you had not brought me up so well, what a wretched thing you would have before you now—instead of what you see in me today!* And to Pauline who had been her "second mother" from her earliest years and who throughout her life had acted toward her with kindness, she said, *You've always acted this way toward me. I cannot express my gratitude to you.* Then drying her tears, she added, *I'm crying because I'm so touched by everything you've done for me since my childhood* (HLC 76).

She was grateful to her extended family and to all the sisters of her Carmelite community for the many temporal gifts they had given her as well as the gifts of example, affirmation, and guidance. But she was also grateful to them as persons for their presence in her life and for the blessings of spirit and faith vision that they had received from God and had shared with her. *Frequently, when I am at the feet of Our Lord*, she wrote to her aunt, *I feel my soul over-flowing with gratitude when I think over the grace He granted me in giving me relatives like the ones I have the happiness to possess* (GC 765). Later she again wrote to her aunt, *Ah! truly I was born under a blessed star, and my heart melts with gratitude to God, who has given me relatives such as are not to be found any longer on earth* (GC 1022).

How great is my gratitude when I consider the kind attention of Jesus!

Circumstances also spoke to her of God's love and evoked her gratitude. She thanked God for the coincidence of snow falling so beautifully and so unexpectedly on the day that she took the religious habit of the Carmelite community. On that particular day, disregarding all the usual signs of mild weather, Thérèse still hoped that it might snow since *when I was small, its whiteness filled me with delight, and one of the greatest pleasures I had was taking a walk under the light snow flakes. Where did this love of snow come from? Perhaps it was because I was a little winter flower* [Thérèse was born on January 2], *and the first adornment with which my eyes beheld nature clothed was its white mantle* (SS 154). Thérèse said that snow falling on that day expressed *thoughtfulness on the part of Jesus! Anticipating the desires of His fiancée, He gave her snow. Snow! What mortal bridegroom, no matter how powerful he may be, could make snow fall from heaven to charm his beloved?* (SS 156). It was a coincidence that spontaneously called forth the expression of Thérèse's gratitude.

Oh! how great is my gratitude when I consider the kind attention of Jesus! What is He reserving for us in heaven if here below His love dispenses surprises so delightful? More than ever, I understand that the smallest events of our life are conducted by God, she wrote several months before she died (GC 1015).

She expressed gratitude even for her difficulties and for sufferings since they allowed her to share in the suffering of Christ from her place at the foot of the cross. She prayed in her Act of Oblation to Merciful Love, *I thank You, O my God! for all the graces You have granted me, especially the grace of making me pass through the crucible of suffering* (SS 277).

The greatest source of Thérèse's suffering during the first years of her life in the convent was not her interactions with Mother Gonzague or with the sisters, however painful some of those experiences were. Her most difficult suffering was the slow mental and physical deterioration of her father. Less than a year after her entrance into Carmel, her "king" suffered a series of strokes and was committed to a mental institution. He remained there for the next three years and was able to visit Thérèse only once more before he died. It was a dreadful three years for Thérèse.

But in addition to suffering the slow, excruciating loss of her beloved father to the isolation of mental illness, there was also the suffering of the gossip that circulated throughout the town and even found a home in Carmel. Her father was said to be in a "lunatic asylum," with the subtle accusation that this had happened because of his sorrow over losing Thérèse to the cloister (HLTT 149). Thérèse suffered in deep anguish and silence.

Years later, however, Thérèse managed to experience a sense of gratitude even for this terrible ordeal: *Yes, Papa's three years of martyrdom appear to me as the most lovable, the most fruitful of my life; I wouldn't exchange them for all the ecstasies and revelations of the saints. My heart overflows with gratitude when I think of this inestimable treasure* (SS 157). This she was able to write only several years after her father's death, and only after she had known in faith that even this crucible of suffering was part of God's providence. Thérèse came to see the countenance of her languishing father reflected in the Holy Face of Jesus, and she believed that he was participating in the suffering of Jesus. Her own sorrow, she believed, was also in union with Christ agonizing over the world (cf. EIG 183ff.).

Weeks before her death, enduring intense physical pain and the isolating suffering of darkness and anguish in the trial of faith, Thérèse wrote, *I cannot say: "The agonies of death have surrounded me," but I cry out in my gratitude: "I have descended into the valley of the shadow of death, nevertheless, I fear no evil because You are with me, Lord!"* [Psalm 18:5; 23:4] (GC 1170). Everything was a display of God's love to be received with gratitude.

Ingratitude, she wrote, *it seems to me this is what He* [Jesus] *must feel the most* (GC 708). She regarded ingratitude as thoughtless disregard for God's love and wanted, by walking the path of love, *to console You for the ingratitude of the wicked* (SS 276; PST 53ff.; cf. GC 682).

Jesus does not demand great actions from us, she had written, summarizing her little way, *but simply surrender and gratitude* (SS 188).

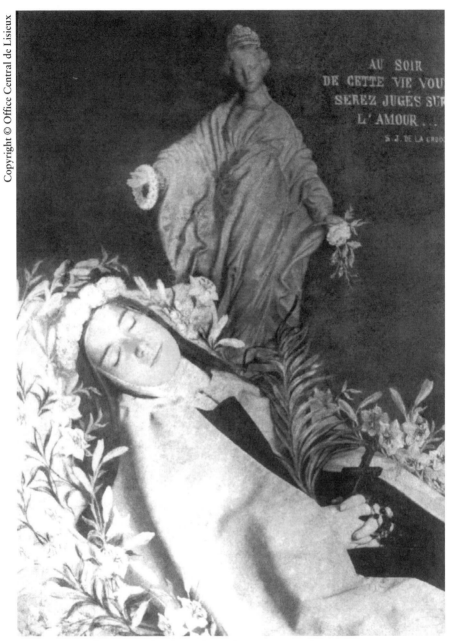

AU SOIR
DE CETTE VIE VOU
SEREZ JUGES SU
L'AMOUR . . .

S. J. DE LA CROIX

Thérèse in death in the infirmary, October 1, 1897

CHAPTER 22

My Vocation Is Love

SUMMARY AND CONCLUDING REFLECTIONS

As we have noted throughout our study, Thérèse continued to deepen her understanding of *the science of love* until her final days, finding in the Sacred Scripture confirmation of her intuitions about the heart qualities of love. Especially important for her were the life and teachings of Jesus as well as St. Paul's description of love and his identification of the fruit of the Spirit (1 Corinthians 13:4-7; Galatians 5:22-23). Neither Jesus nor St. Paul, except in Paul's listing of the fruit of the Spirit, attempt to name the heart qualities of love in a systematic way. Rather, Jesus and St. Paul, as did Thérèse's herself, lived these heart qualities, teaching them mostly by example.

Learning from Jesus and St. Paul

As Jesus lived life in the Spirit of love, he expressed to a remarkable degree the six heart qualities of love that Thérèse discovered on her little way. Confounding the conventional wisdom of his day, Jesus surprised all he encountered, especially his disciples, by his astonishing personal inner freedom, his creative responses, his inclusive compassion, his willingness to not be domineering, his self-surrender to God's will, and his spirit of gratitude to his Father. The Gospels are full of examples.

We can briefly mention that Jesus was uniquely free and creative in his daily life, in his interaction with his questioners, and particularly in his response to the law. One of the reasons his enemies were eventually forced to execute him was because his compassionate response to the poor, outcasts, and sinners, together with his message to love the enemy, challenged the social and religious order of his time. In the Gospels, the word "compassionate" is used in reference only to Jesus, and compassion is the quality that Jesus attributed to his Father.

By Jesus' words and actions, which flowed from his free, creative compassion, he became dangerous to both the Jewish religious establishment and the Roman social structure. At the meeting of the Sanhedrin convened to pass judgment on Jesus, Caiaphas, the Jewish high priest at the time, stated clearly that it would be better that one man should die than for the civic and religious structures of the whole nation to be destroyed (cf. John 11:49-50).

For St. Paul, inner freedom expressed in creative compassion was the essential defining characteristic of the Christian's life in Christ. "For freedom Christ set us free," he wrote to the Galatians who were losing their inner freedom to the bondage of the law and particularly to the slavery of sin (5:1). For St. Paul also, the "old self" (Ephesians 4:22) was the symbol of ingratitude and an absence of willing self-surrender into God's will, a lack that characterized Adam's revolt again the Creator.

Thérèse had meditated on St. Paul's description of love in his First Letter to the Corinthians and his list of the fruit of the Spirit in his Letter to the Galatians. Her understanding of love resonated with the fruit of the Spirit: "love, joy, peace, patience, kindness, generosity, faithfulness, gentleness, self-control" (Galatians 5:22-23). Also, Thérèse's sense that the absence of peace was a sure indicator of the lack of love, as well as her recognition of the six heart qualities of love, encompassed St. Paul's understanding of what love is: "Love is patient, love is kind" (1 Corinthians 13:4).

Moreover, Thérèse's heart qualities can be taken as the positive side of St. Paul's negative description of what love is not: "It is not jealous, [love] is not pompous, it is not inflated, it is not rude, it does not seek its own interests, it is not quick-tempered, it does not brood over injury, it does not rejoice over wrongdoing but rejoices with the truth" (1 Corinthians 13:4-6). Each of these negative indicators that St. Paul named—what love is not—can be seen, on close examination, to be an early sign of the loss of inner freedom, the seed of violence, and the indication of the beginning of conflict. Each of Thérèse's heart qualities of love is a positive indicator of love and a stepping-stone on the little way of love that is without conflict or violence.

Reflecting God's Own Nature

Thérèse recognized that each heart quality of love was a gift of God and had not been achieved by her own willful effort. Together they were a reflection of God's own nature.

She understood that her ability to maintain her inner freedom in difficult circumstances was the grace and manifestation of God's free love in her. Her capacity to be creative was the grace and manifestation of her participation in God's

Spirit of infinite creativity. Her compassion was the grace and manifestation of God's compassion for the world. Her sense of willingness was the grace and manifestation of God's ever-empowering and never-overpowering will. Her spirit of self-surrender into God's arms in every circumstance was the grace and manifestation of God's own self-emptying in Jesus. Her pervading sense of gratitude was the grace and manifestation of God's own joy and delight in creation.

Without these heart qualities, she knew that even her best intentions to love, like her earlier teenage attempts to practice virtue, would be loving *in a strange way* (SS 97). Lacking these dispositions, she knew she was expressing her own self-centeredness, taking selfish care of her own neediness, compensating her excessive feelings, and acting in self-promoting ways. If these heart qualities were absent, she knew she was not welcoming God's grace into her life.

Together these qualities opened her heart to a new depth of God's life in and through her and deployed God's love present and acting in her. They indicated that the supernatural reality of God's Spirit of love was real, present, and empowering her in her very human condition. They proclaimed to her that in the present moment, she was living and moving and having her existence in God's love (Acts 17:28). And they eventually played a very practical role in Thérèse's relationships in ordinary day-to-day life. Most important, they supported the grace of inner peace and prevented Thérèse from moving into any kind of violence—self-violence or violence to others.

We have observed that Thérèse was certain of this truth that God is love and in God there is no violence (1 John 4:7ff.). Thérèse was also convinced that the co-creative human love that participates in divine love, and to which Jesus was inviting her, must also be without hostility. We saw that Thérèse's understanding of *the science of love* was developmental, and she often did not know exactly what the next step on the path of love was, but she was sure that she would not knowingly and willingly step off that path of love onto the path of violence.

Love without Violence

Thérèse did not need any special psychological or spiritual gifts to recognize the heart qualities of love and to notice that they freed her from violence. She recognized this in the honesty of her prayerful reflections during her three formative experiences.

Her teenage conversion had opened her eyes to the possibility of engaging in self-violence. Her struggle to love the sisters with whom she lived in the Carmelite community led her to recognize that violence could poison the heart of a group desiring to live a life of love; in particular, she learned that she herself needed to resist this contamination of her own heart by not cultivating angry and hostile feelings. And as she encountered the popular religious teaching and as her union with God deepened, Thérèse became more aware of how violence had distorted the spirituality of the times and infected the hearts and actions of even religious people wishing to do good, but doing so by violent means.

Thérèse's path of growth returned again and again to the foundational issue that violence in any form is incompatible with love. Her path spiraled downward into a deeper self-awareness of the subtlety of hostility in her own heart. It also simultaneously spiraled upward as she experienced the sublime nature of God's love embracing her and as she saw more clearly the reach of violence in the personal, social, and religious areas of human life.

We can note that Thérèse's experiences with the difficult sisters in the very mundane and even trivial circumstances of her community life are a microcosm, revealing the same dynamics that underpin the larger social issues in which enemies are created and hostility erupts. Thérèse's life and teaching proclaim a wisdom that sheds light on a vision of God's kingdom of love as it could flourish, not only in one-to-one relationships, but also within and among societies and cultures. Thérèse's life and teaching reveal the thoughts, feelings, and dispositions that must prevail in the human heart and become priorities in societies and cultures if God's word of love and peace is to find a home in the world.

A Way That Is New

In her maturity Thérèse came to refer to her path of love as *a little way, a way that is . . . totally new* (SS 207). Her little way is, of course, not new in the sense that it really is "the fundamental mystery, the reality of the Gospel that the Spirit of God allowed her heart to reveal directly to the people of our time," as Pope John Paul II said in proclaiming her a Doctor of the Church (DAS 10).

However, Thérèse's little way can be considered "new," since it is a way of spirituality that had been lost to the common religious teaching of her time. By rediscovering Jesus' spirituality of love, Thérèse has rediscovered the treasure hidden in a field; she has grasped the pearl of great price (Matthew 13:44-46).

Her little way is the newly unearthed cache of gold, the treasure of apostolic faith that had been hidden beneath the misunderstandings of the prevailing spirituality, buried in the field of the common sense of conventional wisdom, the culture of violence and death of our times.

Thérèse's "intimate sense of spiritual realities" provides through the vision and life of a contemporary young woman a new, fresh, creative expression of Jesus' teaching of love without violence. Thérèse's little way offers a new emphasis in the developing understanding of the apostolic faith as that understanding "makes progress in the Church with the help of the Holy Spirit" (DAS 7). Thérèse's little way, therefore, contributes to the Church's development of doctrine in our time by proclaiming a spirituality that negates any violence that might linger in a mistaken understanding of the Church's authentic teaching.

As we noted, Thérèse's spirituality in particular shines the Gospel light on the violence hidden in Jansenism, perfectionism, and Pelagianism. These errors poisoned the spirituality of Thérèse's day and continue in various forms to contaminate religion in our own time. Among other errors, there is a mistaken belief that a "good" or "sacred" violence can be used to end the perceived evil in oneself or others. This "good" violence is often thought to be pleasing to a vengeful, punitive God. Thérèse simply rejected all aspects of these notions.

Specifically, she rejected violence, not violently, but by being more and more available to the source of love. She resisted violence and subverted it, serenely bearing its pain, resisting its contamination, opening herself more fully to God's love, and quietly living and teaching her little way of love.

In her maturity, she managed relationships without the codependency of her youth, setting appropriate boundaries of detachment and self-protection. She avoided violence to herself, fleeing situations that she could not cope with but returning without resentment or revenge. The inevitable violence that she encountered in her life of love—violence that she could not end—she diminished with patience and kindness but without masochism or self-pity. She resisted being violent to others through faith and prayer, not by engaging in rivalry or gossip. When in a position of authority, she acted responsibly but without compulsion or arrogance, requiring obedience but without overpowering. She made judgments without condemning and corrected without retaliation. She avoided the violence of striving for perfectionism and resisted the violence of excessive fear or guilt in failing. Her spiritual discipline was not self-punitive but consisted in maintaining awareness and faith as she established her identity, security, and self-worth in her union with God. In all of this, she combated evil but without using evil's means.

By living a life of love and revealing what loving might feel like and look like, Thérèse has become a "living icon of God," as Pope John Paul II called her. She manifests the feminine face of God, "who shows his almighty power in his mercy and forgiveness" (DAS 8). Her understanding that God desires love without violence is a "new" modern lens through which to read the signs of our time and a light of hope in the darkness of contemporary confusion and conflict.

A Way That Is Little

Thérèse also considered her way to be "little." It is little in the sense that it is easily accessible to anyone who is willing to accept its challenge and in the sense that it does not require great intellectual, religious, or social predispositions or achievements. Or more precisely, Thérèse's little way is for little ones, the ordinary faithful, living as best they can in a way that is not self-centered but grateful in the present circumstances of life, coping with ordinary responsibilities in a spirit of faith, and focusing on doing God's will in the spirit of justice and love that makes life flourish.

Throughout our study, we saw that as Thérèse matured, her human weaknesses decreased, but we also noticed that she never completely transcended the limitations of her excessive feelings. That, of course, is not to say that she was not a saint. But it is to say that she was a human saint, a very human saint. Thérèse is a saint with whom modern people seeking God can identify precisely in their littleness, their insignificance, and especially in their weaknesses of repeated failings, in their inability to acquire the phantom sanctity of perfectionism, and in their unholy feelings.

Thérèse recognized that willingly bearing in faith the trial of having difficult human feelings is a *work of love* and the foundation for cooperating with God's transforming grace. Self-awareness, humble self-acceptance, and self-abandonment into the arms of God, with a willingness to be transformed, became an integral part of her prayer, as a *cry of recognition and of love, embracing both trial and joy* (SS 242). This prayer became her loving response to the Trinity's self-emptying in Christ and to her Beloved's stooping down in divine providence.

A Way That Is Self-Emptying

All the saints have emphasized "orthodoxy," holding right doctrines and orthodox beliefs. All stressed "orthopraxis," doing right works and proper spiritual, charitable practices. Thérèse's little way does this as well, and it also emphasizes quite explicitly the need for cultivating what we might call "orthofeelings"—right feelings, thoughts, and dispositions. Right thoughts and feelings that she harbored in her heart mattered to Thérèse because they contributed to who she was and who she was choosing to become.

Spontaneous feelings and thoughts beyond her control, Thérèse recognized, were sometimes distressing and problematic, often arising from defensive urges. Such reactions were not bad in themselves since they were the spontaneous, unconsidered response of human nature. They also revealed to Thérèse a certain truth about the immediate situation as well as a truth about her own tendencies and feelings that had often lingered from childhood.

These spontaneous feelings were true but not the whole truth. To see the bigger truth, Thérèse needed to empty herself of her expectations and natural desires and preferences. She needed to bring her feelings into the light of faith. Of themselves her feelings were not failings, but without the illumination of faith, they were not reliable guides, and they could not be the basis of sound judgments, proper beliefs, or right works.

We might note that Thérèse's emphasis on cultivating right feelings, thoughts, and dispositions provides an important corrective to a notion that pervades much thinking in our day, even among religious people. It is the assumption that freedom includes the uninhibited and indiscriminate expression of spontaneous, often violent feelings, an assumption that virtually reduces morality to doing what feels good.

Thérèse came to understand that by the self-emptying of faith, she could also cultivate awareness, honesty, trust, appreciation, openness, dialogue, joy, kindness, patient endurance, generosity, reconciliation, mildness, sympathy, inclusivity, gentleness, and all such dispositions and spiritual practices that nourish the heart qualities of love.

These were the dispositions that Thérèse recognized participated in the fruit of the Spirit and allowed her to choose to share in the mystery of Christ, who "emptied himself, taking the form of a slave" (Philippians 2:7). She nourished these dispositions of self-emptying in herself by her devotion to the Christ Child and to the Holy Face. She also saw these feelings and sentiments embraced by her beloved Mother Mary, by Mary Magdalene, by the publican, and by Zacchaeus. They formed the stepping-stones of her downward path of littleness. Thérèse was convinced that *what pleases Him is that He sees me loving my littleness and my poverty, the blind hope that I have in His mercy* (GC 999).

The little way is not a way of achieving holiness with spiritual accomplishments, but a way of being taken into the Heart of Holiness, the Heart of Love. It recognizes that a sure sign of the lack of love is violence to oneself or others, and that such violence is a clear indication of our failure to respond willingly to our call to participate in the self-emptying of Christ in the present moment.

With Empty Hands

The little way is not a way of grasping God, but a way of allowing God to grasp us in our trust and willing receptivity, in our emptiness and spiritual poverty. It is not a way of acquiring and holding on to merits or accomplishments, but a way of giving up all concern about such things. It is not a technique to reach God, since God does not need to be reached. God is already embracing us, for it is in God that "we live and move and have our being" (Acts 17:28). But the little way is an attitude, a spirit of faith and love, focused especially on our call to be available to God's love, repentant in our weakness. It is, therefore, a way of coming to God with empty hands.

We saw that Thérèse could not and did not achieve the holiness associated with the perfectionism taught in the misguided spirituality of her day. Rather, she received authentic holiness by willingly surrendering *without fear in* [the] *Father's arms* (SS 188). She knew that God's arms were already open to her; she was already embraced by God in union with Christ, and all she needed was to be willing to fall into that Love. In her maturity she prayed: *I beg You, O my God! to be Yourself my Sanctity! . . . In the evening of this life, I shall appear before You with empty hands, for I do not ask You, Lord, to count my works. All our justice is stained in Your eyes. I wish, then, to be clothed in Your own Justice and to receive from Your Love the eternal possession of Yourself. I want no other Throne, no other Crown but You, my Beloved!* (SS 276–77; PST 53ff.).

Being before God with empty hands, being clothed in God's justice, and receiving the beginning of the eternal possession of God's life of love even in this life were essential to Thérèse's understanding of *the science of love*. This understanding fundamentally oriented her relationship with God, whom she found waiting to be recognized and loved and who was embracing her at the heart of the ordinary experiences of her life. *I can depend on nothing, on no good works of my own in order to have confidence*, she said as she neared death. *We experience such great peace when we're totally poor, when we depend upon no one except God* (HLC 137).

I go to Him with confidence and love

We noted that Thérèse's Act of Oblation to Merciful Love could be considered an expression of her little way in the form of a prayer and that Jesus' words "Love your enemies" and "Love one another as I have loved you" could be understood as the little way in the form of the Gospel call. We also indicated that the story of the Pharisee and publican could be read as the little way in the form of a Gospel parable and that the account of Zacchaeus is the little way in the form of a Gospel narrative. We pointed out that her expression *How much you have to lose* (MSST 28) could be heard as the little way in the form of a maxim. Her insight that all that God asks is *surrender and gratitude* (SS 188) and that *if you are willing to bear serenely the trial of being displeasing to yourself, then you will be* [for Jesus] *a pleasant place of shelter* (cf. GC 1038) could be understood as a précis of the little way. Now we can suggest that being before God with empty hands is the little way in the form of a grateful gesture of humility, availability, spiritual poverty, confidence, and love.

We can also note that the last statement by which Thérèse concluded her autobiography shortly before her death, *I go to Him with confidence and love* (SS 259), can be understood as the little way in the form of her personal testimony to her fundamental life orientation. Thérèse needed to say nothing more. She could rest in the arms of God. She had learned *the science of love* and had followed her path of love into the Sacred Heart of God, into an *eternal face to face* intimacy with Jesus (SS 277).

She had, at the end of her life, embraced her true identity in her union with God and found, as she said, the reason for her existence: *O Jesus, my Love; . . . I have found it. . . . MY VOCATION IS LOVE! . . . I shall be Love* (SS 194).

Select Bibliography

Bro, Bernard, OP. *St. Thérèse of Lisieux: Her Family, Her God, Her Message*. San Francisco: Ignatius Press, 2003.

Bro, Bernard, OP. *The Little Way: The Spirituality of Thérèse of Lisieux*. London: Darton, Longman, & Todd Ltd., 1997.

Catechism of the Catholic Church. Vatican City: Libreria Editrice Vaticana, 1994.

de Meester, Conrad, OCD, ed. *St. Thérèse of Lisieux: Her Life, Times, and Teaching*. Washington, DC: ICS Publications, 1997.

de Meester, Conrad, OCD. *With Empty Hands: The Message of St. Thérèse of Lisieux*. Washington, DC: ICS Publications, 2002.

Descouvemont, Pierre. *Thérèse of Lisieux and Marie of the Trinity*. New York: Alba House, 1997.

Divine Amoris Scientia: Apostolic Letter of His Holiness Pope John Paul II, October 19, 1997.

Gaucher, Guy, OCD. *The Story of a Life: St. Thérèse of Lisieux*. San Francisco: Harper & Row Publishers, 1987.

Görres, Ida Friederike. *The Hidden Face: A Study of St. Thérèse of Lisieux*. San Francisco: Ignatius Press, 2003.

Jamart, Francois. *Complete Spiritual Doctrine of St. Thérèse of Lisieux*. New York: Alba House, 1961.

O'Mahony, Christopher, OCD, ed. and trans. *St. Thérèse of Lisieux by Those Who Knew Her*. Huntington, IN: Our Sunday Visitor, 1975.

Payne, Steven, OCD. *St. Thérèse of Lisieux: Doctor of the Universal Church*. New York: St. Paul's/Alba House, 2002.

Piat, Stéphane-Joseph. *The Story of a Family*. Rockville, IL: Tan Books and Publishers, Inc., 1994.

Schmidt, Joseph F., FSC. *Everything Is Grace: The Life and Way of Thérèse of Lisieux*. Frederick, Maryland: The Word Among Us Press, 2007.

Six, Jean-Francois. *Light of the Night: The Last Eighteen Months in the Life of Thérèse of Lisieux*. Notre Dame, Indiana: University of Notre Dame Press, 1998.

Sister Geneviève of the Holy Face (Céline Martin). *My Sister St. Thérèse*. Rockford, IL: Tan Books and Publishers, Inc., 1997.

Thérèse of Lisieux. *Collected Letters of St. Thérèse of Lisieux*, trans. F. J. Sheed. New York: Sheed and Ward, 1949.

Thérèse of Lisieux. *Collected Poems of St. Thérèse of Lisieux*, trans. Alan Bancroft. Herefordshire, England: Gracewing, 2001.

Thérèse of Lisieux. *General Correspondence, vols. I and II*, trans. John Clarke, OCD. Washington, DC: ICS Publications, 1982, 1988.

Thérèse of Lisieux. *St. Thérèse of Lisieux: Her Last Conversations*, trans. John Clarke, OCD. Washington, DC: ICS Publications, 1977.

Thérèse of Lisieux. *Story of a Soul*. Trans. John Clarke, OCD. Washington, DC: ICS Publications, 1977.

Thérèse of Lisieux. *The Prayers of St. Thérèse of Lisieux*, trans. Aletheia Kane, OCD. Washington, DC: ICS Publications, 1997.

Index

merciful, *See* **God's love**
path of, *See* **little way**
pure, 15–17, 35, 39, 212–13
self-love, 227, 233
without violence,18, 32, 34, 103, 112, 142, 245, 247–48

Marie (Thérèse's sister), 23, 79–82, 87, 91, 111–12, 150, 183, 198–99, 236, 239
Marie of the Angels, Sr., 116
Martin, Louis (Thérèse's father), 23, 40, 43, 45, 53, 55–57, 59–65, 73, 101, 105, 128, 144, 159, 175, 178–79, 182, 205, 220, 224, 236, 241
Martin, Zélie (Thérèse's mother), 23, 41–47, 49, 53–54, 56, 60, 65, 67, 81, 105, 120, 137, 139, 158, 175, 183, 221, 223
Marx, Karl, 28
Mary Magdalene, St., 48, 50–51, 67, 152, 174, 179, 250
measureless desires (infinite desires), 15, 35, 116, 136, 138, 140, 159, 171, 177
melancholy, 43–45, 47–48, 65, 137, 183, 221, 238
Mother Gonzague, 77, 87–88, 91, 120–22, 130–31, 152, 184, 197, 199, 241
  relationship with Thérèse, 80–83, 86–87, 117
  Thérèse's attachment to, 82–84
  Thérèse's disagreement with, 118–19
motives,19, 40–41, 111, 226–27
  ambiguity of, 15–16, 35, 40, 137, 139
  motivation, 16–17, 33, 39, 59, 76, 85, 122, 150, 155, 191, 212
Nietzsche, Friedrich, 28

non-violent love, *See* **love**, without violence; *See also* **spirituality**, without violence
Pauline (Thérèse's sister), 23, 28, 67, 73–75, 80–82, 87, 91, 99–100, 109, 114, 118, 120, 131, 151, 178, 192–93, 201–3, 208, 221, 224–25, 230, 237
peace, *See* **inner peace**
Pelagianism, 17, 31, 135–36, 147, 154, 171, 190, 192, 247. *See also* **Jansenism; perfectionism**
perfectionism (perfection), 17, 31, 56, 92, 94, 135–36, 138–48, 151, 154, 157, 171, 174–77, 179, 189–93, 223, 225, 231, 236, 247–48, 250. *See also* **Jansenism; Pelagianism**
  striving for perfection, 139–140, 247
Philomena, Sr., 67
Pichon, Fr., 16
Pius X, Pope, 13, 24
Pius XI, Pope, 23
Pranzini, Henry, 79
prayer, 15, 22–23, 28, 33–35, 40, 49, 61–62, 76, 79, 97, 101, 103–5, 109, 111–12, 115–16, 118, 121–22, 130, 145–47, 150–52, 155, 157, 159, 166–69, 171, 174, 176–77, 179, 184–87, 189, 191, 195–97, 203–4, 206, 208, 217, 220, 222, 224, 227–28, 232, 245, 247–48, 251
  community, 94, 155, 166, 187, 196
  devotions, 25, 78, 156, 161, 166, 171, 179, 202, 236, 249
  Oblation to Merciful Love, 165–71, 192, 200, 208, 229, 240, 251
  Thérèse's definition of, 155, 185
Prou, Fr., 16

Scriptural Index

Acknowledgments

Quotations from *Story of a Soul*, translated by John Clarke, OCD. Copyright © 1975, 1976, 1996, by Washington Province of Discalced Carmelites, ICS Publications, 2131 Lincoln Road, N.E., Washington, D.C. 20002-1199 U.S.A. www.icspublications.org. Used with permission.

Quotations from *St. Thérèse of Lisieux: Her Last Conversations*, translated by John Clarke, OCD. Copyright © 1977, Washington Province of Discalced Carmelites, ICS Publications, 2131 Lincoln Road, N.E., Washington, D.C. 20002-1199 U.S.A. www.icspublications.org. Used with permission.

Quotations from *General Correspondence, Volume One*, translated by John Clarke, OCD. Copyright © 1982 by Washington Province of Discalced Carmelites, ICS Publications, 2131 Lincoln Road, N.E., Washington, D.C. 20002-1199 U.S.A. www.icspublications.org. Used with permission.

Quotations from *General Correspondence, Volume Two*, translated by John Clarke, OCD. Copyright © 1988 by Washington Province of Discalced Carmelites, ICS Publications, 2131 Lincoln Road, N.E., Washington, D.C. 20002-1199 U.S.A. www.icspublications.org. Used with permission.

Quotations from *The Prayers of St. Thérèse of Lisieux*, translated by Aletheia Kane, OCD. Copyright © 1997 by Washington Province of Discalced Carmelites, ICS Publications, 2131 Lincoln Road, N.E., Washington, D.C. 20002-1199 U.S.A. www.icspublications.org. Used with permission.

Quotations from *St. Thérèse of Lisieux: Her Life, Times and Teaching*. Copyright © 1998 by Washington Province of Discalced Carmelites, ICS Publications, 2131 Lincoln Road, N.E., Washington, D.C. 20002-1199 U.S.A. www.icspublications. org. Used with permission.

Quotations from the English translation of the *Catechism of the Catholic Church* for use in the United States of America, copyright © 1994, United States Catholic Conference, Inc.—Libreria Editrice Vaticana. Used with permission.

the WORD among us®
The *Spirit* of Catholic Living

This book was published by The Word Among Us. For thirty years, The Word Among Us has been answering the call of the Second Vatican Council to help Catholic laypeople encounter Christ in the Scriptures—a call reiterated by Pope Benedict XVI and a Synod of Bishops.

The name of our company comes from the prologue to the Gospel of John and reflects the vision and purpose of all of our publications: to be an instrument of the Spirit, whose desire is to manifest Jesus' presence in and to the children of God. In this way we hope to contribute to the Church's ongoing mission of proclaiming the gospel to the world and growing ever more deeply in our love for the Lord.

Our monthly devotional magazine, *The Word Among Us*, features meditations on the daily and Sunday Mass readings, and currently reaches more than one million Catholics in North America each year and another 500,000 Catholics in 100 countries. Our press division has published nearly 200 books and Bible studies over the past 12 years.

To learn more about who we are and what we publish, log on to our Web site at **www.wau.org**. There you will find a variety of Catholic resources that will help you grow in your faith.

Embrace His Word, Listen to God . . .

www.wau.org